D1488525

ADVANCES IN SOCIAL COGNITION
VOLUME II

Social Intelligence and Cognitive Assessments of Personality

ADVANCES IN SOCIAL COGNITION, Volume II

Social Intelligence and Cognitive Assessments of Personality

Edited by
ROBERT S. WYER, JR.
THOMAS K. SRULL
University of Illinois, Urbana-Champaign

LEA LAWRENCE ERLBAUM ASSOCIATES, PUBLISHERS
1989   Hillsdale, New Jersey   Hove and London

Lawrence Erlbaum Associates, Inc., Publishers
365 Broadway
Hillsdale, New Jersey 07642

Library of Congress Cataloging in Publication Data

Social intelligence and cognitive assessments of personality / edited
  by Robert S. Wyer, Jr., Thomas K. Srull.
      p.   cm. — (Advances in social cognition, ISSN 0898-2007 ; v.
  2)
    Includes bibliographies and indexes.
    ISBN 0-8058-0506-0. — ISBN 0-8058-0500-1 (pbk.)
    1. Personality and social intelligence.   2. Personality and
  cognition.   3. Personality assessment.   I. Wyer, Robert S.
  II. Srull, Thomas K.   III. Series.
  BF698.9.S64S63   1989
  155.2—dc20   89-7648
                                                  CIP

Printed in the United States of America
10   9   8   7   6   5   4   3   2   1

Contents

Preface

This volume is the second in a new series in *Advances in Social Cognition*. The purpose of the series is to present and evaluate new theoretical advances in all areas of social cognition and information processing. An entire volume is devoted to each theory, thus allowing it to be evaluated from a variety of perspectives and its implications for a wide range of issues to be considered.

The series reflects the two major characteristics of social cognition: the high level of activity in the field and the interstitial nature of the work. Each volume contains a target chapter that is timely in its application, novel in its approach, and precise in its explication. The target chapter is then followed by a set of critical commentaries that represent different theoretical persuasions, different subdisciplines within psychology, and occasionally separate disciplines. We believe that the dialogue created by such a format is highly unusual but, when done with care, extremely beneficial to the field.

Public debates are interesting and informative but they require a special group of people if they are to be productive. In this respect, we want to thank all the contributors. For several years, Nancy Cantor and John Kihlstrom have been developing an entirely new conceptualization of personality and social cognition. Traditional issues are addressed and new ones are raised. They manage to make many of their points with force but, at the same time, acknowledge remaining weaknesses. It is clear that they struggle between being constrained by the data and being bold in their theorizing. Cantor and Kihlstrom work in a tradition that holds great promise but has also become quite uncommon. Agree or disagree, such efforts cannot be ignored. We thank both Nancy and John for their scholarship, for their courage, and for their extraordinarily cooperative style.

The commentators have played an equally important and difficult role. They were asked to prepare chapters that were critical but fair, and ones that were detailed but well reasoned. Readers will find that each of them is insightful, thought provoking, and an important contribution in its own right. We want to extend our sincere appreciation to each of the commentators for being so analytical and clear.

As before, we also want to acknowledge the help of Larry Erlbaum. He is everything one could hope for in a publisher, and a wonderful friend.

Robert S. Wyer, Jr.
Thomas K. Srull

ADVANCES IN SOCIAL COGNITION
VOLUME II

Social Intelligence and Cognitive Assessments of Personality

1 Social Intelligence and Cognitive Assessments of Personality

Nancy Cantor
University of Michigan

John F. Kihlstrom
University of Arizona

Many personality theorists have spoken of the need for more integrated approaches to questions of individual adaptation to the social world. In this chapter, we take the study of human intelligence as source and inspiration for such an integrative endeavor. We have been greatly influenced by recent analyses of intelligence that focus on three aspects of problem solving: expertise, context, and pragmatics. We adopt this perspective in our own treatment of the social intelligence that, in our view, forms the cognitive basis of personality.

Social intelligence is multifaceted, domain and task specific, and reformulated in each significant life context. Therefore, there is little point in making global comparisons of individuals—measuring their "social IQ," as it were. We disavow, explicitly and at the outset, any intention of offering yet another abstract individual-difference dimension for the psychometrician's mill. Nor do we wish to parlay the multidimensional nature of social intelligence into a new taxonomy of people that, like its forebears, will miss the flexibility and discriminative nature of human experience, thought, and action. We assume, by direct analogy to language, that an infinite variety of individual differences can be produced by the interactions among a finite set of general principles encompassing social learning, social cognition, and social interaction. Therefore, our primary task is to describe the general social-cognitive processes out of which human individuality is constructed. In addition, we wish to describe research that indicates how social intelligence is acquired, altered, and utilized in everyday life and clinical situations, throughout the life cycle. We pay particular attention to people's use of social intelligence in dealing with the mundane and monumental problems that they confront in the ordinary course of everyday living.

1

PERSONALITY AND COGNITION: EARLIER TREATMENTS

From a social-cognitive point of view, the study of personality can be viewed as the analysis of the ways in which people interpret situations, set goals within them, and plan and execute behavior that is consistent with these interpretations and goals. This viewpoint is not original to us, of course, and any unique contribution of ours must be viewed in the context of what came before.

Cognitive Styles as Personality

One of the longest standing traditions in personality and cognition has to do with the characteristic styles for perceiving and thinking that people develop (Gardner et al., 1959; Kagan & Kogan, 1970). Whereas these styles are typically measured in impersonal perceptual-cognitive tasks, the assumption is that they generalize to the interpersonal domain as well; that is, the proponents of the cognitive-style approach assume that performance on standard laboratory tasks is indicative of broad personality characteristics that mediate the person's behavior in the social world outside the laboratory. Many early theorists of cognitive style were influenced by psychoanalytic ego psychology, and related various stylistic dimensions to defensive as well as adaptive functions. However, one does not have to embrace psychodynamic theory in any form to appreciate the heritage of cognitive-style theory for modern cognitive approaches to personality. In fact, recent work in the cognitive-style tradition has emphasized the role they play in mediating adaptive social behavior rather than in defending against intrapsychic drives.

This trend is clearly illustrated in work on field embeddedness (also known as field dependence–independence, analytic-global style, and psychological differentiation; see Witkin et al., 1962; Witkin & Goodenough, 1977). In the laboratory, psychological differentiation is measured by a variety of impersonal laboratory tasks such as the Body Adjustment Test, Rod and Frame Test, and Embedded Figures Test. Witkin and Goodenough (1977) argue that there is a complex relationship between psychological differentiation and social behavior. For example, field-dependent people tend to be more conforming, dependent, and other directed than field-independent people. Another popular cognitive style is impulsivity–reflectivity (also called conceptual tempo; see Kagan et al., 1964; Messer, 1976), which describes the individual's tendency to reflect on the validity of the problem-solving process under conditions of uncertainty. Again, the style is typically measured by an impersonal laboratory task, such as the Matching Familiar Figures Test or the Design Recall Task, but performance on these tests is held to predict social behavior. For example, impulsivity predicts aggressiveness, shyness, and attention seeking in children—although not, somewhat paradoxically, risk taking or delay of gratification.

2

Field independence–dependence, impulsivity–reflectiveness, and other cognitive-style constructs have been subject to vigorous criticism (Baron, 1982; Laboratory of Comparative Human Cognition, 1982; Scribner & Cole, 1973). For example, the generality of the supposed cognitive style is often at issue: The various ostensible laboratory measures of psychological differentiation do not intercorrelate highly, and reflectivity does not appear to be consistent across various phases in the problem-solving process. In both cases, external relations with criterion social behaviors have proved difficult to replicate or subject to many qualifications. Moreover, cross-cultural studies often turn up evidence of value bias—who wants to be labelled field dependent or impulsive?—in apparent contradiction to the central tenet of cognitive style that opposite styles are equally adaptive.

The cognitive-styles tradition provides us with some important lessons about possible pitfalls in the study of cognition and personality. First, it is probably fruitless to attempt to develop a small set of basic cognitive styles derived from very abstract individual-difference constructs. Second, there should be no expectation that any aspect of problem solving necessarily will be generalizable across markedly different problem contexts, or different phases in the life cycle. Third, the effectiveness of any mode of thinking must be evaluated not with respect to normative standards within a culture, but rather with respect to the individual's own goals, as perceived within the framework of the life tasks in which he or she is currently engaged.

The Social Cognitivists

A more immediate and substantial source of the social-intelligence view of personality may be found in the work of the major proponents of social-learning theory: Rotter, Bandura, Kelly, and Mischel. We recognize that social-learning theory was originally formulated by Neal Miller and John Dollard. But their account of social learning was so closely tied to Hullian S–R formulations that it cannot be called cognitive in the modern sense. We also recognize that Kelly is not, strictly speaking, a social-learning theorist. In fact, in the preface to his 1955 monograph, he argued for throwing learning theory out altogether. Yet Kelly's theory is clearly social in its scope and clearly has a major learning component to it. Because Kelly's work has been so much of an influence on our own thinking (chiefly through Mischel), we include him in this statement of our intellectual history.

In any history of the development of social-cognitive approaches to personality, pride of place must go to Rotter, who proposed the first theory of social learning to employ cognitive concepts (Rotter, 1954; Rotter, Chance, & Phares, 1972). Rotter broke with the classic behaviorist view of social learning, as represented by the work of Miller and Dollard, in a number of critical respects. Whereas behaviorists defined reinforcements objectively, he defined them subjectively in terms of the value attached to various outcomes; whereas the behaviorists defined reinforcement contingencies objectively in terms of stimulus–response probabilities, he defined them subjectively in terms of the individual's expectations. Whereas the behaviorists defined the situation objectively in terms of the array of stimuli impinging on the individual, he defined it subjectively in terms of the meaning ascribed to stimulus events. The result was an expectancy-value theory of choice, in which the individual regulates his or her own behavior in terms of goals, the expected probability of certain outcomes, and the values attached to them.

Alongside the various ideas pertaining to cognitive style, Rotter's construct of locus of control represents one of the earliest attempts to postulate an explicitly cognitive dimension of individual differences in personality. Somewhat paradoxically, however, the cognitive thrust of Rotter's theory has been obscured somewhat by the later conversion of locus of control into a broad trait-like construct. It is true that Rotter himself postulated individual differences in the person's generalized expectancy and developed a questionnaire measure permitting people to be classified as generally internal or generally external. But it is important to point out that Rotter also argued that the individual's generalized expectancies stood alongside specific expectancies tailored to the particulars of the situation. Moreover, Rotter viewed these expectancies as learned beliefs and thus subject to considerable change as a result of life experiences or therapeutic intervention. Conceptually, then, locus of control should not be viewed as a stable, consistent, trait-like dispositional entity, regulating behavior independent of environmental events and unresponsive to attempts at change.

Rotter's other contribution to the development of a cognitive approach to personality has also been obscured by the later emphasis on locus of control. In the preface to his seminal 1954 book, Rotter explicitly stated that his goal was to produce a social-learning theory of personality that would integrate the theories of Hull and Tolman. In other words, Rotter anticipated current concern with the interaction of cognitive elements such as expectancies with motivational elements such as goals and values. In fact, Rotter postulated a set of secondary psychological needs (including recognition status, dominance, and physical comfort), derived from physiological drives through learning in early childhood, which determine differences in the value attached to various reinforcements. By attending to needs, goals, and values as well as expectations, Rotter anticipated the current emphasis on hot as opposed to cold cognition in the social domain.

Rotter's theory is a theory of choice. It states that choices are determined by expectancies and values, and that expectancies and values are learned. However, despite Rotter's titular emphasis on social learning, he does not delve too much into the learning process itself. This aspect of social-learning theory has been analyzed most thoroughly by Bandura and his colleagues (Bandura, 1977b, 1986; Bandura & Walters, 1963) in terms of the distinction between learning by response consequences and learning by modelling. His emphasis on modelling gave even his earliest theoretical work a clearly cognitive flavor: Knowledge can be acquired through precept and example, simply by observation, without reinforcement (and without repeated exposure). However, even his analysis of learning by response consequences was cognitive in nature: direct experience of reinforcement provided the person with information about environmental outcomes and what must be done to gain or avoid them. As a result of either type of learning, the individual forms mental representations of experience that permit anticipatory motivation in the form of act–outcome expectancies. The cognitive emphasis in Bandura's work is so strong that his most recent statement is of a social-*cognitive* rather than a social-*learning* theory.

More recently, Bandura has moved away from analyses of the social-learning process in general to the more specific topic of the learned expectancies governing behavior. This recent work has focused on the role of self-efficacy expectations in regulating behavior and promoting behavior change. Bandura has distinguished between outcome expectancies—beliefs concerning the consequences of certain actions—and efficacy expectancies—beliefs concerning the ability to perform the actions required to produce certain outcomes. Individuals' expectations about their personal efficacy influence their attempts to perform important tasks, their persistence in the face of failure, and their responses to stress. Within a particular domain, an individual is only as skilled as he or she thinks is the case; performance cannot be optimal without a sense of mastery. Note that self-efficacy is context specific. Thus self-efficacy theory is quite different from more generalized formulations concerning attributional style and locus of control. Note that it is not consistent with Bandura's emphasis to develop a test of *generalized* self-efficacy. Instead, self-efficacy serves as an example of how anticipatory expectations develop and change through social learning.

In keeping with his emphasis on self-efficacy expectancies, Bandura has considered in detail the role of internal standards and self-evaluation processes in motivating performance. Individuals engaged in goal-directed behavior match their progress with an internal standard of performance and evaluate their success or failure in accordance with their perceived self-efficacy at the task at hand. When self-efficacy is high, motivation will also be high even when current performance is substandard. When self-efficacy is low, motivation will be low even when current performance meets relevant standards. Self-regulation is a cyclical process, in which standards are set, performance monitored and evaluated, and standards revised; motivation and self-esteem rise and fall accordingly.

Kelly (1955) was probably the first major theorist to provide a thoroughly cognitive and fully idiographic treatment of personality. He characterized people as naive scientists engaged in explaining events in terms of hypotheses derived from personal constructs about themselves and the world. People differ in the nature of their personal constructs, how many they have available, and which they choose to apply at any given time. This constructive alternativism forms the basis for flexibility in the construal of social situations and events, and thus for discriminativeness in social behavior. Constructs are abstract cognitive frameworks—we might today call them schemata—composed of similarities and contrasts. Once a construct is applied to an object or event, it carries implications that the perceiver can use to anticipate other features or future events. Kelly assumed that individuals develop highly personalized, unique repertoires of personal constructs to interpret situations and events. People cannot understand the world except through their own constructs; but just as important, we cannot understand other people unless we understand the constructs that they bring to bear on the interpretive process.

Just as Rotter's concept of expectancies came to be identified with his construct of generalized locus of control, so Kelly's concept of personal constructs is often identified in terms of cognitive complexity. Some individuals have highly differentiated systems, involving many different constructs and a rich network of relations among them; others have very simple systems consisting of only a few constructs. In some individuals the personal construct system is so simple as to be monolithic. Kelly assumed that a high degree of complexity was characteristic of the personal construct systems of well-functioning adults, in that it afforded more opportunity for constructive alternativism. Following Kelly's own example, a number of investigators have proposed quantitative indices of cognitive complexity (Scott, Osgood, & Peterson, 1979). In a manner reminiscent of the various cognitive styles, and of the abuse of Rotter's concept of generalized locus of control (Rotter, 1975), this attempt to capture the cognitive basis of personality with a single individual-difference dimension seems fundamentally misguided. The core of personal construct theory is best viewed as residing in the *content* of the individual's personal constructs, the uniqueness of which effectively prohibits any simple nomothetic comparisons. Kelly's work is seminal because it showed how a theory of personality could give central weight to the interpretations that people make of their social world without assuming that individuals can be characterized in terms of a small number of enduring cognitive styles or dispositions. Like Allport, he celebrated the uniqueness of the individual personality and preferred idiographic analyses of individuals rather than nomothetic comparisons among people based on widely shared dimensions.

Rotter's emphasis on values and expectancies, Bandura's emphasis on the social-learning process, and Kelly's emphasis on personal constructs are all brought together in Mischel's development of a cognitive social learning theory of personality (Mischel, 1973, 1977, 1979, 1981, 1984). Mischel concluded that the variability of social behavior across situations reflected the fact that people are acutely responsive to small changes from one setting to another. Far from substituting external for internal control, however, Mischel emphasized the determining power of the subjective meaning of the situation, and the ability of people to modify these meanings by means of cognitive transformations. Hence, for Mischel the critical task is to study the cognitive structures and operations that are involved in forming and transforming mental representations of stimulus situations. As an exemplar of cognitive control, Mischel has chosen to study delay of gratification in children; observing that children learn to control their wishes and their environments in large part by thinking in nonconsummatory ways (e.g., Mischel, 1981).

It is important to note that Mischel does not deny the occurrence of cross-situational consistency and temporal stability—although he does tend to view rigidly consistent and thus indiscriminate behavior as rather pathological. However, he does consider these matters to be empirical questions rather than a priori assumptions, and he is at pains to account for both stability/consistency and variability with the same theoretical language. Behavioral consistencies, when they are observed, derive from the consistent application of particular modes of construal. Often, consistency is observed when the person enters an unfamiliar situation and, not knowing what else to do, relies on time-worn strategies of construal and response. Most people, however, retain the ability to alter their construals, as appropriate, and fine-tune their behavior as appropriate (Wright & Mischel, 1987). Similarly, stability is to be found not so much in how people behave in various situations, but in their repertoire of behavioral possibilities. Cognitive and behavioral competencies are not acquired anew every time they are used. Once acquired, they remain available in the subject's repertoire, to be tuned and used as required.

The various social-cognitive treatments of personality seem to agree with the cognitive-style theorists that adaptation involves a process of problem solving, with interpretation and inference at the center. However, cognitive social-learning theory goes beyond the cognitive-style tradition by emphasizing the construal and reasoning process as central to social adaptation. All the social cognitivists provide fairly concrete specifications of the cognitive structures and processes underlying social behavior in particular life domains. Kelly's Role Construct Repertory Test provides an analysis of the context, organization, and complexity of the person's system for categorizing people, situations, and events. Rotter emphasizes both general and specific outcome expectancies, whereas Bandura focuses on people's expectancies concerning themselves. Mischel explicates processes of cognitive transformation and planning that constitute a basis for self-regulation and for taking control over environments.

The social cognitivists differ from the cognitive stylists on a number of dimensions, for example. The first is the level of specificity. Whereas the cognitive stylists postulated abstract, molar dimensions of individual differences with trait-like properties of consistency and stability, the ideas of the social cognitivists are much more concrete and molecular. All avoid the ranking of individuals on continuous dimensions and other classificatory exercises. Rather than emphasizing widely shared and highly generalized cognitive dispositions, they emphasize unique attributes manifested in more or less specific contexts.

The social-cognitive stress on individual learning history provides an account of both personality development and change and provides a basis for understanding the complexity, diversity, and uniqueness of each individual personality. There is also a difference in value. Although the cognitive stylists were at great pains to deny it, one could not help but get the impression that one style—field independence, for example—was better or more adaptive than its opposite member. The social-cognitive approach is rather less judgmental in this respect. In their emphasis on individual differences in goals and values, the social-cognitive theorists are reluctant to characterize any particular response or style as objectively better than another: Value can only be determined with respect to adaptiveness for the individual. If social-cognitive theorists celebrate any value it is flexibility, enabling people to adjust their behavior to the demands and constraints of whatever situations they may encounter. Hence, by implication at least, the social cognitivists place a premium only on "intelligent" thought—intelligent in the sense of being unprogrammed, nonrigid, and creative.

PERSONALITY AND INTELLIGENCE

Adaptive behavior is the natural domain for the study of personality, and adaptive behavior has all the qualities of intelligent action. It is purposive, flexibly attuned to the individual's goals, not rigidly stereotyped or indiscriminate. Our view of personality focuses on human intelligence because we believe that people use their intellectual resources to frame problems and search out solutions, give meaning to their life situations, and adapt to the demands of the settings in which they live. We are aware of the irony in proposing to place intelligence at the center of a cognitive theory of personality. In the past, the analysis of social behavior has often proceeded by analogy to intellectual behavior. Our approach can be misconstrued as postulating a single overarching dimension of social IQ, consistent and stable, on which individuals can be comparatively ranked. As noted earlier, we specifically disavow any such intent. Nevertheless, it does seem to us that any presentation of a social-intelligence view of personality requires some consideration of the ways in which intelligence has been conceptualized in the past.

Conceptualizations of Intelligence

Historically, the most popular construal of intelligence has been psychometric—that is, intelligence has been defined as that which is measured by intelligence tests (Gould, 1981). Psychometricians hold that individuals differ in their capacity to perceive relations, organize and remember information efficiently, draw logical inferences, and reason through problems to solutions. Although they may differ among themselves on the question of whether these abilities cohere to form a single unitary intellectual ability, all agree that intelligence tests provide a means of ranking people with respect to their relative intelligence (Gould, 1981).

A hallmark of the psychometric approach is the assumption that intelligence is an entity that can be measured, largely independent of the individual's specific knowledge about different domains in the real world (Baltes, 1986). Thus, intelligence is commonly tested with items that do not relate to the particular everyday tasks and life goals of the testees. A good example of this tendency is the distinction between fluid and crystallized intelligence (Cattell & Horn, 1978). Fluid intelligence is measured with tests of perception, memory, and reasoning that are assumed to be equally familiar (or unfamiliar) to all testees. Crystallized intelligence is measured by tests of real-world knowledge that is heavily influenced by social and cultural experience. Crystallized intelligence gives form and content to the raw potential of fluid intelligence.

In contrast to the psychometric view is the popular or naive conceptualization of intelligence, which makes no reference to performance on standardized tests but appears to be based on performance in everyday life contexts (Sternberg, Conway, Keton, & Bernstein, 1981). The popular concept classifies intelligence into three categories: practical problem-solving ability, verbal ability, and social competence. The various features associated with these categories are typical rather than defining in nature (Neisser, 1979). The clear implication is that there is no one right way, or even two or three, to be intelligent. Whereas the popular concept is similar to the psychometric one in its emphasis on problem-solving skills and verbal ability, these elements are generally described with reference to social tasks and practical life problems. Moreover, social interaction is given an emphasis in the popular concept that is generally missing in the psychometric approach. Finally, intelligence in the popular sense of the word is inextricably linked to a specific sociocultural environment.

Although people generally feel capable of characterizing social intelligence, and recognizing it when they see it manifested, it has proved difficult to devise any test that adequately captures a person's ability to solve practical problems in ordinary life domains (Denney, 1984; Denney, Pearce, & Palmer, 1982). Part of the problem is that the lay conception of intelligence is more implicit than explicit. Moreover, the problems in social life that tap practical intelligence will vary from one individual to another and are not easy to translate into paper-and-pencil format. Even if one could achieve consensus on the kinds of real-life social situations that tap practical intelligence, the difficult task would remain of specifying the knowledge base and problem-solving skill(s) most appropriate to that situation. Finally, even slight changes in context may result in substantial changes in the individual's preferred approach to a problem. If the assessment of practical intelligence requires systematic in vivo sampling, all hope of comparative ranking vanishes (this, of course, is just as things should be from our perspective).

The psychometric and popular conceptions of intelligence also differ with respect to two central assumptions of the doctrine of traits: stability across time and consistency across contexts. Because psychometricians characterize the individual's basic intellectual resources as a trait analogous to eye color or hair texture, their expectation is that intelligence will remain relatively stable over most of the life-span, perhaps declining in old age. By contrast, the popular conception does not clearly distinguish between a basic intellectual reserve and those skills and knowledge acquired through social experience. Thus, it allows for considerable growth in intelligence over the whole life course. In the face of the individual's growing capacity to confront the problems of life in specific domains, it is difficult to point to a stable core of intelligence that remains unchanged.

Psychometricians, like trait theorists in general, also assume that the individual's characteristic level of intelligence will be displayed consistently across a wide variety of different domains. By contrast, from a popular perspective intellectual performance rests on experiences that are specific to particular domains of social life. Far from being discouraged when people show intelligence in one domain but not another, the intuitive psychologist expects that people will vary in their intelligence across different life domains by virtue of differences in exposure to those domains. In addition, the social ecology in which an individual conducts his or her life will have an enormous impact on intelligent behavior by setting up certain tasks or problems as worthy of attention and certain outcomes as worthy of achievement (Baltes, 1986; Sternberg, 1984).

Intelligence: Expertise, Context, and Pragmatics

In a manner paralleling recent treatments of intelligence in general (e.g., Sternberg, 1982), our analysis of social intelligence borrows from both the psychometric and lay conceptions of intelligence, with an emphasis on the latter. Intelligence is displayed in real-world problem-solving behavior, on tasks related to the goals encouraged by the individual's social-life context. Understanding social intelligence, then, requires some characterization of the expertise that people bring to bear in solving life problems, the contexts that render certain problems more important than others, and the pragmatic considerations that define the goals to be achieved in an intelligent solution.

At the core of any characterization of intelligence is expertise—the repertoire of knowledge used in solutions to problems. Many analyses of this repertoire distinguish between declarative and procedural knowledge (e.g., Anderson, 1981). Declarative knowledge consists of the individual's fund of information concerning real and imagined objects and events in the world. It includes information about facts (or presumed facts), categorical relations, beliefs, and attitudes. Procedural knowledge includes the rules, skills, and strategies available to the person for acquiring, manipulating, storing, and retrieving declarative knowledge—in other words, the basic cognitive operations performed in the course of perceiving, remembering, and thinking. In addition to the formal rules of inductive and deductive reasoning, the procedural knowledge repertoire includes a number of less formal cognitive heuristics that may be applied to judgment and inference (Nisbett & Ross, 1980; Tversky & Kahneman, 1974). Finally, the knowledge repertoire includes a set of higher order "metarules" for planning, monitoring, and making decisions about what problems need to be worked on and how they are best approached (Baron, 1981, 1982).

A central assumption here is that any individual's store of declarative knowledge will be highly elaborate and organized in some domains and rather sparse in others. Selective exposure creates many irregularities in the knowledge base: Children can only acquire expertise about the objects and events that are most familiar to them. Various interests and skills may be differentially encouraged by parents, teachers, peers, and institutions—the 5-year-old's expertise about dinosaurs likely contrasts markedly with her knowledge of other aspects of natural history and is not a product of her genetic endowment. Directed social learning is important (especially once the child gets to school), as are the unintentional communications of informal models and other, even more subtle, environmental influences. Analyses of cognitive development support this domain-specific view of declarative expertise (Keil, 1984, 1986). In addition, experts may execute certain procedures automatically, without conscious attention and effort, even though performance on other tasks may require considerably more cognitive effort (Smith, 1984; Sternberg, 1984). Accordingly, any characterization of intelligence as expertise must be fine-tuned to specific domains. This effectively precludes interindividual comparisons and rankings of the kind commonly associated with the psychometric view of intelligence.

Recent theoretical approaches to intelligence also reflect a concern that intelligence be measured on tasks that are relevant to the contexts in which individuals live their lives (Baltes, 1986; Denney, 1984; Neisser, 1976; Sternberg, 1984). This argument is familiar from life-span developmental psychology (Erikson, 1950; Ryff, 1982): The life tasks of a child or adolescent are different from those of a young adult or a retiree. Along the same lines, we must recognize the different life tasks that confront urban and rural dwellers, people in 19th and 20th century, people in the First and Third Worlds. Expertise, and the opportunity to acquire and display it, will naturally vary according to the contexts to which people are exposed.

Recognition of this fact leads to a concern with the features that differentiate contexts. Veroff (1983) has suggested five major contextual determinants of personality: historical, cultural, developmental, organizational, and interpersonal. Similarly, Baltes and his colleagues (Baltes, Dittman-Kohli, & Dixon, 1984) have proposed that life tasks are age graded, history graded, and non-normative. These life contexts shape not only the general problem domains that people emphasize but also constrain their levels of expertise. Optimal task performance may only be achieved when a problem is framed in such a way that it taps into the person's current life experience.

Motivation and choice play an important role in intellectual performance

(Baron, 1982; Sternberg, 1984). Optimal task performance can only be evaluated with reference to the life goals of the individual. Long ago, Simon (1955) argued that the maximal value was not necessarily optimal; in many circumstances, the optimal outcome is one that is merely satisfactory. Personal goals distinguish between important problems and trivial ones, and between preferred and undesirable solutions. Thus, analyses of intelligence must be relativistic, recognizing that intelligent solutions will differ from time to time, place to place, and person to person.

It follows from an emphasis on real-life contexts and personal goals that intelligence can only be assessed with tasks that are familiar to the individual. The seeming paradox here is that both the psychometric and popular conceptions of intelligence involve the ability to handle novel tasks or circumstances. Moreover, we have defined intelligent behavior as that which is flexible and sensitive to varying circumstances—which cannot be demonstrated if subjects focus exclusively on the familiar. Thus, efforts at assessment must achieve some balance between familiarity and novelty. Tasks must be familiar enough to tap the individual's expertise; but they must be novel enough to give the person an opportunity to adjust to new demands and feedback. This may be accomplished by allowing the person to practice a novel task, or to place a familiar task in a novel context. Periods of life transition provide a nice real-world analogue to a laboratory task that balances familiarity and novelty of demands (Stewart & Healy, 1985).

When analyses of intelligence are directed at the tasks of social life, the question arises whether social intelligence is an entity separate from academic intelligence (Neisser, 1976). Guilford (1967), like Thorndike (1920), answered in the affirmative and proposed that social intelligence be measured with tests that tap social perceptiveness—the ability to identify the feelings, traits, and actions of other people. Unfortunately, in psychometric terms the various attempts to describe a distinct and coherent set of social abilities independent of academic intelligence have met with little success. Tests designed to measure social intelligence do not hang together as they should; and social intelligence tests are not better than academic intelligence tests at predicting criteria of social effectiveness (Keating, 1978).

Rather than concluding that the concept of social intelligence has no (discriminate) validity, we conclude (with, among others, Ford & Tisak, 1983) that people draw on the same set of intellectual resources to solve the problems of both academic and social life. Whatever differential validity social-intelligence tests prove to have may be due to the fact that the tests themselves more closely resemble the criteria of behavioral effectiveness and social functioning (e.g., Ford & Tisak, 1983). Even this difference may disappear as tests of nonsocial intelligence attend more to real-world problem-solving contexts. As the distinction between academic and social intelligence gets ever more fuzzy, social intelligence remains a distinct repertoire only because its relevant knowledge base is explicitly and importantly interpersonal.

Social Intelligence: Expertise, Context, and Pragmatics

The concept of *social* intelligence is a convenient organizing principle; we believe it does not necessarily involve any unique cognitive structures and processes. The social-intelligence repertoire contains declarative and procedural knowledge relevant to, and directed at, the tasks of social life (Cantor & Kihlstrom, 1987). It consists of concepts about ourselves, other people, and the social situations in which we encounter them, including a more or less continuous historical record as well as more abstract descriptive information; the rules governing impression formation, causal attribution, and other social judgments and inferences; and problem-solving metaknowledge used in goal setting, planning, monitoring, and evaluating action. There are no a priori reasons for thinking that these mental structures and processes are any different from those applied in the nonsocial domain. Social knowledge seems unique because of its immediacy and salience to us as social creatures, the pressure created by the interactional contexts in which it is used, its ability to elicit strong feelings in us, and —perhaps—the consequences of making mistakes. From this perspective, nonsocial knowledge may be defined as information whose content, contexts of application, and pragmatics of usage are less directly and less obviously linked to personal and social approval (if not survival).

We realize that our emphasis on the continuity between social and nonsocial intelligence risks ignoring the important emotional and motivational sources of social behavior (Isen & Moore, 1987). The risk is exacerbated by the strong emphasis in laboratory studies on cold, dry social cognition (cf. Fiske, 1982). Yet, as cognitivists, we are not at all uninterested in emotions and motives. Rather, we start by viewing emotions and motives as integrated within cognitive structures and processes of life-task problem solving (Showers & Cantor, 1985). For the present, we simply wish to explicitly recognize these reciprocal relations between cognition and emotion: Emotions are subject to cognitive construction and control, but cognitions are clearly influenced by emotional and motivational processes (e.g., Isen, Daubman, & Nowicki, 1987; Niedenthal, 1987). Although some theorists have raised the possibility of emotion without cognition (Zajonc, 1980b), it is virtually impossible to consider cognition and emotion separately when discussing life-task problem solving (Norem & Cantor, 1988). People are emotionally involved in their life tasks: They are highly motivated to solve them, and they achieve their solutions through the application of social-cognitive structures and processes. In the process of analyzing (''cold'') social intelligence, we must not simply analyze the social knowledge stored in the mind, in a vacuum; we must also identify the critical *social tasks* and *life contexts* in which this knowledge is used and has meaning, as well as the individual *purposes* to which it is put. The intelligent person is one who can employ social knowledge flexibly and adaptively to meet personal goals and create good feelings. Intelligent people know their limits, and shape and select environments in which they can act competently and feel efficacious (Emmons, Diener, & Larsen, 1986).

13

Assessment of Social Intelligence

In this vein, the assessment of social intelligence centers on the problems or *life tasks* on which an individual sees himself or herself as working in a particular period in life; the *self-concepts and personal memories* that constitute an important part of the expertise for those life tasks; and the *cognitive strategies* or preferred procedures for implementing one's goals in specific life-task contexts. Because we believe that all personality assessment procedures should begin with a search for general principles and processes of social thought and behavior, our assessments start with the life tasks, concepts and memories, and problem-solving strategies that characterize a group of people undergoing a shared life experience, moving to patterns of individual differences only after a "normative" social-intelligence portrait has been developed.

For example, Cantor and her colleagues (Cantor et al., 1987) have studied the interpersonal and achievement life tasks of college students, following these students as they navigate relevant tasks over 4 years of college life. Students in this longitudinal sample typically appraised their interpersonal life tasks as far less threatening and more rewarding than their achievement life tasks, brought to bear self-concepts and plans that differed in content and in complexity when thinking about their social and academic activities and involvements at college, and reacted to discrepancies between their "actual" and "ideal" standards for personal performance in the two domains with opposite patterns of thoughts, feelings, and effort. Their "social" self-concepts indicated far more confidence and control over these life tasks than did their "student" self-concepts. Accordingly, they worried more about the achievement domain and had more detailed and intricately thought-through plans for how to handle those situations, as compared with their plans for social situations. Self-concept discrepancy seemed to serve as an inspiration to these students in the social domain, and as a debilitating reminder of anxiety in the achievement domain. For one group of (21) students, for example, activity, energy, and feelings of satisfaction experienced at an on-campus social event, were positively related to self-concept discrepancy (after Higgins, Klein, & Strauman, 1985) in their "social" self-concepts. In contrast, across the full longitudinal sample of 147 students (and for those same 21 students), self-concept discrepancy in their images of actual and ideal "student" self was strongly related to feelings of life stress and anxiety measured at the end of a college grading period. Moreover, these general patterns of life-task appraisal, self-evaluations, and performance strategies characterized the students' specific ("on-line") reactions to academic and social-life activity, as measured by experience sampling (Hormuth, 1986).

Additionally, within any one domain of life-task activity, different strategies emerged to characterize students' approaches to their shared life-task concerns. For example, whereas all the students appraised their achievement tasks as more threatening and less immediately rewarding than their interpersonal task activity, some students worked to cast as optimistic a light as possible on those academic pursuits, and other students—the ''defensive pessimists'' in the sample— seemed to actually emphasize, even exaggerate, the negative when facing achievement tasks. Each groups' strategic construction of the achievement-task context seemed to serve them well, as students in both groups initially maintained their excellent records of achievement; but the path to success differed markedly across these groups. The defensive pessimists did well to the extent that they reflected in detail about forthcoming hurdles in the achievement domain; so much so that for them, self-concept discrepancy in the ''student'' self domain was actually positively related to academic performance success. Optimists, in contrast, excelled by framing their achievement tasks in a relatively rosy light, and they did best when not reflecting much before these tasks and when the discrepancy between actual and ideal ''student'' self-concepts was only minimal. These students had strikingly different ways of handling their anxieties in the achievement domain, although their thoughts, feelings, and actions in the social life-task domain did not differ (see Cantor et al., 1987 for a detailed report of these data).

This portrait of shared life tasks and individualized strategies evoked in the transition to college life illustrates several general features of a social-intelligence assessment. Unlike the cognitive-styles tradition that precedes this work, we look for patterns of problem solving in social-life contexts that are highly specific to the nuances of those contexts and to the goals of the individuals as they face those particular life tasks. Adaptiveness is judged relative to the nature of the ''problems'' (as framed by the participants themselves) inherent in each context. As such, it is not necessarily ''good'' or ''bad'' to perceive self-concept discrepancy or to have complex plans across all life-task situations; the adaptiveness of this social intelligence depends on the particular demands that these individuals see in their social and achievement activity and on the specifics of their self-appraised expertise for handling those problems.

As one illustration of the relativity of standards for effective life task problem solving, consider the different role played by expectations, plans, and self-concept ideals in the case of optimists and defensive pessimists. As noted previously it is not always the case that reflecting in detail about the potential risks in a task, or setting seemingly unwarranted, low expectations for self-performance at a task, is always self-defeating—the utility of these strategic task constructions can only be judged in the context of the particular individual's ''problems'' in the situation at hand. For defensive pessimists in our studies (Norem & Cantor, 1986 a, b), it has been critical to their academic success that they are afforded the opportunity to ''harness'' anxiety by engaging in negative task construals and self-assessments of precisely this (counterintuitive) kind. Of course, the pessimists' strategy is not without its costs, for it is a stress-engendering one that takes a toll in other aspects of the pessimists' well-being, even while serving a positive function in the achievement domain (Cantor & Norem, 1988).

Each strategy has its own way of handling the shared aspects of these students' life tasks, and yet the key to the adaptiveness of these strategies is that they each also address the unique version of these shared achievement tasks, as cognitively constructed by the pessimists and the optimists. For optimists and defensive pessimists, the strategic process of task construal, effort modulation, and self-evaluation works in very different ways to maintain motivation, self-esteem, and successful task performance in achievement contexts.

A central feature of the social-intelligence framework for the analysis of personality is that it provides a set of criteria for judging "intelligence" that are importantly different from those applied before in the evaluation of the desirability of different cognitive styles. In this regard, one standard for intelligent action is whether the person can select and shape a living environment in which he or she can effectively carry out a preferred strategy, without incurring social censure or jeopardizing other personal goals. Defensive pessimists, for example, seem to find a comfortable social-support network of very close friends who apparently allow the pessimists to engage in "worst-case" anticipatory reflections without interference (Cantor & Norem, 1988). As such, the "pessimists" can embrace their rather odd but effective achievement strategy and still feel good about their social-life interactions. The same successful selection of a comfortable environment is not typically observed in the case of individuals who embrace a strategy of "self-focused depression" (e.g., Pyszczynski & Greenberg, 1987). In that case, the response of the social environment is often quite negative, perpetuating a debilitating cycle of self-censure for the "depressed" individual. This standard for intelligent action recognizes, therefore, the existence of considerable variation in strategy by environment fit: Some environments simply do not allow or reward some strategies; some strategies have very particular requirements for a comfortable environment. Individuals must, with some measure of self-awareness, find ways to maximize the match between their preferred strategies and their life environments.

A related criterion for "intelligent" action assesses the sensitivity to feedback, to the costs and benefits of embracing different strategies in different task contexts, which an individual exhibits. For example, although defensive pessimists seem quite aware of their need to find environments that will quietly support their preparatory cognitive work, they appear to be less consistently in tune with the potential costs (in emotional wear and tear and motivation) of continued use of such a confrontive, troubleshooting strategy. Defensive pessimists are good at finding ways to use their strategy, but they may well miss signals as to *overuse* of the strategy, with subsequent losses in life satisfaction, intrinsic task motivation, and, sometimes, even in performance itself (Norem, 1987). In fact, our longitudinal data suggest that over time defensive pessimism generates its own set of negative feedback in feelings of exhaustion, overpreparation, and stress, perhaps watering down any ultimate enjoyment of the achievement success (Cantor & Norem, 1988). In that respect, intelligent responding would dictate that the individual greatly restrict use of such a strategy to a select set of truly threatening and risky life-task events—an aspect of social intelligence that one suspects is not routinely exhibited.

SOCIAL CONCEPTS AND INTERPRETIVE RULES

From a cognitive point of view, the structure of personality is identified with the social intelligence repertoire used in interpersonal problem solving. Just as traditional approaches to personality are concerned with the nature and organization of personality traits and motives, so the cognitive approach is concerned with the nature and organization of social knowledge. In this way basic research on social cognition, once thought of as belonging to the domain of social psychology, becomes part and parcel of the psychology of personality. Defined in this way, however, one despairs of ever distilling personality structure into a few basic trait dimensions or type categories. Some simplification may be achieved by assuming a high degree of continuity between social and nonsocial knowledge—an assumption that is admittedly controversial (Lingle, Altom, & Medin, 1983; Ostrom, 1984; Zajonc, 1980a). So much work in social cognition is derived from the efforts of our nonsocial colleagues. However, there are reasons for thinking that the investigation of social cognition may reveal, or at least highlight, aspects of cognition in general that are obscured when social knowledge is ignored.

In keeping with the continuity assumption we have adopted the distinction, articulated in the nonsocial domain, between declarative and procedural knowledge. The social-intelligence repertoire contains both concepts about the social world and rules for manipulating and transforming this conceptual information, and putting it to work. For the present we confine ourselves to knowledge of others and the situations in which we encounter them; a later section is devoted to knowledge of ourselves.

Conceptual Knowledge of People, Situations, and Events

Building on the insights of Kelly (1955), we accord privileged status to the social concepts that organize our knowledge about kinds of people, situations, and events encountered in everyday life. The most familiar examples of such conceptual knowledge are social stereotypes based on race, gender, religious or ethnic background, and social status (Deaux & Lewis, 1984; Hamilton, 1981). They also include personality types such as workaholics and yuppies (Andersen & Klatzky, 1987; Cantor & Mischel, 1979), psychiatric diagnoses such as neurotic and psychopath (Cantor & Genero, 1986), broad classes of social situations such as dates and parties (Cantor, Mischel, & Schwartz, 1982; Pervin, 1976), trait-based categories of social behavior such as dominance and nurturance (Buss & Craik, 1983; Hampson, 1982), and generic scripts for social interactions

(Abelson, 1981; Forgas, 1982). (Social scripts are unique in the social-knowledge repertoire in that they have both declarative and procedural status: As declarative knowledge structures, they help us identify situations we find ourselves in and anticipate what will happen next; as procedural knowledge structures, they serve as guides to action.)

It is generally acknowledged that conceptual knowledge is not organized into proper sets, with singly necessary and jointly sufficient defining features, perfect vertical nesting and sharp horizontal boundaries, and homogeneity of instances. Social concepts, like natural concepts generally, comprise fuzzy sets, with central and peripheral characteristic features, imperfect nesting, variations in typicality, and heterogeneity of instances. Whereas there remains a dispute between prototype and exemplar forms of representation (Smith & Medin, 1981), we do not wish to take sides in this argument. Because exemplars can be imaginary, it seems reasonable to conclude that whether a concept is organized around a single prototype or multiple exemplars is an empirical question that must be answered anew for each particular case.

Although concepts about people, situations, and events are probably organized in a similar manner, they certainly differ with respect to content. Concepts of all kinds, of course, carry information concerning attributes that are characteristic of the category in question. Rather than being simple features lists, moreover, categories serve as schemata by preserving information about co-occurrence relations among these attributes—information that can serve as the basis for inference and prediction.

With respect to persons, these attributes are often expressed in terms of physical and psychological traits—for example, the "Big Five" of extraversion, agreeableness, conscientiousness, emotional stability, and culturedness (Norman, 1963). These broad trait dimensions might be considered "blind date questions"—the basic information that we would want about a stranger with whom we have to interact. Person categories also carry information about general evaluation, goals, and intentions (Hoffman, Mischel, & Mazze, 1981).

Whereas the study of social knowledge has traditionally focused on persons, more recently attention has turned to situations as well (Fredericksen, 1972; Moos, 1973). Situation categories contain information about the local physical environment, as well as the types of behaviors that are appropriate to the context: situations both constrain and elicit behavior (Price & Bouffard, 1974). They also carry affective and evaluative information. There is an interesting symmetry between person and situation categories, in that person categories contain information about the kinds of situations in which various types of people are likely to be found, whereas situation categories contain information about the kinds of people likely to be encountered in various settings (Cantor, Mischel, & Schwartz, 1982).

Our intuitive knowledge of persons and situations is united in our knowledge of interpersonal events—a knowledge that gives life to these otherwise static concepts (Zuroff, 1982). In navigating the social world, people are guided by their knowledge of typical interpersonal behaviors and common social tasks. Social events can be described in terms of the motives or needs that are involved in them, and the different social domains in which they are played out; the roles played by the various participants, the individual plans and scripts that they follow, and the norms that regulate their interactions (Trzebinski, McGlynn, Gray, & Tubbs, 1985). Event concepts also carry affective meaning, and their invocation is an occasion for emotional arousal (Fehr & Russell, 1984; Plutchik, 1980; Shaver, Schwartz, O'Connor, Kirson, Marsh, & Fischer, 1985). Some event concepts pertain to the mundane episodes and rituals that consume the everyday life and have clear and well-practiced behavioral scripts associated with them. Others concern more monumental activities, such as the "basic evolutionary tasks" of Plutchik (1980): establishing dominance and maintaining control (over something), exploring one's territory, finding out who we are and where we belong, and coping with separation and loss. These are less well-defined problems that admit of many different representations, and many different solutions. And these events are especially revealing of the individual's social intelligence.

As noted earlier, social concepts are structured as fuzzy sets organized around typical examples or summary prototypes (Holyoak & Gordon, 1984; Lingle et al., 1983; Smith & Medin, 1981). It seems possible that the representation of concepts may shift from exemplars to prototypes and (perhaps) back again, as a person accrues relevant social experience (e.g., Homa, Sterling, & Trepel, 1981). In any event, social concepts must be represented in such a way as to highlight the central tendency of the category but not obscure variability that characterizes its constituent instances—for the simple reason that people routinely make use of both types of information. The internal structure must also permit people to retrieve information (or make judgments about) the typicality of different category members.

Although social concepts contain information about the affective connotations of category members, most models represent this information in relatively cold, static form—as features linked to concepts (e.g., Bower, 1981). However, the activation of social concepts frequently evokes actual feelings in terms of specific patterns of vascular and motor activity. Recently, some models have argued for a more dynamic representation of affect—that is, as a set of motor procedures that will actually produce the corresponding emotion when a concept is activated in memory (Gilligan & Bower, 1984; Lang, 1979; Leventhal, 1984). In other words, "hot, wet" content may be represented directly in the formerly "cold, dry" conceptual structure (Zajonc & Markus, 1985). Such models remain to be fully developed, but the effort may result in a radical departure from the propositional, list-structure form often assumed in models of concept representation (Holyoak & Gordon, 1984).

Social construal is so complex because people must bring so many different concepts to bear when making sense of a particular person, situation, or event (Srull & Wyer, 1980). Therefore, it is important to consider the relations among concepts, both within and across these domains. Some of these relations within domains include level of abstraction, class inclusion, perceived similarity. Of particular interest, from the point of view of personality, are the idiosyncratic relations among concepts not generally thought to be related. These descriptive and evaluative associations derive from the person's unique experience (direct and vicarious) with the categories in question (Wyer & Srull, 1981). They cannot be predicted from the dictionary or common meanings of the category labels, and they are the basis for many of the surprises and misunderstandings that occur in social intercourse.

An important question in both social and nonsocial domains concerns the existence of a preferred or basic level of categorization: Is there a level, somewhere in the tangled hierarchy of superordinate and subordinate concepts, that provides particularly rich, distinctive, vivid, and easily accessible category labels for social entities (Hampson, John, & Goldberg, 1986)? Probably not. The preferred level of categorization necessarily depends on the individual's processing goals, as well as his or her particular areas of expertise and ignorance. Nevertheless, something about "basic levels" seems right. Individuals do seem to have preferred levels of categorization, even if these levels are not widely shared. Perhaps, in turn, analysis of these preferred levels can serve as the basis for describing the expertise and processing goals that characterize the individual in their respective domains.

Person and situation concepts have implications for each other, and both have implications for behavior. Therefore it is also important to examine the relations among concepts across as well as within domains. Concepts from the three domains may be united by virtue of their shared association with different life tasks. For example, dominance tasks involve, among other things, power-hungry people, the settings where interpersonal conflict occurs, and the ways in which conflict is displayed and resolved. Accordingly, a key to understanding the tangled webs of people's individual social-knowledge repertoires is to understand the life tasks that they confront.

The uniqueness of life experiences and of life tasks raises the problem of individual differences in social concepts and how they are to be construed. As Kelly (1955) pointed out, individuals differ in their construals in large part because they differ in the content and organization of their personal construct systems. One way to characterize these individual differences, as noted earlier, is in cognitive complexity (e.g., Linville, 1985). Another way is in social expertise (Showers & Cantor, 1985). Expertise may be manifested in the degree to which particular concepts are elaborated within the declarative knowledge system, greater elaboration permitting the person to make finer distinctions; in the number of levels available in the hierarchy within various domains, more levels permitting more flexibility in construal; and in the number of links across conceptual domains, a greater density of connections permitting the person to see the implications of various social entities for his or her current life tasks.

Interpretive Rules in Social Construal

In addition to social concepts, the social-intelligence repertoire consists of the interpretive rules by which we make sense of social experience. However, although people can often articulate their declarative knowledge of the social world, we seem to have little or no direct introspective access to procedural knowledge (Kihlstrom, 1984; Nasby & Kihlstrom, 1986). A major portion of research within cognitive social psychology is devoted to uncovering the implicit rules that govern social categorization (Cantor & Mischel, 1979), inferences concerning dispositional traits and emotional states (Jones & Davis, 1965; Shaver et al., 1985; Weiner, Frieze, Kukla, Reed, Rest, & Rosenbaum, 1972), evaluating likability (Anderson, 1974; Fiske & Pavelchak, 1986), making attributions of causality (Kelley, 1967, 1972) and other judgments (Nisbett & Ross, 1980), testing hypotheses (Skov & Sherman, 1986; Snyder, 1981b), and processing social memories (Hastie, 1981).

The earliest research in this domain appeared to suggest that procedural knowledge involves fairly extensive information integration and complicated calculations—as in Anderson's cognitive algebra or Kelly's ANOVA cube. More recently, however, the field has recognized the degree to which people may deviate from potentially time-consuming algorithms and rely instead on more efficient shortcuts, as in Tversky and Kahneman's (1974) quartet of heuristics: representativeness, availability, simulation, and anchoring. Such procedural economies have now been identified in practically every domain of social perception, memory, and judgment (Nisbett & Ross, 1980). The field has also come to appreciate the liabilities associated with the use of judgmental heuristics, as exemplified by the "fundamental attribution error" (Ross, 1977). Nevertheless, on balance these heuristic principles appear to serve us rather well, as evidenced by the frequency with which they are used (Miller & Cantor, 1982). The paradox of social judgment is that people get along rather well with procedures that, in normative terms, are nonoptimal and prone to bias and error.

It may be, as some have suggested, that a reliance on heuristic principles signals a lapse of normative rationality, and our poor ability to test hypotheses effectively prevents us from becoming aware of our errors. It may also be that this reliance is dictated by the nature of the declarative knowledge base on which procedural knowledge must operate. The network of social knowledge is very rich, but it is also very tangled and sports many informational gaps. Moreover, the variability of human social behavior presents the observer with stimulus information that is often fragmentary, inconsistent, and ambiguous. Under these circumstances it might be inordinately time-consuming to have to analyze all the possibilities and implications, and more efficient instead to render a quick judgment—especially if there are few important consequences of making a mistake (Hogarth, 1981).

Now that many judgmental heuristics have been identified, the major task remains to determine the circumstances in which they are evoked, and the actual consequences of overreliance on them (e.g., Borgida & Howard-Pitney, 1983). Our reading of the literature in several different areas suggests that certain shortcut procedures are often quite efficient modes of social information processing. For example, in the face of a continuously shifting social episode, it may be adaptive to deploy attention away from a person who is behaving in accordance with expectations. Reliance on inferential activity to fill in the resultant memory gaps may occasionally lead to judgmental error, but it will also free processing resources for use in the event that something surprising occurs (Hastie, 1984; White & Carlston, 1983).

Whereas most social psychological research has examined the general processes underlying social perception, memory, and judgment, some investigators have begun to document consistent individual differences in the manner in which people process social information. In addition to the literature on attributional style and complexity (Fletcher et al., 1986; Metalsky & Abramson, 1981), there have been studies of evaluative styles (Ostrom & Davis, 1979), styles of attentional focus (Carver & Scheier, 1981), and coping styles (Miller & Mangan, 1983). The link to the earlier literature on cognitive styles is tempting. Nevertheless, it is important to note that the more recent work does not employ tasks lacking social content to make predictions about personality and social behavior. Rather, the instruments by which these individual differences are assessed make explicit (and usually exclusive) reference to social content. Moreover, some of the new processing styles pertain to rather narrow domains, rather than possessing trait-like generality across situations.

One important dimension of procedural individual differences concerns the degree of effort required to invoke various processing routines. By virtue of extended practice, some procedures become automatic and effortless. They are invariably invoked by certain environmental events, and their execution consumes little or no processing capacity. Automaticity in the procedural domain, like elaboration in the declarative, is an index of differential expertise. Experts may also differ in their tendency to utilize diagnostic information when it is available, rather than relying on stereotypes and other abstract categorical knowledge (Higgins & Bryant, 1982; Linville & Jones, 1980); and in the intensity of their response to social events (Linville, 1982).

A final dimension is personal involvement. Under conditions of low motivation, involvement, or commitment people may be content to rely on judgmental heuristics and other processing shortcuts. Involved, motivated, committed people may perform more careful, systematic cognitive analyses of events (Borgida & Brekke, 1981; Borgida & Howard-Pitney, 1983). Of course, from a social-cognitive point of view people cannot be characterized as more or less motivated, involved, or committed *in general*. Rather, these features will vary according to the setting in which the person is observed. As in the domain of declarative knowledge, procedural expertise, context, and pragmatics are closely linked.

SELF-KNOWLEDGE AND SELF-REFLECTION

The cognitive basis of personality is found in the mental structures that represent information about persons, situations, and events, and the mental processes that operate on them in the course of adaptive problem solving. Although oneself is a person like other people, the self also has a special status, being subject and object simultaneously; that is, personality involves mental representations of the self as well as others, but it is the self that is doing the representing. Because of this special status, the self deserves separate treatment.

Knowledge about the self can be classified in the same manner as other knowledge: declarative and procedural, episodic and semantic (Kihlstrom & Cantor, 1984; Kihlstrom, Cantor, Albright, Chew, Klein, & Niedenthal, 1988). Semantic self-knowledge is what is generally meant by the self-concept: It is the mental representation of one's own personality—and, we might add, one's own body. Episodic self-knowledge consists of the continuous record of auto-biographical memory. Procedural self-knowledge includes the skills, rules, and strategies that we employ to process information about ourselves.

Concepts of the Self

The self-concept is the person's mental representation of his or her own personality, but it is selective and not an exhaustive list of features. A number of theorists have attempted to characterize this selectivity by asserting that the self includes only stable characteristics (Snygg & Combs, 1949), those over which the person has control (Rogers, 1951), or those that are generalized across situational contexts (Allport, 1955). Based on recent theories of categorization, however, we can say that the self-concept qua concept consists of those features that distinguish oneself from other people—that is, features that are highly characteristic of oneself but not highly characteristic of others. This means that the self-concept encodes the uniqueness of the personality that it represents. One implication of this point of view is that people actively construct their self-concepts by comparing themselves to others (McGuire, 1984). Another is that the self-concept encodes only those personality features of which the individual is aware—although nonconscious self-concepts may be observed in certain forms of psychopathology such as fugue or multiple personality (Kihlstrom, 1984).

Traditional approaches generally assume that the self is a unitary structure—a kind of "one person, one self" rule. However, some social psychologists have raised the possibility that each person has many selves, corresponding to different social roles or contexts (Cooley, 1902; Gergen, 1971; Mead, 1934; Sarbin, 1952). Our view of the self as a concept leads us to endorse a version of the multiplicity view. Natural concepts are arranged in hierarchies, and if the self functions as a concept it must also be part of a hierarchy. Of course, the unitary self could be one element in a hierarchy of persons. But we suspect that there is a tangled hierarchy of selves, each specific to a different situational context. There is no reason to think that the self-concept does not incorporate information about the discriminativeness and flexibility of the person's social behavior. Furthermore, the self includes not only those features that comprise the personality—the actual self—but also those features that the person wants to have—the ideal self—as well as those that others want the person to have—the ought self (Higgins, Strauman, & Klein, 1986). Possible selves are objects of both hope and fear, and they lend a strong motivational quality to the self-concept (Markus & Nurius, 1986). Finally, great diversity is given to the self-concept by the availability of autobiographical memory, which provides the possibility for retaining mental representations of oneself at different periods of life.

The multiplicity of selves does not mean that the self is fragmentary or incoherent. The self is a family of selves, related to each other through family resemblance: each self shares some feature overlap with other selves (Rosenberg & Gara, 1985). The unity of self comes from these overlapping resemblances. Some selves may be central, by which we mean that they share many features with other selves; others may be peripheral, sharing relatively few features. Further, at least in well-adjusted individuals, there may be considerable overlap between the actual, ideal, and ought selves. A sense of unity may also be given by the existence of a basic level of self-conception—that is, a level at which people prefer to focus their self-awareness. Alternatively, at the very top of the hierarchy there may well be a superordinate self-concept whose features show the most overlap across the various context- and epoch-specific selves. Further unity to the self is given by the autobiographical record, which preserves the transitions from one self to another and provides the person with memories of the actions and experiences of his or her various selves: This continuous autobiographical record is what is missing in fugue, multiple personality, and other cases of the divided self (Kihlstrom, 1984).

The self-concept raises the same questions concerning internal structure and interconcept organization that were addressed in our discussion of other people. Again, we feel that there is no reason to take a position in the exemplar-prototype debate; but for purposes of simplicity we assume that each entry in the self-concept repertoire is a summary prototype abstracted from memories of the self in specific situations and at specific times. The features of this prototype are those that distinguish (or, more properly, are perceived as distinguishing) oneself from others in that setting (McGuire & Padawer-Singer, 1976). The extent to which these self-concepts are elaborated is determined by the amount of experience in relevant settings, and by the amount of processing devoted to the task of distinguishing self from others.

As noted earlier, not all attributes of personality feature in the self-concept, and the features linked to the self-concept vary in centrality. A person is self-schematic with respect to some feature when he or she defines that feature as somehow important to his or her own self-concept. Self-schematic (Markus, 1977) features are, obviously, central features of the self-concept; they may also be features of the "prototypical" self and figure prominently at the "basic" level of the self-concept hierarchy. Viewed in terms of associative network theory, self-schematic features are those linked directly to the node representing the self, permitting rapid access without intervening inferential activity (Kihlstrom & Cantor, 1984; Kihlstrom et al., 1988).

Like social behavior itself, the self is flexible. Of all the available self-concepts, only one—the working self-concept (Markus & Nurius, 1986)—will be the focus of attention at any particular time. Precisely which self is activated may be determined by personal goals—the life tasks that the person confronts at any particular time. In addition, certain self-concepts may be primed by contextual cues in the immediate social setting (Bargh, 1982). Alienation may occur when a person is forced to adopt a view of self that is nonpreferred or inconvenient. By the same token, flexibility in self-construal permits people to try out new identities in various situations. Throughout, however, the prototypical or basic-level self may serve as an anchor in a variety of social interactions (Lewicki, 1984).

Memories of the Self

Although psychologists have been studying episodic memory since the time of Ebbinghaus (Tulving, 1972), we know surprisingly little about the structure and organization of the continuous record of autobiographical memory (Neisser, 1982). In principle, episodic memories contain three different types of information: a raw description of some event in the person's history; a description of the spatiotemporal context in which that event occurred; and some reference to the self as the agent or experiencer of that event. Personal recollections tend to be hot and wet rather than cold and dry: They often involve vivid images and feelings that are lacking in the raw factual material drawn up from semantic memory. Consider, for example, our remarkably vivid and detailed flashbulb memories that preserve highly salient, unexpected, emotionally arousing events (Brown & Kulik, 1977). Of course, not all autobiographical memories have all these features: It often occurs that we remember something that we cannot date or locate precisely; and we may be uncertain whether something actually happened or we merely imagined it. And not all personal experiences are recorded in auto-biographical memory, as indicated by the childhood amnesia that typically covers the first 5 to 7 years of life (Kihlstrom & Harackiewicz, 1982).

The contextual specificity of autobiographical memory gives it an organizational structure that is lacking in purely semantic memory; that is, autobiographical memory is temporally organized to provide a sense of continuity across the life-span (Kihlstrom & Evans, 1979). This is not to say that one's personal recollections are encoded in an unbroken stream, like a videotape. The temporal stream may well be segmented into salient epochs marked by salient transitions—for example, entering school (Brim & Ryff, 1980; Cohler, 1982). But temporal sequencing does not preclude other schemes from organizing memory as well. Events may be categorized by the contexts in which they occurred, the personality traits they exemplified, the feelings they evoked, or the goals they served. In any case, there seems to be a sense of narrative integrity to auto-biographical memory, with people able to reflect on the beginning, middle, and potential end of their life stories. Gaps in the record may be filled in, and other events set aside, to enhance the person's sense of continuity (Greenwald, 1980). One's history, however inchoate it may appear at the moment, makes sense in retrospect: Whereas it may have a linear component, the personal narrative is also woven around personal goals and life tasks (Levinson, 1978; Valliant & McArthur, 1972). Far from being an unbiased record, autobiographical memory is an important clue to what the person considers to be important in his or her own life. The subjective history of the personality is the personality (Murray, 1938).

Interpretive Rules for Self-Reflection

Finally we turn to procedural aspects of selfhood: the skills, rules, and strategies employed in processing information about oneself. Some of these procedures have already been touched on in our discussion of the semantic and episodic aspects of declarative self-knowledge. For example, we seem to selectively encode those aspects of ourselves that distinguish us from others (McGuire & Padawer-Singer, 1976). We tend to ignore or reconstrue information that is incongruent and focus on information that is congruent, with our preferred self-concepts (Markus, 1977). We tend to focus on information and events with positive rather than negative emotional connotations (Matlin & Stang, 1978). A number of processing strategies are revealed in self-evaluation—whether in the literature on the self–other differences in causal attribution (Jones & Nisbett, 1972), self-efficacy (Bandura, 1977a, 1982), social comparison (Tabachnik, Crocker, & Alloy, 1983), self-evaluation maintenance (Tesser & Campbell, 1983), and the various illusions that surround the self (Alloy & Abramson, 1979; Lewinsohn, Mischel, Chaplain, & Barton, 1980).

A question remains whether any of this procedural knowledge is unique to the self. The same processing principles might apply to any other person whom we liked, and with whom we were intimately familiar. A case in point is the self-reference effect in memory (Greenwald, 1981; Kihlstrom, 1981; Kuiper & Derry, 1981; Rogers, 1981), which was once thought to indicate that the self was a uniquely rich and elaborate memory structure. It now appears that the self-reference effect has little specifically to do with either the self as a memory structure or self-reference as a processing strategy but rather reflects more familiar principles of organization and elaboration (for reviews see Kihlstrom et al., 1988; Klein & Kihlstrom, 1986).

One feature of self-knowledge that is distinctive results from our privileged access to information about our own internal thoughts and feelings, as well as the availability of memories from our personal past. Although there are limitations on this access (Nisbett & Wilson, 1977), and the information retrieved is not always reliable (Greenwald, 1980), there is growing evidence that people make use of their privileged data base of self-knowledge when making judgments and inferences about themselves (e.g., Andersen, 1984; Andersen & Ross, 1984). For example, one reason for the actor–observer difference in causal attribution may be that people have access to more information about the contextual variability of their own behavior than is available to an external observer; alternatively, people may act on their awareness of discrepancies between situational constraints and their own internal goals and intentions. But access does not require use. There appear to be marked individual differences in the focus of attention toward, or away from, the internal, subjective self (Carver & Scheier, 1981; Snyder, 1979).

LIFE TASKS AND PROBLEM-SOLVING STRATEGIES

Social knowledge is employed in interpreting and solving life tasks, and these life tasks provide the unit of analysis in understanding the application of social intelligence in everyday problem solving. Some life tasks are freely undertaken, others are imposed on us by our life situations, but all are highly salient, attention-consuming problems that possess motivational properties for individuals and offer goal states around which large portions of life are organized (Klinger, 1975, 1977). Thus, the life task of "being productive at work" may be a self-imposed "desire," whereas the "demand" of "getting tenure" is a salient, institutionally imposed life task for most academicians (Reich & Zautra, 1983). As a starting position, we assume that these life tasks are relatively accessible to awareness, although people do not think about them all the time, and they may need some help in articulating them. Life tasks vary from long-term, abstract goals to short-term, concrete ones: Effective research depends on selecting tasks of appropriate size for analysis (Goldfried, 1983; McFall, 1982). Some life tasks of territoriality, identity, hierarchy, and safety may well be universal, whereas others may be specific to particular cultures or subcultures (cf. Plutchik, 1980; Veroff, 1983); each individual, of course frames these shared life tasks in a unique manner. If we are lucky, they do not become full-fledged crises. As ill-defined problems, however, they admit of many different solutions, all potentially acceptable from the point of view of adaptation.

Some theorists have argued that there exists a set of universally experienced psychological needs that motivate goal-directed human behavior. Accordingly, everyone works on the same life tasks throughout their lives, although there are individual differences in the salience of various categories of needs and goals (Maslow, 1968; Murray, 1938; Plutchik, 1980; Rogers, 1951; Rotter, 1954). Others have argued that life tasks are linked to stages or epochs in the life-span (Erikson, 1950; Levinson, 1978). We are particularly interested in those life tasks that confront us at particular epochs in the life course; tasks for the recent retiree, for example, of "enjoying leisure time," "feeling connected to people," "finding 'jobs' to do" (Ryff, 1982). These seem to provide an appropriate balance of characteristics for research purposes: They are relatively universal, relatively significant, relatively concrete, relatively enduring, relatively frequent in appearance.

The concept of life task is not new with us. One of its origins is Adler's (1931) notion of "style of life," by which he meant the individual's characteristic pattern of approach to feelings of inferiority. Another is Klinger's (1977) concept of "current concerns": the goals to which people commit themselves, and which give meaning to their lives. More recently, Little (1983) has developed the concept of "personal projects," around which people organize their daily lives. Little asserts: "A personal project is a set of interrelated acts extending over time, which is intended to maintain or attain a state of affairs foreseen by the individual" (pp. 276). Similarly, Emmons (1986) has investigated "personal strivings," such as "finding intimacy" or "being less competitive," that provide future-states towards which individuals strive. Individuals select their personal strivings or projects, but these selections are constrained by the opportunities afforded them by their environments. Still, most people have a wide range of options available to them, and their choices both reveal and shape their personalities.

A person's current life tasks may be defined as those that the person perceives to be central and important to him or herself during a specified period in life (Cantor & Kihlstrom, 1985b, 1987). They are defined by individuals themselves as self-relevant, time consuming, and meaningful: They cannot be defined for individuals by external authorities. Nevertheless, life tasks are responsive to the structures, demands, and constraints of the social environment. In fact, such tasks, by their very nature, tend to crop up at particular periods in the person's life. Times of life transition into new age subcultures or new social relationships provide an impetus to the individual to reconsider his or her pressing concerns (Veroff, 1983). When the school-age child becomes the high school adolescent, there are new expectations of "future careers" and "close relationships" to embrace (Higgins & Parsons, 1983). Similarly, joining the marriage partnership cannot help but force on one a host of salient life tasks; those that vary from the mundane chores of "financial management" to the existential tasks of "achieving equity in the relationship." Still, although external and uncontrollable factors of social development may pose tasks for people, individuals still do select those that they will solve, and in what order.

If infancy prepares the child for working intentionally toward self-understanding (Kopp, 1982), then childhood prepares the adolescent for selecting and defining his or her own life tasks (Harter, 1983). With an organized and differentiated self-awareness, the adolescent has what it takes to turn shared demands into personal projects. Adolescents (at least late adolescents!) are able to use themselves as reference points without imposing their own perspectives on others (Bannister & Agnew, 1977; Higgins, 1981); they are able to see themselves as others do, or might (Nicholls, 1984), and to evaluate themselves as they might other people (Ruble & Rholes, 1981). Their feelings of self-efficacy are highly differentiated, and they are able to reflect on the logic and appropriateness of their own internal processes (Flavell & Ross, 1981). With these skills in hand, adolescents are able to confront their age-graded normative tasks. Having spent so many years of social learning, they are exceptionally well versed in the demands of their family, peer, and school cultures; and they know enough about themselves to want a uniquely defining set of life tasks. The late adolescent seems ready to be an intentional social problem solver, ready to construct and achieve and avoid his or her own cherished set of possible selves (Markus & Nurius, 1986).

Social Learning and Life-Task Choices

The study of life-task problem solving involves therefore the interplay between environmentally and biologically given tasks, and the individual's own version of those shared demands as he or she actually experiences them. In this regard, it is critical to acknowledge our cognitive-social-learning orientation: Social interactions provide the context in which social intelligence is acquired and life tasks are selected and negotiated, and this principle extends even to the earliest exchanges between parent and infant (Hay, 1986). Bruner (1981), for example, has shown how mothers pose ever more complex developmental tasks of role playing, intentionality, and self-correction, by speaking to their toddlers in language that is always just one step beyond the current expertise of the child (see Vygotsky, 1962)—social environments keep even the youngest of children goal directed and channel their energy towards the "right" life tasks. And, despite Piaget's emphasis on egocentricity, even very young children are responsive to the goals and values of their parents; as Rheingold (1982) has demonstrated in her insightful analysis of the beginnings of prosocial behavior in little children's participation in household chores. For older children and young adults, as Higgins and Parsons (1983) suggest, the messages as to age-appropriate life tasks are much less subtle—practically all adolescents know that they are supposed to be "struggling to achieve an independent identity," even before they read it in the popular press or see it portrayed on "family ties." As Bandura (1977b) outlined, children learn a great deal in a very short period of time about the morays of their culture, from a diverse set of messages provided through direct and indirect tutelage.

Whereas it is in fashion these days to take some of the burden (of social tutelage) off parental caregivers and teachers and peer models by stressing the biological and genetic basis of personality development (Goldsmith, 1983), it is wise not to forget that the social environment has the power to solidify and even exaggerate those behavioral tendencies in the process of "teaching" individuals about themselves. Patterns of individual differences in temperament and in gender differentiation are likely candidates for such social influence because there exist widely shared implicit theories about the behavioral correlates of infant reactivity (see Lewontin, Rose, & Kamin, 1984) and of gender (Frieze et al., 1978). These social influences are especially important in the present account of life-task problem solving precisely because parents and teachers and peers can "help" to pose the child's life tasks by their emphasis on certain features of personality that they presume to be givens for that person. The child who is constantly told that he or she is "naturally" high strung will likely look for outlets for that energy in tasks that are compatible with this personality. Significant figures in a social environment sometimes strongly shape behavior simply by their messages about the tasks for which a person is so "uniquely" well suited!

There is one major way in which the social-intelligence perspective, as a cognitive-social learning theory, does very definitely relieve parents and teachers and peers of the onus in individuals' choices of life tasks to embrace. Consistent with literature on cognitive-social development (e.g., Higgins, Ruble, & Hartup, 1983), we assume that the child (and adolescent and adult) plays an active and selective role in his or her own social learning (Bandura, 1977b, 1986). There is, for example, rarely complete overlap between the child's "theory of self" and the parents' view of their child's personality, intelligence, and life goals (Harter, 1983). Individuals develop their own reading of their life experience, self-attributes, and the values of their subculture, and those autobiographical narratives (Cohler, 1982) and self-theories (Epstein, 1973) are the critical forces behind their choices of tasks to pursue. The social environment can lay out the possibilities, but the individual does the ultimate selecting, with or without full awareness of that responsibility. The highly able child, in a family of achievement-oriented parents and siblings, who persists in viewing his or her successful performances as reflective of effort rather than of ability (Phillips, 1984), is unlikely to gravitate towards high-pressure achievement life tasks, even in the face of parental messages to the contrary. That "obstinate" child may well have developed a personal theory of intelligence—one that construes intelligence to be a fixed entity, perhaps—such that pursuit of those highly valued life-task goals is believed to lead to a punishing dead end (Dweck, 1986). In this way, a more complete account of individual's choices of life tasks resides in their theories and perceptions of self and of others, the autobiographical baggage that sets the tone for how they address those environmentally and biologically given life tasks.

Uncovering Life Tasks

The possibilities for alternative readings of life tasks present both advantages and disadvantages for empirical analysis of personality, as many have noted. One clear disadvantage is that it is easy to become overwhelmed with the idiographic complexity of individuals' unique construals and difficult to find simplifying dimensions that capture the richness of those personal construals. Several solutions to this idiographic/nomothetic dilemma are currently being pursued, with reasonable success. Typically, the aim is to find a group of people who, at some level, share a common task or problem or goal in a particular environment, and then to see how individuals within the group diverge in their specific construals of, and strategies for handling, the problem to be addressed. In our own work, for example, we have chosen to study life tasks in periods of life transition, in the hopes that times of transition present individuals with relatively clear normative demands, such as the message experienced by most first-year college students to "be independent" and to "carve a career goal" (Cantor et al., 1987; see also, Stewart & Healy, 1985; Veroff, 1983). In a similar vein, Oyserman and Markus (1987) have studied the possible selves of a group of juvenile delinquents coping with the shared burden of enforced detention; whereas Fincham and his colleagues (e.g., Fincham, Beach, & Nelson, 1987) have investigated differences in couples' construals of their marriage situation, holding relatively constant certain basic parameters of the interpersonal intimacy context.

Another familiar hurdle posed by the multiplicity and complexity of construals is that individuals will not always be able to, or find it easy to, report on "problems" to which their efforts are addressed in any given context. One way around the limitations of introspective access is to use methods that are not directly dependent on self-reports of task construal. In this regard, Eric Klinger's work on current concerns, in which he analyzes the focus of attention, fantasy life, and conversations that tap into the incentives that motivate action for different individuals in similar situations, is a model program of research (Klinger, 1975, 1977). Similarly, Higgins and his colleagues (e.g., Higgins, King, & Mavin, 1982) have used nonobvious priming techniques and free-recall measures to make inferences about individuals' chronically accessible constructs. Another approach to this obstacle in the investigation of life tasks is to combine data on self-articulated tasks or constructs or projects with data gathered from experience-sampling studies in which on-line behavior, mood, and activity reports can serve as a validity check on self-reports collected "out of context" (Hormuth, 1986). Emmon's (1986) work on personal strivings, as well as our own investigations of the life-task activity of college students, suggests that experience-sampling techniques are very useful in mapping the goal-directed activity of individuals.

Cantor et al. (1987) found six categories of life-task activities—"making friends," "being on own," "working on identity," "getting good grades," "choosing a career," "handling time-management"—that accounted for 88% of the activities reported by their college student sample in an experience-sampling study. Moreover, the students' mood–emotion profiles in different activity contexts reported in the experience-sampling study converged with life-task appraisals that they had provided one year earlier: achievement life tasks were appraised in general as much more stressful and threatening than were social-life tasks, and the on-line mood reports paralleled those appraisals. The convergence between life-task appraisals and on-line mood reports was also strong with regard to patterns of individual differences—defensive pessimists, for example, who appraised their achievement life tasks as especially more threatening than their social-life tasks also showed significantly greater mood variability than did optimists in the experience-sampling study (Cantor & Norem, 1988). Such methods are especially effective in capturing fluctuations in mood and appraisal over time and across situations; providing a window on the dynamics of person-in-situation interactions (e.g., Larsen, 1987).

Strategies for Problem Solving in Life Tasks

Analyzing personality in terms of life tasks permits the investigator to draw on concepts familiar in the literature on nonsocial problem solving (Abelson, 1981; Gagne, 1984). Each life task begins at some starting state; there is some goal state to be attained; and there are operations that will move the individual from Point A to Point B, usually by proceeding through a hierarchy of subgoals. A critical feature of this approach is that it also encourages an emphasis on *processes* that translate those goals into action in specific situations. Individuals' construals of situations in terms of personal projects or current concerns or life tasks set up problems to be addressed, from which strategies of action follow to insure preferred outcomes and insure against undesirable outcomes (Bruner, Goodnow, & Austin, 1956; Showers & Cantor, 1985).

Cognitive strategies, as patterns of thoughts, feelings, and effort, before, during, and after events, serve as important guides to action in many arenas of personality functioning (Kuhl & Beckmann, 1985). For example, cognitive strategies, such as those that characterize illusory-glow optimism or self-handicapping or self-focused depression, play a significant role in achievement behavior

(Norem & Cantor, 1986a, b; C. R. Snyder, 1985) and often set the tone for important interpersonal interactions (Pyszczynski & Greenberg, 1987). These strategies involve both interpreting the problem and planning the solution. Problem-solving strategies involve the coordination of declarative and procedural knowledge.

One of the most common ways in which people begin working on a problem is to simulate a number of possible outcomes or endstates (D'Zurilla & Nezu, 1980; Kahneman & Tversky, 1982). As the simulation unfolds various hypotheses may be tested—often by searching autobiographical memory for similar episodes in one's own past, or by searching semantic memory for comparable situations about which something is known. After playing through several outcomes, one may formulate a plan, carry it into action, and monitor the results (Spivak, Platt, & Shure, 1976). Sometimes, of course, this process of anticipatory strategizing is actually reversed: A person finds him or herself having performed a particular strategy that in turn leads then to the acknowledgment of an "appropriate" goal (Vallacher & Wegner, 1985). In any case, the challenges involved in planning social interaction are increased by the fact that others may not cooperate, requiring frequent revisions. In contrast to nonsocial problem solving, social problem solving is inherently interactive: Each participant's plans must be coordinated with the others'. Things are guaranteed to run smoothly only when all participants are executing well-defined scripts—in which case, of course, little or no planning is needed.

Throughout the social problem-solving cycle each person has to monitor the success of his or her plans, the discrepancy between intended goals and actual outcomes, and the responses of the other people involved (D'Zurilla & Goldfried, 1971). The monitoring process is complicated by the richness of even mundane social interactions: There is so much to attend to, including the costs as well as the benefits associated with potential outcomes, and the fluctuating values attached to various goals. Much of the cognitive activity that occurs during problem solving involves understanding the causes of the various behaviors observed, evaluating the person's level of control over outcomes, and reviewing past events that are similar to the current situation. The demands of these activities can be reduced considerably by various heuristics and other shortcut procedures. Accordingly, people may develop habitual strategies for allocating resources to various sources of information, or they may learn to shift attention back and forth between sources. Of course, as various procedures become highly practiced, progressively fewer attentional resources are required, and much monitoring can proceed outside of conscious awareness (Kihlstrom, 1984).

Nevertheless, it is also very effective, as a self-regulatory aid, to maintain heightened self-awareness in key problem-solving contexts (Duval & Wicklund, 1972). Despite the existence of individual differences in self-awareness (Fenigstein, Scheier, & Buss, 1975; Snyder, 1979), self-awareness can also be increased for everyone by arranging to be reminded of a particular intention

(Abelson, 1982; Fazio & Zanna, 1978); by selectively inhabiting situations that are closely related to one's self-concept (Markus, 1983), or by creating a critical audience—either in fact or in fantasy (Baldwin & Holmes, 1987). When people fail to reach their goals, they may engage in symbolic self-completion, finding alternative outlets through which to solidify a treasured identity, attitude, or skill (Gollwitzer & Wicklund, 1985). Kuhl (1985) describes a set of such self-regulatory strategies that people can use in action control, maintaining intentions in the face of obstacles and competing interests by, for example, enlisting social support for one's objectives or observing "stop-rules" that prevent endless rumination and instead provoke action. In many contexts, there is this need for conscious self-regulation to "keep on track," and to stay away from distractions or debilitating cycles of self-criticism (Nolen-Hoeksema, 1987).

Although the strategies just described lead to successful self-regulation, a number of other processes can lead to failure (we leave aside those failures that are due to low motivation or uncontrollable contingencies). Intentional self-control can be broken down when the person relies mindlessly on familiar, automatized patterns (Langer, 1987; cf. Langer & Piper, 1987). On other occasions, the person's own thoughts or mood can interfere with performance (Kuhl, 1985; Salovey & Rodin, 1985). Negative mood states are especially disruptive (Carver & Scheier, 1981), especially when they reinforce negative views of self and self-efficacy. Conditions that encourage external orientations and focus on performance evaluation can also diminish feelings of competence and self-efficacy (Deci & Ryan, 1980; Harackiewicz, Manderlink, & Sansone, 1984). Finally, the motivation for intentional self-regulation can be impaired when people perceive obstacles to be insurmountable or events to be uncontrollable. Such conditions, when combined with a proclivity for rumination, self-focus, or self-defeating attributions, may lead to depression and withdrawal of effort (Abramson, Seligman, & Teasdale, 1978; Peterson & Seligman, 1984; Pyszczynski & Greenberg, 1987).

Individual Differences in Preferred Strategies

Another way in which people can reduce the cognitive demands of life-task problem solving is by relying on a small number of preferred strategies. Such reliance obviously obviates the need to solve each problem anew. Analyses of achievement behavior offer a good opportunity for observing these kinds of individual differences (Dweck, 1983; Klinger, 1977; Nicholls, 1984; Weiner, 1985). Most achievement situations invoke competing goals—succeeding at the task, or at least avoiding failure, are the most obvious; others involve enhancing feelings of competence or self-esteem. The relative salience of these goals will differ from problem to problem; but once evoked, they may lead to consistent patterns of goal-directed activity.

Perhaps the most commonly described strategy is optimism based on positive past experiences and the desire to support a self-image of high competence. The confident optimist selects tests carefully to maximize not just the probability of success but also the diagnosticity of success with regard to true ability (Jones & Pittman, 1982; Trope, 1986). Having selected a task in light of expected outcome and its attributional consequences, the optimist must then adjust his or her effort in response to actual progress and ultimately cope with actual success or failure by asserting or denying personal control over the outcome. In other contexts, the desire to protect a sense of competence may overwhelm the desire to attain success. In this case, some self-protective strategies are available to cushion blows to self-esteem before the fact (Showers & Cantor, 1985)—for example, self-handicapping (Jones & Berglas, 1978) and defensive pessimism (Norem & Cantor, 1986a, b). Self-handicapping and defensive pessimism do not lead people to be happy or satisfied with failure. Nevertheless, self-handicapping will enhance self-esteem in the event of success, whereas defensive pessimism may motivate increased effort. Thus, even though they look self-defeating, both strategies may reflect quite adaptive problem-solving behavior.

In this regard, cognitive strategies are best viewed as *patterns* of cognition–effort–action that follow from characteristic construals of particular situations as presenting particular problems, rather than as isolated tendencies to make certain kinds of interpretations or attributions. Illusory glow optimism, for example, involves the following cognitive maneuvers that present the self in a rather rosy light as well as maintaining perceptions of control and motivation for a task: positive self-appraisals and expectations, self-serving excuses, strategic effort withdrawal, self-enhancing performance evaluations and attributions (Taylor & Brown, 1988). Defensive pessimism, in contrast, seems also to be an effective strategy for handling achievement pressures, but it follows a very different pattern: In this case, the bulk of the protective and motivating cognitive work occurs *before* the event, as the (successful) "pessimist" anticipates the possibility of negative, rather than positive outcomes, and reflects in detail about ways to cope with the impending task (Cantor et al., 1987).

These divergent paths to success in the achievement domain make most sense (and the action appears most coherent) when considered in light of the *problems* to which they seem to be addressed, i.e., in terms of the individual's construal of the life task. For example, experimental work has shown that subjects using defensive pessimism have higher levels of test anxiety than subjects using illusory glow optimism, even in the face of equivalently good records of past performance success (Norem & Cantor, 1986b). Managing this anxiety thus seems to be part of the problem for the defensive pessimists more so than for the optimists. For defensive pessimists the problem is one of approaching the task itself, whereas optimists seem to focus more on evaluations of performance *after* the task has been completed. Optimists are managing their own and others' reactions to performance (Snyder, Stephan, & Rosenfield, 1978); pessimists are guarding against immobilizing anxiety and/or effort withdrawal that would interfere with the task process. Pessimists are worried about *how* the task works; optimists are worried about *what* the outcome will look like. It is not that pessimists do not care about evaluation, or that optimists do not need to stay motivated and relaxed during the task itself; but each group has an overriding concern that is apparent in their task construals and that gives their strategic work its special purpose. In this way, the strategy analysis provides insight into the coherence of actions and also makes apparently irrational behavior seem somewhat more understandable, in light of its strategic function for the individual.

Strategies and Dispositions

It would be easy to reify strategies such as self-handicapping and defensive pessimism into trait-like dispositional dimensions. It would also be wrong. Self-handicapping and defensive pessimism are available to everyone, and a pessimist in one situation is often an optimist in another. Our data support the discriminative use of strategies within the life-task contexts for which they are intended: Academic defensive pessimists look very different from optimists in terms of their characteristic thoughts, feelings, and actions in achievement situations, and, yet, they overlap substantially on these measures with their optimist peers in social situations (Cantor & Norem, 1988). These are not simply "moderate" pessimists; they are extremely "pessimistic" prior to academic tasks and quite "optimistic" in their approach to social task situations. Typically, there is only a modest correlation (around .30) in our college student samples between self-reported use of defensive pessimism in academic and in social situations (see Showers, 1986 for a discussion of a negative thinking strategy in social contexts).

More to the point, the defensive-pessimist strategy shares features of both the negative-thinking characteristic of dispositional pessimism and the confrontive-coping activity that typically characterizes an optimistic orientation (Scheier, Weintraub, & Carver, 1986). Whereas there is nothing in principle that precludes dispositional pessimists from using defensive pessimism to overcome immobilizing self-doubts, the academic defensive pessimists whom we have been studying are not those individuals—they acknowledge their past successes, take control of their current anxieties via use of the strategy, and are indistinguishable from optimists on measures of generalized hopelessness (see Cantor & Norem, 1988). In fact, we assume that the functional character of this strategy is intimately related to its *selective* use in appropriate contexts—to the extent that defensive pessimism as a strategy devolves into real pessimism as a generalized negative orientation to all problems in living, then, indeed, it puts the individual at risk for depression and distress (Scheier & Carver, 1985).

Rigid and overgeneralized reliance on a single strategy as a "solution" to diverse life-task problems constitutes a failure of intelligent action, in our opinion. Intelligent use of strategies like defensive pessimism or self-handicapping is better reflected in the behavior of students who learn, over time, to restrict their strategic negativity (for defensive pessimists) or excuses (for self-handicappers) to a few critical situations that present sure risks to self-esteem (Norem, 1987; C. R. Snyder, 1985). Of course, this theoretical standard for intelligent behavior may not always be realized in the reactions of real people in the face of real threats and anxieties; yet neither is there reason to assume instead that people inevitable rely rigidly on generalized coping strategies—as with most answers to questions of human behavior, both the strategic and the dispositional models provide reasonably good descriptions of some people's ways of coping.

ASSESSING INDIVIDUALS' LIFE TASKS
AND STRATEGIES

Every program for personality assessment involves building a story about particular individuals working on their own version of common life tasks. Our assessment program (Cantor & Kihlstrom, 1985a, 1985b, 1987) applies an intelligence model—of context, expertise, and pragmatics—to the study of individuals by searching for connections between the individual's particular reading of life tasks, relevant perceptions of self and family life, and preferred strategies (for regulating thoughts, feelings, and effort) to address those life tasks *as he or she "sees" them*. In this regard we have found it useful to focus attention on groups of individuals who show a decidedly distinctive or "deviant" pattern of life-task appraisal, relative to the modal perceptions of people in the same life-transition period. We look for meaningful deviations (from the norm) in feelings about a life task, assuming that behind these deviant appraisals are unique versions of common life-task problems; versions that derive from the specifics of the person's self-knowledge and personal experiences. These unique "problems," in turn, are likely to bring forth unique strategies in relevant task contexts, and the strategies will have particular consequences for personality adjustment. Our aim is to trace a path from life-task appraisal to cognitive strategy to consequences for adjustment and functioning in that life-transition period. In evaluating those consequences, we try to take a relativistic attitude toward standards of performance and adjustment: The strategy has to fit the individual's version of the normative life-task problem, as well as address more widely held goals of social functioning and personal health. It is not always the case that the "objectively" best solution to a common life task serves the individual as an answer to his or her particular set of current concerns.

To illustrate the process of building personal stories in the present approach, we draw again from the longitudinal study of the transition to college life, as described earlier (Cantor et al., 1987). Whereas most students in that sample entered college with relatively positive appraisals of the ease, rewardingness, and potential for progress of their *social*-life tasks, one group of (27) students was clearly distinguishable from a (modal) group (of 84 students) by their tendency to see these social-life tasks as more threatening than rewarding (Langston & Cantor, 1988). The distinctive reaction of these same students was also reflected in their strategy for working on social-life tasks: These students favored a highly constrained interaction strategy in which they frequently considered the possibility of "social failure," evaluated their specific social-life tasks as very difficult and stressful to handle, felt inhibited in initiating actions in social situations and looked to the guidance of others, and focused on the self after disappointing social interactions. These same students were *not* more likely to embrace an ineffective strategy in the academic domain, nor were they diffusely more immobilized, defeated, or prone to withdraw effort from their life-task activities. (Characterization of the strategy emerged from Q-sort ratings provided by trained judges on the basis of videotaped interviews with the students about their current social and academic life-task activities, goals, successes, and failures. The Q-sort deck was comprised of 92 items constructed to represent the specific elements in a variety of well-researched self-regulatory strategies. Each item in the deck was phrased in a way that mapped onto these students' current college life experiences in achievement and social-life domains. See Norem (1987) for a detailed description of the Q-sort deck and rating procedure.)

Specification of these students' problem-solving strategy for social interactions is a very basic ingredient of the social-intelligence assessment. The strategy, which we label as a *social constraint* strategy, contained a diverse set of 19 Q-sort items that cohered well in ratings of these students (alpha = .91) and also decomposed well into four subscales that seemed to constitute the components of a strategic approach to social-life tasks. The strategy components included: task appraisal (e.g., "finds social tasks stressful"), self-appraisal (e.g., "sees discrepancy between actual and ideal social self-concepts"), self-in-action (e.g., "picks friends to facilitate goals" as uncharacteristic), and relations to groups and to others ("comfortable with structure imposed by others"). Importantly, the strategy was comprised of elements of thoughts, feelings, and actions that spanned a temporal period before, during, and after relevant events. Moreover, whereas the elements had some functional coherence in that they all, in one way or another, addressed the social life-task goals of these students, their descriptive content came from many traditional dispositional categories (e.g., anxiety, shyness, conformity, and so forth). The strategy description captured the diversity and richness of these students' approach to their pressing problems, without sacrificing a handle on coherences in their personalities that were predictive of adjustment.

In turn, students who fit the profile of the social-constraint strategy were experiencing significantly more stress and dissatisfaction with their social lives at college, although they were performing on par with the typical Honors student in their academic endeavors. The appraisal–strategy–outcome relations were quite clearly defined within the social-life arena. A path model performed on data from the sample as a whole over 3 years at college, tracing a causal-temporal chain from appraisal of social-life tasks (gathered in the first year at college) to degree of endorsement of the social-constraint strategy (gathered from observer ratings of interviews in sophomore year) to adjustment outcomes of perceived daily life stress and social-life satisfaction (gathered in the junior year at college), provided a good fit to these patterns of personality functioning. Most importantly, the social-constraint strategy provided the key link between life-task appraisal (e.g., balance of reward to threat) and the adjustment outcomes, as measured 2 years later; the more direct links between goals and outcomes were not significant in these path models. In other words, students' appraisals impacted on their subsequent adjustment to college life via the problem-solving strategies that those individuals embraced when they confronted those life tasks. It is not sufficient for personality prediction to know that an individual has framed a pressing life task in a particularly negative or positive light; rather, the task appraisal provides insight into the likely strategy for working on the task, which, in turn, provides the clearer path to particular (good or bad) outcomes.

The social-constraint strategy seems to have had rather specific consequences for social adjustment. Students in the "deviant" group in this sample appraised the social-life tasks as important and engaging, but difficult to master; as if they felt ineffective and worried about making interpersonal mistakes. They embraced a strategy of self-focused humility in which they were predominantly guided by others in their "actions" in social contexts–a strategy that may well have made sense as a reflection of their unique concerns, but one that was not likely to be personally very satisfying in the long run. As such, these data raise a central question in the social-intelligence analysis: *Why* exactly do (otherwise) competent individuals embrace seemingly self-defeating strategies, such as this one, as they work on specific life tasks?

To address this question it is important to consider the individual's own version of each relevant life task, and, in this regard, we look to people's autobiographical knowledge and experiences to provide special insight into the personal rationale for a seemingly self-defeating strategy. For example, the perceptions of family life reported by the students in this sample provided a view of the unique "problems" of social relations that those with the deviant pattern of life-task appraisals may well have felt the need to address in social life at college. Students in the deviant appraisal group, in contrast with the other (modal) group of students, perceived their families to be relatively nonexpressive in interpersonal interactions and affectively inhibited with family members, especially when provocative issues arose at home (as measured on the Expressiveness Subscale of the Moos Family Environment Scale, 1974). They were more likely than their peers to endorse items of the following kind in describing their family life: "It's hard to "blow off steam" at home without upsetting somebody"; "We are usually careful about what we say to each other"; "We tell each other about our personal problems (negatively scaled)." In turn, recall that the central theme of their strategic approach to social life seemed to be one of constraint, inaction, and otherdirectedness; a theme that at the least fits well with this portrait of a somewhat inhibited and affectively restrained family-life atmosphere.

Of course, these data on perceptions of family interactions can not stand on their own in tracing the etiology of these students' self-defeating strategy in social-life contexts. Without behavioral observation data in the family context it is difficult to assess the accuracy of the students' retrospective reports. However, from our perspective, these data provide valuable insight into the "cognitive baggage" that the students bring with them to college; baggage that is likely to influence their reading of college-life tasks regardless of the actual truth-value of these beliefs. For example, it may well be that the inhibition in action and affective expression that these particular students perceived in their family lives set the tone for their perceptions of difficulty in actively structuring their own social environments in an assertive and rewarding fashion. In other words, the salient "problem" for these students may have been that they felt a lack of skill and control in the social domain, an inability to "make social life work for them," and, perhaps in reaction to this perception, they embraced a rather self-deprecating strategy of otherdirectedness and restrained action (or, rather, inaction). From this perspective, the social-constraint strategy, whereas certainly not optimal as a solution to their broader life-task goals, may have felt rather "obligatory" to these individuals as a temporary solution to their more specific perceptions of social incompetence and fear of embarrassment in social relations—in this very narrow way, the strategy "makes sense" for their subjectively conceived "problem."

As Baumeister and Scher (1988) point out in their recent analysis of self-defeating strategies, quite frequently individuals trade off broader adjustment goals for answers to more pressing, specific needs. Of course, solutions to these pressing, local problems may entail further unanticipated costs that only seem worthwhile when the strategy brings more immediate rewards (e.g., defensive pessimists pay a price for their success, but they do at least succeed). These students who embraced the social-constraint strategy were not likely to feel good about their chosen strategic trade-off; the costs in subjective stress and social satisfaction were relatively heavy given that the benefit was itself only an implied one, i.e., avoiding social embarrassment. Yet, satisfied or not, they may well have perceived the strategy as the only available path towards their broader social goals. And such a restricted vision of one's strategic alternatives speaks poorly to the effectiveness of their social intelligence. Intelligent action implies a level of problem-solving flexibility and innovation that does not appear to exist for these particular students as they approach problems in their social life-task domain. In fact, assessments of strategies in different life-task contexts suggest a potential for nonrigid problem solving, but a strong pull towards routinization, with nonoptimal consequences for personality growth and change (Nasby & Kihlstrom, 1986).

ASSESSMENT FOR CHANGE

From a cognitive point of view, maladaptive behavior occurs because the social intelligence used to interpret situations and plan actions is somehow inadequate or inappropriate to the task. Corrective change—whether incidentally evoked in the course of social interaction or more deliberately elicited in therapeutic encounters—requires articulation of the person's repertoire of social knowledge so that it can be critically examined and revised. In a series of papers, we have outlined a clinical assessment technology based on experimental tasks familiar in the laboratory study of social cognition (Kihlstrom & Nasby, 1981; Nasby & Kihlstrom, 1986). Some of these tasks are intended to tap consciously accessible declarative knowledge, whereas others are intended to permit valid inferences about unconscious procedural knowledge.

Self Awareness and Corrective Change

The first step in clinical assessment should be to determine the life tasks in which the person is currently engaged, placing them into the twin contexts of the individual's personal history and the demands of the external social world. Fortunately, people apparently find it rather easy to articulate their life tasks by means of simple and direct self-reports (Emmons, 1986; Little, 1983). If there are concerns about the validity of self-reports, it is possible to employ more direct time-sampling methods to gain an "on-line" picture of the distribution of the person's daily thoughts and activities (Diener & Larsen, 1984; Nezlek, Wheeler, & Reis, 1983). In addition, Little (1983) has proposed a method for assessing the degree to which each current life task facilitates or impairs progress on each of the others; the same kind of technique could be used to assess conflict between two different individuals' life tasks. Using techniques for probing autobiographical memory (Robinson, 1976), clients can be asked to recall incidents that are relevant to their life tasks. And using a free-listing method for assessing situations (Pervin, 1976), they can be asked to indicate how their life tasks interact with the settings in which they commonly find themselves.

Life tasks are approached through the individual's fund of declarative social knowledge. Procedures such as Kelly's (1955) Role Construct Repertory Test (and its more current, high-tech variations: Pervin, 1976; Rosenberg, 1977; Rosenberg & Gara, 1985) capitalize on the person's ability to articulate the meanings they attribute to the people and events they encounter. For example, subjects might be asked to list and freely describe the people they know (Rosenberg, 1977), the situations they encounter (Pervin, 1976), or the identities they experience and present to others (Rosenberg & Gara, 1985). Each is then freely described, and then every target (person, for example) is rated on every descriptor. The resulting cluster analysis shows how that aspect of the person's social world is organized. Other investigators have proposed similar techniques for assessing possible selves (Markus & Nurius, 1986) and self-ideal discrepancies

(Higgins, Straumann, & Klein, 1986). Quantitative analyses can be applied to index the complexity of the mental representations, their agreement with cultural consensus, and the like.

Where direct introspective reports are undesirable (perhaps because of the possibility that some declarative social knowledge is not accessible to consciousness or easily put into words; Shevrin, 1986) the social cognition laboratory provides other procedures that can be adapted to the purposes of individual assessment: Priming tasks can assess the accessibility of declarative knowledge, whereas divided-attention tasks can determine the degree to which social-stimulus information is processed automatically (e.g., Bargh, 1982). Similarly, clustering in free recall can be used to index the organization of social knowledge (Kihlstrom, 1981). The yield from such procedures may be of interest to the assessor. But our (admittedly limited) experience suggests that many of them are also intrinsically interesting to clients and provide a valued opportunity for self-reflection.

Uncovering procedural social knowledge involves special problems precisely because it is not consciously accessible to clients (Kihlstrom, 1984; Nisbett & Wilson, 1977). For this reason, self-report methodologies are obviously of no use. Nevertheless, it is possible to produce tasks that assess attentional selectivity in response to positive and negative feedback (Mischel, Ebbesen, & Zeiss, 1972), hypothesis-testing strategies (Fong & Markus, 1982; Riggs & Cantor, 1982; Snyder, 1981b), styles of planfulness (Frese, Stewart, & Hannover, 1987), and attributional style (Metalsky & Abramson, 1981). Unobtrusive measures of response latency and incidental memory may be useful in assessing the degree to which these individual differences reflect truly automatized procedures (Nasby & Kihlstrom, 1986)—thus giving some indication of how hard they might be to correct.

Effecting Change

Change, after all, is the major purpose of assessment. We see little point in assessment as an academic exercise in person ranking; careful assessment is arduous for subject and investigator alike, expensive and time consuming, and should be reserved for those occasions where the results will be put to useful purpose. Change may be directed toward developing new life tasks, finding new solutions to old ones, or embracing new possibilities for the self. None of this is going to be easy. Even maladaptive social intelligence developed because it was once useful (or promised to be), and much of the person's expertise is going to be firmly entrenched and difficult to correct. In fact, the social-knowledge repertoire seems structured in such a manner as to resist revision—except, perhaps, by adding knowledge to the repertoire. The situation is especially bleak for procedural expertise, because conscious awareness would seem to be a prerequisite for conscious control and deliberate restructuring. Still, because new knowledge creates new possibilities for constructive alternativism, and thus for behavioral change, adding rather than eliminating social intelligence may be enough—provided that others in the person's social environment are also open to change. If the expectations of others are firmly entrenched, expectancy confirmation may outweigh self-verification (Swann & Ely, 1984). The self-fulfilling prophecy can be a powerful adversary.

We are not clinicians, though one of us has clinical training and both of us work with clinical psychologists and clinical social workers. Still, from a cognitive perspective the techniques of cognitive therapy (or cognitive behavior modification) seem the best approach to affecting adaptive change in client's personalities (Meichenbaum, 1977; Wilson & Franks, 1982). These techniques work by altering the client's repertoire of social knowledge, and helping the client to acquire new behavioral routines based on what he or she has learned. For example, new images of a "perfect relationship" can be considered, hopefully overwhelming the client's prior, self-defeating standards (Ruhrold, 1986). Video reconstruction of a marital "debate" can help a client to "see" his or her dysfunctional interaction strategies. Through active intervention efforts the client is then taught to develop and master new scripts for social interaction (Jacobson, 1984), and to avoid slipping into old ones (Meichenbaum & Cameron, 1982). Relapses are to be expected, in part because many procedures are automatically executed, but the clinician actively encourages the client to persist in self-reflection and efforts to change (Meichenbaum & Cameron, 1982).

CONSISTENCY AND INTELLIGENCE

The major issue in personality is consistency. Traditionally, consistency in experience, thought, and action has served as prima facie evidence that people have personalities. The social-intelligence approach involves many different types of consistency, but the most important of these is the consistency of action with perceptions and intentions (Kuhl & Beckmann, 1985). Intentional consistency is apparent when people express their life goals and strive to achieve them, and when people act in accordance with their subjective impressions of the situation. People construct consistency in their lives, but this consistency is not always readily apparent to an external observer. Rather, it can only be appreciated from the point of view of the actor.

The life-task strategy approach should give additional insight into these regions of intentional consistency in personality functioning because it forces a rather fine-tuned person-by-situation analysis (e.g., Wright & Mischel, 1987). Such an approach asks direct questions about the person in that situation: What is this person likely to see as the problem to be addressed in this situation? How does he/she typically try to address such a problem? What patterns of strategic effort will this situation afford or allow? These are all questions of strategy-by-environment fit that recognize both the propensity of individuals to select person- ally compatible environments (Emmons, Diener, & Larsen, 1986; Snyder, 1981a) and the constraints placed on effective action by the "rules" implicit in most social contexts (Argyle, 1981). For example, Smith and Rhodewalt (1986) suggest that a key ingredient to understanding "Type A" behavior is the map- ping of patterns of construal and of situation choice: Type A individuals con- sistently choose to be in stress-engendering task contexts; moreover, they "see" competition and the need for an assertive (i.e., stress-engendering) response where others might not, and in contexts in which a competitive response will not always be rewarded.

A thorough analysis of the opportunities afforded by certain environments for certain forms of strategic work, or, on the other hand, of the problems most likely to be engendered by particular people's favorite strategies in particular environments, would perhaps give us a better sense of the limits on personality change and consistency. One could ask of a person whether he or she managed to find sufficiently encouraging environments for preferred strategies; or, whether particular environments came to bend the rules to allow a broader range of "acceptable" responses. The emphasis on the "fit" or match between particular construals and strategies on one hand and particular environments on the other, recognizes a value system for personality functioning, without being overly specific or constraining as to a standard for "normal" or "good" behavior.

Too much consistency—of the wrong kind—can be a bad thing. People can persist in self-defeating patterns of construal and action. Or, a strategy like defensive pessimism or self-handicapping that is functional in some contexts can be rigidly embraced, creating a set of undesirable "side-effects" over time (Berglas, 1985; Cantor & Norem, 1988). Even a highly beneficial orientation to life-task problem solving, such as the ego-protective optimism observed to pro- mote mental health (Scheier & Carver, 1985; Taylor & Brown, 1988), can be detrimental to adjustment if it precludes personality growth in reaction to social feedback. Intentional consistency is adaptive only insofar as the person possesses a knowledge base broad enough to permit flexibility in constructive alter- nativism—the ability to view things from different perspectives, and to entertain alternative hypotheses. This cognitive flexibility, and the resulting flexibility of action and potential for self-correction, makes the difference between adaptive and maladaptive social intelligence.

Social Intelligence and Personality Change

Cognitive approaches to personality, in which goals and self-concepts and per- sonal memories and strategies for self-regulation and self-fulfillment, take center stage, are by no means new. However, there is a renewed interest in this tradi- tion, with excitement about pursuing the cognitive representation of goals (Per- vin, 1988), the dynamics of a "cognitive self" and of autobiographical narratives (Cohler, 1982; Markus & Wurf, 1987), and cognitive strategies for protecting self-esteem and bolstering persistence towards goals (Bandura, 1986; Kuhl & Beckmann, 1985). This interest is flourishing in large part because of trends in cognitive-social psychology to "heat up" the study of social cognition (e.g., Fiske, 1982; Isen & Moore, 1988), and to show ways in which social cognition impacts on (and is then shaped by) motivation in central domains of social life (Sorrentino & Higgins, 1986). These trends increase the attractiveness of social intelligence as a centerpiece for personality, because the study of lives and of people must, almost by definition, be primarily concerned with personal adjustment and growth—concerns that until relatively recently seemed far from the purview of the laboratory study of cognition.

In turn, these cognitive models of personality enable us to join once again in common cause with clinical psychologists, as the limits of self-control and mutability of personality are tested (Ingram, 1986). As we have noted throughout this chapter, there are in our opinion two main ways in which the constructs that are popular with today's cognitivists differ, at least in principle, from the cognitive styles of past theorists: concepts of self, autobiographical memories, life tasks and strategies, are *specific* to particular life contexts (in the past, present, or future); and they should be *mutable*. Our review (Cantor & Kihlstrom, 1987) of experimental literature in social cognition and personality uncovered many reasons to be optimistic about the specificity and mutability of social intelligence. Of course, we also found many less encouraging signs, and much future work to be done in assessing the potential for personal growth.

On the side of mutability. The store of multiple self-concepts, each characterizing different context-specific aspects of personality (Kihlstrom & Cantor, 1984), and the record of autobiographical memories which provides the basis for a multiplicity of event-specific feelings of self-efficacy and inefficacy (Bandura, 1982), serve as critical resources for self-reflection and self-change—grist for the mill of cognitively oriented therapists (e.g., Segal, 1988). Unfortunately, these diverse aspects of self are often buried somewhat under the weight of a few chronically accessible constructs (Higgins, King, & Mavin, 1982), and there is a strong pull towards overgeneralizations about self-esteem that mask the specificity of feelings of self-efficacy (Harter, 1983). Nevertheless, it is encouraging that such a diverse base of self-knowledge can be uncovered, and the more that one's life situations can be varied too, the more likely that these distinct aspects of self will be evoked as guides to behavior; providing the basis for ever-more positive feedback to bolster efforts at self-change. Major life transitions provide such arenas for self-reflection and growth (Levinson, 1978), but even routine variations in everyday life activities can be used to facilitate recognition of new aspects of self and remembrance of easily forgotten selves (Wilson & Franks, 1982).

On the side of rigidity. There is little reason to doubt that this process of bolstering a "mutable self" is a very difficult one indeed. Even when we do uncover or recover hidden selves, the tendency is to quickly incorporate them neatly into a smoothed-over personal narrative, thus missing the opportunity to intentionally mark a change of course in one's old routines. There may well be many selves stored in memory, but a few selves are always accorded special attention, always elaborated with special associations, and always most likely to push to the forefront of consciousness (Markus, 1977). These special selves are also most often connected to well-learned behaviors. Part of the "double-edge" of expertise is that it is so very easy to use (Smith, 1984), and so very comfortable for others to incorporate (Nasby & Kihlstrom, 1986). Other people expect that we will be this same person at all times, rewarding routines, even when they leave everyone feeling badly (Barnett & Gotlib, 1988). As any family visit so vividly demonstrates, it takes an act of will to break out of well-worn habits and scripted patterns of social interaction (Carlson, 1981).

The reality of compromise. The entrenched expertise of self-knowledge and of social scripts should not entirely be cause for pessimism, for it also sometimes provides the personal motivation, and some of the necessary knowledge, to change and to develop new life patterns. When, for example, the "shy schematic" decides to work on assertiveness, a new possible self (as the life of the party) is probably embellished with knowledge from that old shy self-schema (Markus & Wurf, 1987). Similarly, self-defeating routines, when they are brought to conscious attention by someone else's remark or through personal retrospection, can serve as a basis for acknowledging possible benefits of new interaction strategies (Goldfried, 1983). Of course, people can also make themselves feel very discouraged by focusing on the discrepancy between their current existence and an ideal future state (e.g., Higins et al., 1985); but it is also the case that sometimes that knowledge can provide the impetus for constructive action, especially when an alternative, more positive possible self seems feasible to attain (Markus & Nurius, 1986). Although, these efforts to try on "new faces" (Hochschild, 1979) are clearly risky, and they sometimes seem more likely to promote self-deception than self-understanding and growth (Wilson & Stone, 1985), they also provide the only real avenue for self-change because personal expertise is not easily banished or even modified. Behavior *modification* is probably only achieved through more indirect routes of cognitive-behavior *supplementation*—the old knowledge doesn't go away, it just gets used less and less often, in fewer and fewer life contexts. And we, as researchers, do not really know yet how often the process of supplementation occurs, or, how well it works, as people try to master their life tasks with ever new strategic solutions. The future holds, we hope, new methods for testing this critical aspect of social intelligence.

To date the accessible database on the mutability of strategies, and on the proclivity of individuals to try to control and diversify their habitual ways of solving life tasks, remains sketchy. Still, the important contribution of current cognitive-assessment approaches is to force a more detailed consideration of the ways in which people actually try to achieve goals, and of their reactions to failures to do so (e.g., Dweck, 1986; Kuhl & Beckman, 1985). It is surprising that so little literature has accumulated on how (and whether) ''normal'' individuals try to modify self-defeating and disappointing behavior patterns in the course of everyday life; personality psychologists have been too ready to leave questions of mutability and flexibility in the hands of clinicians. Instead, we have focused almost exclusively on questions of structure and of stability in personality, often at the expense of thorough analyses of processes that guide actions, and reactions to feedback, in specific life situations. This imbalance of attention needs to change, for as Allport (1937) said some time ago, personality *is* something and personality *does* something. It seems to us that our field knows too little about what personality does, and about how it changes when those ''doings'' do not lead to satisfactory outcomes.

ACKNOWLEDGMENTS

This chapter is based in large part on thinking developed in a monograph entitled *Personality and Social Intelligence* by Nancy Cantor and John F. Kihlstrom, published by Prentice–Hall in 1987. The research was supported in part by Grant #BNS84-11778 (Cantor & Korn) and by Grant #8718467 (Canton & Noren) from the National Science Foundation and by Grant #MH35856 (Kihlstrom) from the National Institutes of Health.

We wish to thank the editors of this volume, Robert Wyer and Thom Srull, and the commentators, for their thoughtful comments; as well as members of our research groups: Lucy Canter Kihlstrom, Douglas J. Tataryn, Betsy A. Tobias, and James M. Wood; and Aaron Brower, Christopher A. Langston, Paula Niedenthal, Julie K. Norem, Carolin Showers, and Sabrina Zirkel. Nancy G. Exelby provided invaluable technical assistance.

REFERENCES

Abelson, R. (1981). Psychological status of the script concept. *American Psychologist, 36,* 715–729.

Abelson, R. (1982). Three modes of attitude–behavior consistency. In M. P. Zanna, E. T. Higgins, & C. P. Herman (Eds.), *Consistency in social behavior: The Ontario symposium* (Vol 2, pp. 131–146). Hillsdale, NJ: Lawrence Erlbaum Associates.

Abramson, L. Y., Seligman, M. E. P., & Teasdale, J. D. (1978). Learned helplessness in humans: Critique and reformulation. *Journal of Abnormal Psychology, 87,* 49–74.

Adler, A. (1931). *What life should mean to you.* Boston: Little, Brown.

Alloy, L. B., & Abramson, L. Y. (1979). Judgment of contingency in depressed and nondepressed students: Sadder but wiser? *Journal of Experimental Psychology, 108,* 441–487.

Allport, G. W. (1937). *Personality: A psychological interpretation.* New York: Holt.

Allport, G. W. (1955). *Becoming.* New Haven Yale University Press.

Andersen, S. M. (1984). Self-knowledge and social inference: II. The diagnosticity of cognitive/affective and behavioral data. *Journal of Personality and Social Psychology, 46,* 294–307.

Andersen, S., & Klatzky, R. (1987). Traits and social stereotypes: Levels of categorization in person perception. *Journal of Personality and Social Psychology, 53*(2), 235–246.

Andersen, S. M., & Ross, L. (1984). Self-knowledge and social inference: I. The impact of cognitive/affective and behavioral data. *Journal of Personality and Social Psychology, 46,* 280–293.

Anderson, J. R. (1981). *Cognitive psychology and its implications.* San Francisco: Freeman.

Anderson, N. H. (1974). Cognitive algebra: Integration theory applied to social attribution. In L. Berkowitz (Ed.), *Advances in experimental social psychology* (Vol 7, pp. 1–101). New York: Academic Press.

Argyle, M. (1981). The experimental study of the basic features of situations. In D. Magnusson (Ed.), *Toward a psychology of situations: An interactional perspective* (pp. 63–83). Hillsdale, NJ: Lawrence Erlbaum Associates.

Baldwin, M. W., & Holmes, J. G. (1987). Salient private audiences and awareness of the self. *Journal of Personality and Social Psychology, 52*(6), 1087–1098.

Baltes, P. B. (1986). *The aging of intelligence: On the dynamics between growth and decline.* Unpublished manuscript, Max Planck Institute, Berlin.

Baltes, P. B., Dittman-Kohli, F., & Dixon, R. A. (1984). New perspectives on the development of intelligence in adulthood: Toward a dual-process conception and a model of selective optimization with compensation. In P. B. Baltes & O. G. Brim, Jr. (Eds.), *Life-span development and behavior* (Vol. 6, pp. 33–76). New York: Academic Press.

Bandura, A. (1977a). Self-efficacy: Toward a unifying theory of behavioral change. *Psychological Review, 84,* 191–215.

Bandura, A. (1977b). *Social learning theory.* Englewood Cliffs, NJ: Prentice-Hall.

Bandura, A. (1982). Self-efficacy mechanism in human agency. *American psychologist, 37,* 122–147.

Bandura, A. (1986). *Social foundations of thought and action: A social cognitive theory.* Englewood Cliffs, NJ: Prentice-Hall.

Bandura, A., & Walters, R. H. (1963). *Social learning and personality development.* New York: Holt, Rinehart, & Winston.

Bannister, D., & Agnew, J. (1977). The child's construing of self. In J. K. Cole (Ed.), *Nebraska symposium on motivation 1976* (Vol. 24, pp. 99–125). Lincoln: University of Nebraska Press.

Bargh, J. A. (1982). Attention and automaticity in the processing of self-relevant information. *Journal of Personality and Social Psychology, 43,* 425–436.

Barnett, P. A., & Gotlib, I. H. (1988). Psychosocial functioning and depression: Distinguishing among antecedents, concomitants, and consequences. *Psychological Bulletin, 104*(1), 97–126.

Baron, J. (1981). Reflective thinking as a goal of education. *Intelligence, 5,* 291–309.

Baron, J. (1982). Personality and intelligence. In R. Sternberg (Ed.), *Handbook of human intelligence* (pp. 308–352). Cambridge: Cambridge University Press.

Baumeister, R., & Scher, S. (1988). Self-defeating behavior patterns among normal individuals: Review and analysis of common self-destructive tendencies. *Psychological Bulletin, 104*(1), 3–22.

Berglas, S. (1985). Self-handicapping and self-handicappers: A cognitive/attributional model of interpersonal self-protective behavior. In B. Maher (Ed.), *Perspectives in personality* (Vol. 11, pp. 235–370). Greenwich, CT: JAI Press.

Borgida, E., & Brekke, N. (1981). The base rate fallacy in attribution and prediction. In J. Harvey, W. Ickes, & R. F. Kidd (Eds.), *New direction in attribution research* (Vol. 3, pp. 63–96). Hillsdale, NJ: Lawrence Erlbaum Associates.

Borgida, E., & Howard-Pitney, B. (1983). Personality involvement and the robustness of perceptual salience effects. *Journal of Personality and Social Psychology, 45,* 560–570.

Bower, G. H. (1981). Mood and memory. *American Psychologist, 36*, 129–148.

Brim, O. G., Jr., & Ryff, C. D. (1980). On the properties of life events. In P. B. Baltes & O. G. Brim, Jr. (Eds.), *Life-span development and behavior* (Vol. 3, pp. 367–388). New York: Academic Press.

Brown, R., & Kulik, J. (1977). Flashbulb memories. *Cognition, 5*, 73–99.

Bruner, J. S. (1981). Intention in the structure of action and interaction. *Advances in Infancy Research, 1*, 41–56.

Bruner, J. S., Goodnow, J. J., & Austin, G. A. (1956). *A study of thinking*. New York: Wiley.

Buss, D. M., & Craik, K. H. (1983). The act frequency approach to personality. *Psychological Review, 90*, 105–126.

Cantor, N., & Genero, N. (1986). Psychiatric diagnosis and natural categorization: A close analogy. In T. Millon & G. Klerman (Eds.), *Contemporary issues in psychopathology* (pp. 233–256). New York: Guilford Press.

Cantor, N., & Kihlstrom, J. F. (1985a). Social intelligence and personality. In J. T. Spence & C. E. Izard (Eds.), *Motivation, emotion, and personality* (pp. 3–24). New York: Elsevier.

Cantor, N., & Kihlstrom, J. F. (1985b). Social intelligence: The cognitive basis of personality. *Review of Personality and Social Psychology, 6*, 15–33.

Cantor, N., & Kihlstrom, J. F. (1987). *Personality and social intelligence*. Englewood Cliffs, NJ: Prentice-Hall.

Cantor, N., & Mischel, W. (1979). Prototypes in person perception. In L. Berkowitz (Ed.), *Advances in experimental social psychology* (Vol. 12, pp. 3–52). New York: Academic Press.

Cantor, N., Mischel, W., & Schwartz, J. (1982). A prototype analysis of psychological situations. *Cognitive Psychology, 14*, 45–77.

Cantor, N., & Norem, J. K. (1988 in press). Defensive pessimism and stress and coping. *Social Cognition*.

Cantor, N., Norem, J. K., Niedenthal, P. M., Langston, C. A., & Brower, A. M. (1987). Life tasks, self-concept ideals, and cognitive strategies in a life transition. *Journal of Personality and Social Psychology, 53*(6), 1178–1191.

Carlson, R. (1981). Studies in script theory: 1. Adult analogs of a childhood nuclear scene. *Journal of Personality and Social Psychology, 40*, 501–510.

Carver, C. S., & Scheier, M. F. (1981). *Attention and self-regulation: A control-theory approach to human behavior*. New York: Springer-Verlag.

Carver, C. S., & Scheier, M. F. (1985). A control-systems approach to the self-regulation of action. In J. Kuhl & J. Beckmann (Eds.), *Action control* (pp. 237–265). New York: Springer-Verlag.

Cattell, R. B., & Horn, J. L. (1978). A check on the theory of fluid & crystallized intelligence with description of new subtest designs. *Journal of Education Measurement, 15*, 189–264.

Cohler, B. (1982). Personal narrative and life course. In P. Baltes & O. Brim, Jr. (Eds.), *Life-span development and behavior* (Vol. 4, pp. 205–241). New York: Academic Press.

Cooley, C. (1902). *Human nature and the social order*. New York: Scribner.

Deaux, K., & Lewis, L. L. (1984). The structure of gender stereotypes: Interrelationships among components and gender label. *Journal of Personality and Social Psychology, 46*, 991–1004.

Deci, E. L., & Ryan, R. M. (1980). The empirical exploration of intrinsic motivational processes. In L. Berkowitz (Ed.), *Advances in experimental social psychology* (Vol. 13, pp. 39–80). New York: Academic Press.

Denney, N. (1984). A model of cognitive development across the life span. *Developmental Review, 4*, 171–191.

Denney, N. W., Pearce, K. A., & Palmer, A. M. (1982). A developmental study of adults' performance on traditional and practical problem-solving tasks. *Experimental Aging Research, 8*, 115–118.

Diener, E., & Larsen, R. J. (1984). Temporal stability and cross-situational consistency of affective, behavioral, and cognitive responses. *Journal of Personality and Social Psychology, 47(4),* 871–883.

Duval, S., & Wicklund, R. *(1972). A theory of objective self-awareness.* New York: Academic Press.

Dweck, C. (1983). Achievement motivation. In P. H. Mussen (Ed.), *Handbook of child psychology: Ed. 4 Socialization, Personality and social development* (Vol. 4, pp. 644–691). New York: Wiley.

Dweck, C. (1986). Motivational processes affecting learning. *American Psychologist, 41*(10), 1040–1048.

D'Zurilla, T. J., & Goldfried, M. R. (1971). Problem solving and behavior modification. *Journal of Abnormal Psychology, 78,* 107–126.

D'Zurilla, T. J., & Nezu, A. (1980). A study of the generation-of-alternatives process in social problem solving. *Cognitive Therapy and Research, 4,* 67–72.

Emmons, R. A. (1986). Personal strivings: An approach to personality and subjective well-being. *Journal of Personality and Social Psychology, 51*(5), 1058–1068.

Emmons, R. A., Diener, E., & Larsen, R. J. (1986). Choice and avoidance of everyday situations and affect congruence: Two models of reciprocal interactionism. *Journal of Personality and Social Psychology, 51,* 815–826.

Epstein, S. (1973). The self-concept revisited, or a theory of a theory. *American Psychologist, 28,* 404–416.

Erikson, E. H. (1950). *Childhood and society.* New York: Norton.

Fazio, R., & Zanna, M. (1978). Attitudinal qualities relating to the strength of the attitude–behavior relationship. *Journal of Experimental Social Psychology, 14,* 398–408.

Fehr, B., & Russell, J. A. (1984). Concept of emotion viewed from a prototype perspective. *Journal of Experimental Psychology: General, 113,* 464–486.

Fenigstein, A., Scheier, M. F., & Buss, A. H. (1975). Public and private self-consciousness: Assessment and theory. *Journal of Consulting and Clinical Psychology, 43,* 522–527.

Fincham, F. D., Beach, S., & Nelson, G. (1987). Attribution processes in distressed and nondistressed couples: 3. Causal and responsibility attributions for spouse behavior. *Cognitive Therapy and Research, 11*(1), 71–86.

Fiske, S. T. (1982). Schema-triggered affect: Applications to social perception. In M. S. Clark & S. T. Fiske (Eds.), *Affect and cognition: The 17th annual Carnegie symposium on cognition* (pp. 55–78). Hillsdale, NJ: Lawrence Erlbaum Associates.

Fiske, S. T., & Pavelchak, M. A. (1986). Category-based versus piecemeal-based affective responses: Developments in schema-triggered affect. In R. M. Sorrentino & E. T. Higgins (Eds.), *Handbook of motivation and cognition* (pp. 167–203). New York: Guilford Press.

Flavell, J. H., & Ross, L. (1981). *Social and cognitive development: Frontiers and possible future.* New York: Cambridge University Press.

Fletcher, G., Danilovics, P., Fernandez, G., Peterson, D., & Reeder, G. (1986). Attributional complexity, an individual differences measure. *Journal of Personality and Social Psychology, 51*(4), 875–884.

Fong, G. T., & Markus, H. (1982). Self-schemas and judgments about others. *Social Cognition, 1,* 191–205.

Ford, M. E., & Tisak, M. S. (1983). A further search for social intelligence. *Journal of Education Psychology, 75*(2), 196–206.

Forgas, J. (1982). Episode cognition: Internal representations of interaction routines. *Advances in Experimental Social Psychology, 15,* 59–101.

Fredericksen, N. (1972). Toward a taxonomy of situations. *American Psychologist, 27,* 114–123.

Frese, M., Stewart, J., & Hanover, B. (1987). Goal orientation and planfulness: Action styles as personality concepts. *Journal of Personality and Social Psychology, 52,* 1182–1194.

Frieze, I. H., Parsons, J. E., Johnson, P. B., Ruble, D. N., & Zellman, G. L. (1978). *Women and sex roles: A social psychological perspective*. New York: Norton.

Gagne, R. M. (1984). Learning outcomes and their effects: Useful categories of human performance. *American Psychologist, 39,* 377–386.

Gardner, R. W., Holzman, P. S., Klein, G. S., Linton, H. B., & Spence, D. P. (1959). Cognitive control. *Psychological Issues, 1*(4), (Monograph).

Gergen, K. J. (1971). *The concept of self.* New York: Holt, Rinehart, & Winston.

Gilligan, S. G., & Bower, G. H. (1984). Cognitive consequences of emotional arousal. In C. E. Izard, J. Kagan, & R. B. Zajonc (Eds.), *Emotions, cognition, and behavior* (pp. 547–588). New York: Cambridge University Press.

Goldfried, M. R. (1983). History of behavioral assessment. In A. E. Kazdin (Chair.), *Behavioral assessment: Historical developments, advances, and current status.* Symposium conducted at the meeting of the World Congress of Behavior Therapy, Washington, DC.

Goldsmith, H. (1983). Genetic influence on personality from infancy & adulthood. *Child Development, 54,* 331–355.

Gollwitzer, P. M., & Wicklund, R. A. (1985). The pursuit of self-defining goals. In J. Kuhl & J. Beckmann (Eds.), *Action control from cognition to behavior* (pp. 61–85). Heidelberg: Springer-Verlag.

Gould, S. J. (1981). *The mismeasure of man.* New York: Norton.

Greenwald, A. G. (1980). The totalitarian ego: Fabrication and revision of personal history. *American Psychologist, 35,* 602–618.

Greenwald, A. G. (1981). Self and memory. In G. H. Bower (Ed.), *The psychology of learning and motivation* (Vol. 15, pp. 202–236). New York: Academic Press.

Guilford, J. (1967). *The nature of human intelligence.* New York: McGraw-Hill.

Hamilton, D. L. (1981). *Cognitive processes in stereotyping and intergroup behavior.* Hillsdale, NJ: Lawrence Erlbaum Associates.

Hampson, S. E. (1982). *The construction of personality: An introduction.* London: Routledge & Kegan Paul.

Hampson, S. E., John, O. P., & Goldberg, L. R. (1986). Category breadth and hierarchical structure in personality: Studies of asymmetries in judgments of trait implications. *Journal of Personality and Social Psychology, 51*(1), 37–54.

Harackiewicz, J., Manderlink, G., & Sansone, C. (1984). Rewarding pinball wizardry: Effects of evaluation and cue value on intrinsic interest. *Journal of Personality and Social Psychology, 47*(2), 287–300.

Harter, S. (1983). Developmental perspectives on the self-system. In P. H. Mussen (Ed.), *Handbook of child psychology: Ed. 4 Socialization, personality and social development* (Vol. 4). New York: Wiley.

Hastie, R. (1981). Schematic principals in human memory. In E. T. Higgins, C. P. Herman, & M. P. Zanna (Eds.), *Social cognition: The Ontario symposium* (Vol. 1, pp. 39–88). Hillsdale, NJ: Lawrence Erlbaum Associates.

Hastie, R. (1984). Causes and effects of casual attribution. *Journal of Personality and social Psychology, 46*(1), 44–56.

Hay, D. F. (1986). Infancy. In M. Rosenzweig & L. W. Porter (Eds.), *Annual reviews of psychology* (Vol. 37, pp. 135–161). Palo Alto, CA: Annual Reviews.

Higgins, E. T. (1981). The "communication game": Implications for social cognition and persuasions. In E. T. Higgins, C. P. Herman, & M. P. Zanna (Eds.), *Social cognition: The Ontario symposium* (Vol. 1, 343–391). Hillsdale, NJ: Lawrence Erlbaum Associates.

Higgins, E. T., & Bryant, S. (1982). Consensus information and the fundamental attribution error: The role of development and in-group versus out-group knowledge. *Journal of Personality and Social Psychology, 43,*(5), 889–900.

Higgins, E. T., & Parsons, J. C. (1983). Social cognitions and the social life of the child: Stages as subcultures. In E. T. Higgins, D. N. Ruble, & W. W. Hartup (Eds.), *Social cognition and social development: A socio-cultural perspective* (pp. 15–62). New York: Cambridge University Press.

Higgins, E. T., Ruble, D. N., & Hartup, W. W. (Eds.). (1983). *Social cognition and social development*. New York: Cambridge University Press.

Higgins, E. T., Strauman, T., & Klein, R. (1986). Standards and the process of self-evaluation: Multiple affects from multiple stages. In R. Sorrentino & E. Higgins, *Handbook of motivation and cognition: Foundation of social behavior* (pp. 23–63). New York: Guilford.

Higgins, E. T., King, G., & Mavin, G. (1982). Individual construct accessibility and subjective impressions and recall. *Journal of Personality and Social Psychology, 43*(1), 35–47.

Higgins, E. T., Klein, R., & Strauman, T. (1985). Self-concept discrepancy theory: A psychological model for distinguishing among different aspects of depression and anxiety. *Social Cognition, 3*, 51–76.

Hochschild, A. R. (1979). Emotion work, feeling rules, and social structure. *American Journal of Sociology, 85*, 551–575.

Hoffman, C., Mischel, W., & Mazze, K. (1981). The role of purpose in the organization of information about behavior: Trait-based versus goal-based categories in person cognition. *Journal of Personality and Social Psychology, 40*, 211–225.

Hogarth, R. M. (1981). Beyond discrete biases: Functional and dysfunctional aspects of judgmental heuristics. *Psychological Bulletin, 90*, 197–217.

Holyoak, K. J., & Gordon, P. C. (1984). Information processing and social cognition. In R. S. Wyer, Jr., T. K. Srull, & J. Hartwick (Eds.), *Handbook of social cognition* (Vol. 1, pp. 39–70). Hillsdale, NJ: Lawrence Erlbaum Associates.

Homa, D., Sterling, S., & Trepel, L. (1981). Limitations of exemplar-based generalizations and the abstraction of categorical information. *Journal of Experimental Psychology: Human Learning and Memory, 7*, 418–439.

Hormuth, S. (1986). The random sampling of experiences in situ. *Journal of Personality, 54*, 262–293.

Ingram, R. (Ed.). (1986). *Information processing approaches to psychopathology and clinical psychology*. New York: Academic Press.

Isen, A. M., Daubman, K. A., & Norwicki, G. (1987). Positive affect facilitates creative problem solving. *Journal of Personality and Social Psychology, 52*(6), 1122–1131.

Isen, A., & Moore, B. (Eds.). (in press). *Affect and social behavior*. New York: Academic Press.

Jacobson, N. S. (1984). The modification of cognitive processes in behavioral marital therapy: Integrating cognitive and behavioral intervention strategies. In K. Hahlweg & N. S. Jacobson (Eds.), *Marital interaction: Analysis and modification* (pp. 285–308). New York: Guilford Press.

Jones, E. E., & Berglas, S. (1978). Control of attributions about the self through self-handicapping strategies: The appeal of alcohol and the role of underachievement. *Personality and Social Psychology Bulletin, 4*, 200–206.

Jones, E. E., & Davis, K. E. (1965). From acts to dispositions: The attribution process in person perception. In L. Berkowitz (Ed.), *Advances in experimental social psychology* (Vol. 2, pp. 219–266). New York: Academic Press.

Jones, E. E., & Nisbett, R. E. (1972). The actor and the observer: Divergent perceptions of the causes of behavior. In E. E. Jones, D. E. Knouse, H. H. Kelley, R. E. Nisbett, S. Valins, & B. Weiner (Eds.), *Attribution: Perceiving the causes of behavior* (pp. 79–94). Morristown, NJ: General Learning Press.

Jones, E. E., & Pittman, T. S. (1982). Toward a general theory of strategic self-presentation. In J. Suls (Ed.), *Psychological perspectives on the self* (Vol. 1, pp. 231–262). Hillsdale, NJ: Lawrence Erlbaum Associates.

Kagan, J., & Kogan, N. (1970). Individual variation in cognitive processes. In P. Mussen (Ed.), *Carmichael's manual of child psychology* (Vol. 1, pp. 1273–1365). New York: Wiley.

Kagan, J., Rosman, B. L., Day, D., Albert, J., & Phillips, W. (1964). Information processing in the child: Significance of analytic and reflective attitudes. *Psychological Monographs, 78*, (I, Whole No. 578).

Kahneman, D., & Tversky, A. (1982). The stimulation heuristic. In D. Kahneman, P. Slovic, & A. Tversky (Eds.), *Judgment under uncertainty: Heuristics and biases* (pp. 201–208). New York: Cambridge University Press.

Keating, D. P. (1978). A search for social intelligence. *Journal of Educational Psychology, 70*(2), 218–223.

Keil, F. C. (1984). Transition mechanisms in cognitive development and the structure of knowledge. In R. Sternberg (Ed.), *Mechanisms of cognitive development* (pp. 81–99). San Francisco: Freeman.

Keil, F. C. (1986). The acquisition of natural kind and artifact terms. In W. Demopoulos & A. Marras (Eds.), *Language learning and concept acquisition.* Norwood, NJ: Ablex.

Kelley, H. (1967). Attribution theory in social psychology. In D. Levine (Ed.), *Nebraska symposium on motivation 1967 (Vol. 15, pp. 192–240). Lincoln: University of Nebraska Press.*

Kelley, H. (1972). Causal schemata and the attribution process. In E. E. Jones, D. Kanouse, H. Kelley, R. Nisbett, S. Valins, & B. Weiner (Eds.), *Attribution: Perceiving the causes of behavior* (pp. 151–174). Morristown, NJ: General Learning Press.

Kelly, G. (1955). *The psychology of personal constructs.* New York: Norton.

Kihlstrom, J. F. (1981). On personality and memory. In N. Cantor & J. F. Kihlstrom (Eds.), *Personality cognition, and social interaction* (pp. 123–149). Hillsdale, NJ: Lawrence Erlbaum Associates.

Kihlstrom. J. F. (1984). Conscious, subconscious, unconscious: A cognitive perspective. In K. Bowers & D. Meichenbaum (Eds.), *The unconscious reconsidered* (pp. 149–211). New York: Wiley.

Kihlstrom, J. F., & Cantor, N. (1984). Mental representations of the self. In L. Berkowitz (Ed.), *Advances in experimental social psychology* (Vol. 17, pp. 1–47). New York: Academic Press.

Kihlstrom, J. F., Cantor, N., Albright, J. S., Chew, B., Klein, S., & Niedenthal, P. M. (1988). Information processing and the study of the self. In L. Berkowitz (Ed.), *Advances in experimental social psychology* (Vol. 21, pp. 145–180). New York: Academic Press.

Kihlstrom, J. F., & Evans, F. (1979). Memory retrieval processes in posthypnotic amnesia. In J. Kihlstrom & F. Evans (Eds.), *Functional disorders of memory* (pp. 179–218). Hillsdale, NJ: Lawrence Erlbaum Associates.

Kihlstrom, J. F., & Harackiewicz, J. (1982). The earliest recollections: A new survey. *Journal of Personality, 50,* 134–148.

Kihlstrom, J. F., & Nasby, W. (1981). Cognitive tasks in clinical assessment: An exercise in applied psychology. In P. Kendall & S. Hollon (Eds.), *Cognitive-behavorial interventions: Assessment methods* (pp. 287–317). New York: Academic.

Klein, S. B., & Kihlstrom, J. F. (1986). Elaboration, organization, and the self-reference effect in memory. *Journal of Experimental Psychology: General, 115,* 26–38.

Klinger, E. (1975). Consequences of commitment to and disengagement from incentives. *Psychological Review, 82,* 1–25.

Klinger, E. (1977). *Meaning and void: Inner experience and the incentives in people's lives.* Minneapolis: University of Minnesota Press.

Kopp, C. B. (1982). Antecedents of self-regulation: A developmental perspective. *Developmental Psychology, 18,* 199–214.

Kuhl, J. (1985). From cognition to behavior: Perspectives for future research on action control. In J. Kuhl & J. Beckmann (Eds.), *Action control from cognition to behavior* (pp. 267–275). New York: Springer-Verlag.

Kuhl, J., & Beckmann, J. (Eds.). (1985). *Action control from cognition to behavior*. New York: Springer-Verlag.

Kuiper, N. A., & Derry, P. A. (1981). The self as a cognitive prototype: An application to person perception and to psychopathology. In N. Cantor & J. F. Kihlstrom (Eds.), *Personality, cognition, and social interaction* (pp. 215–232). Hillsdale, NJ: Lawrence Erlbaum Associates.

Laboratory of Comparative Human Cognition. (1982). Culture and intelligence. In R. Sternberg (Ed.), *Handbook of human intelligence* (pp. 642–719). Cambridge: Cambridge University Press.

Lang, P. J. (1979). Language, image & emotion. In P. Pliner, K. R. Plankstein, & J. M. Spigel (Eds.), *Perception of emotion in self and others* (pp. 107–117). New York: Plenum.

Langer, E. J. (in press, 1987). *Mindlessness/mindfullness*. Reading, MA: Addison-Wesley.

Langer, E., & Piper, A. (1987). The prevention of mindlessness. *Journal of Personality and Social Psychology, 53*(2), 280–287.

Langston, C. A., & Cantor, N. (in press 1988). Social anxiety and social constraint: When "Making friends" is hard. *Journal of Personality and Social Psychology*.

Larsen, R. J. (1987). The stability of mood variability: A spectral analytic approach to daily mood assessments. *Journal of Personality and Social Psychology, 52*(6), 1195–1204.

Levenson, H. (1972). *Distinction within the concept of internal–external control*. Paper presented at the American Psychological Association Convention, Washington, DC.

Leventhal, H. (1984). A perceptual-motor theory of emotion. In L. Berkowitz (Ed.), *Advances in experimental social psychology* (Vol. 17, pp. 118–182). New York: Academic Press.

Levinson, D. J. (1978). *The seasons of a man's life*. New York: Balantine.

Lewicki, P. (1984). Self-schema and social information processing. *Journal of Personality and Social Psychology, 47*(6), 1177–1190.

Lewin, K. (1935). *A dynamic theory of personality*. New York: McGraw-Hill.

Lewinsohn, P., Mischel, W., Chaplain, W., & Barton, R. (1980). Social competence and depression: The role of illusory self-perceptions. *Journal of Abnormal Psychology, 89*, 203–212.

Lewontin, R. C., Rose, S., & Kamin, L. J. (1984). *Not in our genes*. New York: Pantheon.

Lingle, J. H., Altom, M. W., & Medin, D. L. (1983). Of cabbages and kings: Assessing the extendibility of natural object concept models to social things. In R. S. Wyer, Jr., T. K. Srull, & J. Hartwick (Eds.), *Handbook of social cognition* (Vol. 1, pp. 71–118). Hillsdale, NJ: Lawrence Erlbaum Associates.

Linville, P. W. (1982). Affective consequences of complexity regarding the self and others. In M. Clark & S. Fiske (Eds.), *Affect and cognition: The 17th Annual Carnegie Symposium on cognition* (pp. 79–109). Hillsdale, NJ: Lawrence Erlbaum Associates.

Linville, P. W. (1985). Self-complexity and affective extremity: Don't put all of your eggs in one cognitive basket. *Social Cognition, 3*(1), 94–121.

Linville, P. W., & Jones, E. E. (1980). Polarized appraisals of outgroup members. *Journal of Personality and Social Psychology, 38*, 689–703.

Little, B. (1983). Personal projects—A rationale and methods for investigation. *Environmental Behavior, 15*, 273–309.

Markus, H. (1977). Self-schemata and processing information about the self. *Journal of Personality and Social Psychology, 35*, 63–78.

Markus, H. (1983). Self-knowledge: An expanded view. *Journal of Personality, 51*, 543–565.

Markus, H., & Nurius, P. (1986). Possible selves. *American Psychologist, 41*(9), 954–969.

Markus, H., & Wurf, E. (1987). The dynamic self-concept: A social psychological perspective. In M. R. Rosenszweig & L. W. Porter (Eds.), *Annual review of psychology* (Vol. 38, pp. 299–337). Palo Alto, CA: Annual Reviews.

Maslow, A. (1968). *Toward a psychology of being*. New York: Van Nostrand.

Matlin, M., & Stang, D. (1978). *The Pollyanna principle*. Cambridge, MA: Schenkman.

McFall, R. (1982). A review and reformulation of the concept of social skills. *Behavioral Assessment, 4*, 1–33.

McGuire, W. J. (1984). Search for the self: Going beyond self-esteem and the reactive self. In R. A. Zucker, J. Arnoff, & A. I. Rubin (Eds.), *Personality and the prediction of behavior* (pp. 73–120). New York: Academic Press.

McGuire, W. J., & Padawer-Singer, A. (1976). A trait salience in the spontaneous self-concept. *Journal of Personality and Social Psychology, 33,* 743–754.

Mead, G. (1934). *Mind, self, and society.* Chicago: University of Chicago Press.

Meichenbaum, D. (1977). *Cognitive behavior modifications: An integrated approach.* New York: Plenum.

Meichenbaum, D., & Cameron, R. (1982). Cognitive-behavior therapy. In G. T. Wilson & C. M. Franks (Eds.), *Contemporary behavior therapy: Conceptual and empirical foundations* (pp. 310–338). New York: Guilford.

Messer, S. (1976). Reflection–impulsivity: A review. *Psychological Bulletin, 83*(6), 1026–1052.

Metalsky, G. I., & Abramson, L. Y. (1981). Attributional styles: Toward a framework for conceptualization and assessment. In P. C. Kendall & S. D. Hollon (Eds.), *Cognitive-behavioral intentions: Assessment methods.* New York: Academic Press.

Miller, G., & Cantor, N. (1982). Review of human inference: Strategies and shortcomings of social judgment. *Social Cognition, 1,* 83–93.

Miller, S., & Mangan, C. (1983). Interacting effects of information and coping style in adapting to gynecologic stress: Should the doctor tell all? *Journal of Personality and Social Psychology, 45,* 223–236.

Mischel, W. (1973). Toward a cognitive social learning reconceptualization of personality. *Psychological Review, 80,* 252–283.

Mischel, W. (1977). The interaction of person and situation. In D. Magnusson & N. Endler (Eds.), *Personality at the crossroads: Current issues in interaction psychology.* Hillsdale, NJ: Lawrence Erlbaum Associates.

Mischel, W. (1979). On the interface of cognition and personality. *American Psychologist, 34,* 740–754.

Mischel, W. (1981). Metacognition and the rules of delay. In J. Flavell & L. D. Ross (Eds.), *Social cognitive development: Frontiers and possible futures* (pp. 240–271). New York: Cambridge University Press.

Mischel, W. (1984). Convergences and challenges in the search for consistency. *American Psychologist, 39,* 351–364.

Mischel, W., Ebbesen, E. B., & Zeiss, A. R. (1972). Cognitive and attentional mechanisms in delay of gratification. *Journal of Personality and Social Psychology, 21,* 204–218.

Money, J., & Ehrhardt, A. A. (1972). *Man and woman, boy and girl: Differentiation and dimorphism of gender identity from conception to maturity.* Baltimore: Johns Hopkins University Press.

Moos, R. H. (1973). Conceptualizations of human environments. *American Psychologist, 28,* 652–665.

Moos, R. H. (1974). *Family environment scale (Form R).* Palo Alto, CA: Consulting Psychologists Press.

Murray, H. (1938). *Explorations in personality.* New York: Oxford Press.

Nasby, W., & Kihlstrom, J. F. (1986). Cognitive assessment of personality and psychopathology. In R. E. Ingram (Ed.), *Information-processing approaches to psychopathology and clinical psychology* (pp. 217–239). New York: Academic Press.

Neisser, U. (1976). General academic, and artificial intelligence. In L. B. Resnick (Ed.), *The nature of intelligence* (pp. 240–271). Hillsdale, NJ: Lawrence Erlbaum Associates.

Neisser, U. (1979). The concept of intelligence. *Intelligence, 3,* 217–227.

Neisser, U. (1982). *Memory observed.* San Francisco: Freeman.

Nezlek, J. B., Wheeler, L., & Reis, H. T. (1983). Studies of social participation. *New directions for methodology of social and behavioral science, 15,* 57–73.

Nicholls, J. G. (1984). Achievement motivation: Conceptions of ability, subjective experience, task choice, and performance. *Psychological Review, 91*(3), 328–346.

Niedenthal, P. M. (1987). *Unconscious affect in social cognition*. Unpublished doctoral dissertation, University of Michigan, Ann Arbor.

Nisbett, R. E., & Ross, L. (1980). *Human inference: Strategies and shortcomings in social judgment*. Englewood Cliffs, NJ: Prentice-Hall.

Nisbett, R. E., & Wilson, T. (1977). Telling more than we can know: Verbal reports on mental processes. *Psychological Review, 84*, 231–259.

Nolen-Hoeksema, S. (1987). Sex differences in unipolar depression: Evidence and theory. *Psychological Bulletin, 101*(2), 259–282.

Norem, J. K. (1987). *Strategic realities: Optimism and defensive pessimism*. Unpublished doctoral dissertation, University of Michigan, Ann Arbor.

Norem, J. K., & Cantor, N. (1986a). Anticipatory and post hoc cushioning strategies: Optimism and defensive pessimism in "risky" situations. *Cognitive Therapy and Research, 10*(3), 347–362.

Norem, J. K., & Cantor, N. (1986b). Defensive pessimism: "Harnessing" anxiety as motivation. *Journal of Personality and Social Psychology, 51*(6), 1208–1217.

Norem, J. K., & Cantor, N. (in press, 1988). Capturing the "flavor" of behavior: Cognition, affect and interpretation. In A. Isen & B. Moore (Eds.), *Affect & social behavior*. New York: Academic Press.

Norman, W. (1963). Toward an adequate taxonomy of personal attributes: Replicated factor structures in peer nomination personality ratings. *Journal of Abnormal and Social Psychology, 66*, 574–583.

Ostrom, T. (1984). The sovereignty of social cognition. In R. S. Wyer & T. K. Srull (Eds.), *Handbook of social cognition* (Vol. 1, pp. 1–38). Hillsdale, NJ: Lawrence Erlbaum Associates.

Ostrum, T., & Davis, D. (1979). Idiosyncratic weighting of trait information in impression formation. *Journal of Personality and Social Psychology, 37*(11), 2025–2043.

Oyserman, D., & Markus, H. (1987). *Possible selves and delinquency*. Unpublished manuscript, University of Michigan, Ann Arbor.

Pervin, L. (1976). A free-response description approach to the analysis of person–situation interaction. *Journal of Personality and Social Psychology, 34*(3), 465–474.

Pervin, L. (1988). *The goals concept in personality and social psychology*. Hillsdale, NJ: Lawrence Erlbaum Associates.

Peterson, C., & Seligman, M. (1984). Causal explanations as a risk factor for depression: Theory and evidence. *Psychological Review, 91*(3), 347–374.

Phillips, D. (1984). The illusion of incompetence among academically competent children. *Child Development, 55*, 2000–2016.

Plutchik, R. (1980). A general psychoevolutionary theory of emotion. In R. Plutchik & H. Kellerman (Eds.), *Emotion: Theory research and experience* (pp. 3–33). New York: Academic Press.

Price, R., & Bouffard, D. L. (1974). Behavioral appropriateness and situational constraint as dimensions of social behavior. *Journal of Personality and Social Psychology, 30*, 579–586.

Pyszczynski, T., & Greenberg, J. (1987). Self-regulatory perseveration and the depressive self-focusing style: A self-awareness theory of reactive depression. *Psychological Bulletin, 102*(1), 122–138.

Reich, J. W., & Zautra, A. J. (1983). Demands and desires in daily life: Some influences on well-being. *American Journal of Community Psychology, 1*, 41–58.

Rheingold, H. (1982). Little children's participation in the work of adults: A nascent prosocial behavior. *Child Development, 53*, 114–125.

Riggs, J., & Cantor, N. (1982). Getting acquainted: The role of self-concept and preconceptions. *Personality and Social Psychology Bulletin, 10*(3), 432–446.

Robinson, J. A. (1976). Sampling autobiographical memory. *Cognitive Psychology, 8*, 578–595.

Rogers, C. R. (1951). *Client-centered therapy.* New York: Houghton–Mifflin.

Rogers, T. B. (1981). A model of the self as an aspect of human information processing. In N. Cantor & J. Kihlstrom (Eds.), *Personality, cognition, and social interaction system* (pp. 193–214). Hillsdale, NJ: Lawrence Erlbaum Associates.

Rosenberg, S. (1977). New approaches to the analysis of personal constructs in person perception. *Nebraska symposium on motivation 1976* (Vol. 24, pp. 179–242). Lincoln: University of Nebraska Press.

Rosenberg, S., & Gara, M. A. (1985). The multiplicity of personal identity. In P. Shaver (Ed.), *Review of personality and social psychology* (Vol. 6). Beverly Hills: Sage.

Ross, L. (1977). The intuitive psychologist and his shortcomings: Distortions in the attribution process. In L. Berkowitz (Ed.), *Advances in experimental social psychology* (Vol. 10, pp. 173–220). New York: Academic Press.

Rotter, J. B. (1954). *Social learning and clinical psychology.* Englewood Cliffs, NJ: Prentice-Hall.

Rotter, J. B. (1975). Some problems and misconceptions related to the construct of internal versus external control of reinforcement. *Journal of Consulting and Clinical Psychology, 48,* 56–67.

Rotter, J. B., Chance, J. E., & Phares, E. J. (1972). *Applications of a social learning theory of personality.* New York: Holt, Rinehart, & Winston.

Ruble, D. N., & Rholes, W. S. (1981). New development of children's perceptions and attributions about their social world. In J. H. Harvey, W. Ickes, & R. F. Kidd (Eds.), *New directions in attribution research* (Vol. 3). Hillsdale, NJ: Lawrence Erlbaum Associates.

Ruhrold, R. (1986). *Differentiation of social knowledge structures and skill in marital problem-solving.* Unpublished doctoral dissertation, University of Michigan, Ann Arbor.

Ryff, C. D. (1982). Successful aging: A developmental approach. *The Gerontologist, 22,* 209–214.

Salovey, P., & Rodin, J. (1985). Cognitions about the self: Connecting feeling states and social behavior. In P. Shaver (Ed.), *Review of personality and social psychology* (Vol. 6, pp. 143–166). Beverly Hills: Sage.

Sarbin, T. R. (1952). A preface to a psychological analysis of the self. *Psychological Review, 59,* 11–22.

Scheier, M. F., & Carver, C. S. (1985). Optimism, coping and health: Assessment and implications of generalized outcome expectancies. *Health Psychology, 4,* 219–247.

Scheier, M. F., Weintraub, J. K., & Carver, C. S. (1986). Coping with stress: Divergent strategies of optimists and pessimists. *Journal of Personality and Social Psychology, 51*(6), 1257–1264.

Scott, W., Osgood, D., & Peterson, C. (1979). *Cognitive structure: Theory and measurement of individual differences.* Washington, DC: Winston.

Scribner, S., & Cole, M. (1973). Cognitive consequences of formal and informal education. *Science, 182,* 553–559.

Segal, Z. (1988). Appraisal of the self-schema construct in cognitive models of depression. *Psychological Bulletin, 103*(2), 147–162.

Shaver, P., Schwartz, J., O'Connor, C., Kirson, D., Marsh, C., & Fischer, S. (1985). *Emotions and emotion knowledge: A prototype approach.* Unpublished manuscript, University of Denver.

Shevrin, H. (1986). *The role of consciousness, motivation, and level of organization in person schemata.* Presented at Program on Conscious and Unconscious Mental Processes of the John O. and Katherine T. MacArthur Foundation, Center for the Advanced Study in the Behavioral Sciences, Stanford, CA.

Showers, C. J. (1986). *Anticipatory cognitive strategies: The positive side of negative thinking.* Unpublished doctoral dissertation, University of Michigan, Ann Arbor.

Showers, C., & Cantor, N. (1985). Social cognition: A look at motivated strategies. In M. Rosenzweig & L. W. Porter (Eds.), *Annual review of psychology* (Vol. 36, pp. 275–305). Palo Alto, CA: Annual Reviews.

Simon, H. (1955). A behavioral model of rational choice. *Quarterly Journal of Economics, 69,* 99–118.

Skov, R. B., & Sherman, S. J. (1986). Information-gathering processes: Diagnosticity, hypothesis-confirmatory strategies, and perceived hypothesis confirmation. *Journal of Experimental Social Psychology, 22,* 93–121.

Smith, E. (1984). A model of social inference processes. *Psychological Review, 91*(3), 392–413.

Smith, E., & Medin, D. (1981). *Categories and concepts.* Cambridge, MA: Harvard University Press.

Smith, T. W., & Rhodewalt, F. (1986). On states, traits, and processes: A transactional alternative to the individual difference assumptions in Type A behavior and physiological reactivity. *Journal of Research in Personality, 20*(3), 229–251.

Snyder, C. R. (1985). The excuse: An amazing grace? In B. Schlenker (Ed.), *The self and social life* (pp. 235–261). New York: McGraw-Hill.

Snyder, M. (1979). Self-monitoring processes. In L. Berkowitz (Ed.), *Advances in experimental social psychology* (Vol. 12, pp. 85–128). New York: Academic Press.

Snyder, M. (1981a). On the influence of individuals on situations. In N. Cantor & J. Kihlstrom, *Personality, cognition, and social interaction* (pp. 309–329). Hillsdale, NJ: Lawrence Erlbaum Associates.

Snyder, M. (1981b). Seek, and ye shall find: Testing hypotheses about other people. In E. T. Higgins, C. P. Herman, & M. P. Zanna (Eds.), *Social cognition: The Ontario symposium on personality and social psychology* (Vol. 1, pp. 277–304). Hillsdale, NJ: Lawrence Erlbaum Associates.

Snyder, M. L., Stephan, W. G., & Rosenfield, D. (1978). Attributional egotism. In J. Harvey, W. Ickes, & D. Kidd (Eds.), *New directions in attribution research* (Vol. 2, pp. 91–117). Hillsdale, NJ: Lawrence Erlbaum Associates.

Snygg, D., & Combs, A. W. (1949). *Individual behavior.* New York: Harper & Row.

Sorrentino, R. M., & Higgins, E. T. (Eds.). (1986). *Motivation and cognition: Foundations of social behavior.* New York: Guilford Press.

Spivak, G., Platt, J., & Shure, M. (1976). *The problem-solving approach to adjustment.* San Francisco: Jossey-Bass.

Srull, T. K., & Wyer, R. S., Jr. (1980). Category accessibility and social perception: Some implications for the study of person memory and interpersonal judgments. *Journal of Personality and Social Psychology, 38,* 841–856.

Sternberg, R. J. (1982). The nature of intelligence. *New York University Education Quarterly, 12,* 10–17.

Sternberg, R. J. (1984). Toward a triarchic theory of human intelligence. *The Behavioral and Brain Sciences, 7,* 269–315.

Sternberg, R. J., Conway, B., Keton, J., & Berstein, M. (1981). People's conceptions of intelligence. *Journal of Personality and Social Psychology, 41*(1), 37–55.

Stewart, A. J., & Healy, J. M., Jr. (1985). Personality and adaptation to change. In R. Hogan & W. Jones (Eds.), *Perceptives on personality: Theory, measurement, and interpersonal dynamics* (pp. 117–144). Greenwich, CT: JAI Press.

Swann, W., & Ely, R. (1984). A battle of wills: Self-verification versus behavioral confirmation. *Journal of Personality and Social Psychology, 46,* 1287–1302.

Tabachnik, N., Crocker, J., & Alloy, L. (1983). Depression, social comparison, and the false-consensus effect. *Journal of Personality and Social Psychology, 45,* 688–699.

Taylor, S. E., & Brown, J. (1988). Illusion and well being: Some social psychological contributions to a theory of mental health. *Psychological Bulletin, 103*(3), 193–210.

Tesser, A., & Campbell, J. (1983). Self-definition and self-evaluation maintenance. In J. Suls & A. G. Greenwald (Eds.), *Psychological perspectives on the self* (Vol. 2, pp. 1–31). Hillsdale, NJ: Lawrence Erlbaum Associates.

Thorndike, E. (1920). Intelligence and its uses. *Harper's Magazine, 140,* 227–235.

Trope, Y. (1986). Self-enhancement and self-assessment in achievement behavior. In R. Sorrentino

& E. Higgins (Eds.), *Handbook of motivation and cognition: Foundations of social behavior* (pp. 350–378). New York: Guilford.

Trope, Y., & Bassock, M. (1983). Information-gathering strategies in hypothesis-testing. *Journal of Experimental Social Psychology, 19,* 560–576.

Trzebinski, J., McGlynn, R., Gray, G., & Tubbs, D. (1985). The role of categories of an actors's goals in organizing inferences about a person. *Journal of Personality and Social Psychology, 48*(6), 1387–1397.

Tulving, E. (1972). Episodic and semantic memory. In E. Tulving & W. Donalson (Eds.), *Organization of memory* (pp. 382–404). New York: Academic Press.

Tversky, A., & Kahneman, D. (1974). Judgment under uncertainty: Heuristics and biases. *Sciences, 185,* 1124–1131.

Vallacher, R. R., & Wegner, D. M. (1985). *A theory of action identification.* Hillsdale, NJ: Lawrence Erlbaum Associates.

Valliant, G., & McArthur, C. (1972). Natural history of male psychologic health. I: The adult life cycle from 18–50. *Seminars in Psychiatry, 4,* 415–427.

Veroff, J. (1983). Contextual determinants of personality. *Personality and Sociaı Psychology Bulletin, 9,* 331–344.

Vygotsky, L. S. (1962). *Thought and language.* Cambridge, MA: MIT Press.

Weiner, B. (1985). An attributional theory of achievement motivation and emotion. *Psychological Review, 92*(4), 548–573.

Weiner, B., Frieze, I., Kukla, A., Reed, L., Rest, S., & Rosenbaum, R. (1972). Perceiving the causes of success and failure. In E. Jones, D. Kanouse, H. Kelley, R. Nisbett, S. Valins, & B. Weiner (Eds.), *Attribution: Perceiving the causes of behavior* (pp. 95–120). Morristown, NJ: General Learning Press.

White, J., & Carlston, D. (1983). Consequences of schemata for attention, impressions, and recall in complex social interactions. *Journal of Personality and Social Psychology, 45*(3), 538–549.

Wilson, G. T., & Franks, C. (Eds.). (1982). *Cognitive behavior therapy.* New York: Guilford.

Wilson, T., & Stone, J. I. (1985). Limitations of self-knowledge: More on telling more than we can know. In P. Shaver (Ed.), *Review of personality and social psychology* (Vol. 6, pp. 167–183). Beverly Hills: Sage.

Witkin, H., & Goodenough, D. (1977). Field dependence and interpersonal behavior. *Psychological Bulletin, 84*(4), 661–689.

Witkin, H. A., Dyk, R. B., Faterson, H. F., Goodenough, D. R., & Karp, S. A. (1962). *Psychological differentiation.* Hillsdale, NJ: Lawrence Erlbaum Associates.

Wright, J., & Mischel, W. (1987). The conditional approach to dispositional constructs: The local predictability of social behavior. *Journal of Personality and Social Psychology, 53*(6), 1157–1177.

Wyer, R. S., & Srull, T. K. (1981). Category accessibility: Some theoretical and empirical issues concerning the processing of social stimulus information. In E. T. Higgins, C. P. Herman, & M. P. Zanna (Eds.), *Social cognition. The Ontario symposium* (Vol. 1, pp. 161–197). Hillsdale, NJ: Lawrence Erlbaum Associates.

Zajonc, R. B. (1980a). Cognition and social cognition: A historical perspective. In L. Festinger (Ed.), *Four decades of social psychology.* Oxford: Oxford University Press.

Zajonc, R. B. (1980b). Feeling and thinking: Preferences need no inferences. *American Psychologist, 35,* 151–175.

Zajonc, R. B., & Markus, H. (1985). Must all affect be mediated by cognition? *Journal of Consumer Research, 12,* 363–364.

Zuroff, D. C. (1982). Person, situation, and person-by-situation interaction components in person perception. *Journal of Personality, 50,* 1–14.

2 Why a Theory of Social Intelligence Needs a Theory of Character

Jonathan Baron
University of Pennsylvania

Cantor and Kihlstrom argue that the adequacy of personality and social intelligence must be judged with respect to the individual's own goals and environment. A style or habit that is good for one person in one environment may be bad for a person with different goals or one in a different environment. Individuals have many goals and function in several environments (situations) simultaneously, and they must learn to achieve their goals in each environment. We can expect successful adaptations to be specific to certain kinds of situations. General dispositions that cut across environments, when they exist, are likely to be unsuccessful in some of these environments. The adequacy of a person's adaptation should be assessed in environments that are somewhat familiar. The study of personality is best carried out by examination of homogeneous groups of people who are all trying to solve similar problems.

I agree with most of this. For example, I applaud the inclusion of personal goals as well as environmental demands in the definition of social intelligence. Too many definitions of various forms of intelligence (e.g., Sternberg, 1985) speak of adaptation as if goals did not exist or were the same for all individuals in a given environment.

I begin this response with a couple of quibbles about the generality–specificity issue. Then I sketch my own theory of social intelligence and personality, which is in the same spirit as that of Cantor and Kihlstrom.

First, the quibbles. One concerns the argument about specificity. Surely it is true that habits and styles may be specific to people's goals in certain situations, so they may not be completely general. Such specificity, however, may also be the result of a superficial analysis of habits and styles. At a deeper level, consistency might be found. (Or it might not be found.) We cannot just assume that lack of generality is, so to speak, a general rule of human functioning.

For example, take the style dimension of reflection–impulsivity in problem solving, cited by Cantor and Kihlstrom. The usual definition of this dimension is that reflectives are those who are slow in order to be careful and impulsives are fast and careless. Thus, the dimension may be measured by subtracting an individual's rank (or z score) on errors within some reference group from his rank on time in some problem-solving task.

Baron, Badgio, and Gaskins (1986) have proposed an alternative definition, in which the dimension is defined in terms of the optimal amount of time a person ought to spend, given the person's own goals and abilities in the task. The time a person ought to spend is dependent on her desire to be correct, her personal cost for the time spent, and the expected effect of extra time on accuracy (which, in turn, depends on ability).

A child may be fast and inaccurate in one situation but slow and careful in another, yet equally reflective in both, by the new definition. In the first situation, the child may have low ability, so that spending extra time is useless, or no interest in the task. By this (arguably) less superficial definition of reflectiveness, consistency may be found across situations, even if it is not found with the traditional measures. I know of no evidence on this point (except for the findings of Baron et al., 1986, which show only that the new and old dimensions are not identical). It is just a possibility that should be explored.

I think that Cantor and Kihlstrom might be sympathetic to this possibility, because it fits with their own emphasis on looking at adaptation with respect to a person's goals in the situation. The point is that, when we do that, consistencies may emerge that were not apparent beforehand.[1]

I must set the stage for my second quibble by introducing some distinctions that will also be important later, those among normative, prescriptive, and descriptive theories (Baron, 1985a, 1986, 1988a, in press). A *normative* theory, in the present context, is a general standard that tells us what good adaptation is. It is a criterion by which we evaluate specific cases. For example, to say that a good adaptation is one that is likely to help someone achieve their goals is an (incomplete) normative theory. It tells us what we need to do to evaluate a particular person's adaptation, namely, discover what their goals are, what their habits and styles are, and how likely these habits and styles are to succeed, compared to the alternatives. Another normative theory is the statement that the amount of time a child spends on a problem should maximize the expected attainment of the child's goals (Baron et al., 1986).

A *descriptive* theory or account describes what an individual, or some group,

---

[1]Cantor and Kihlstrom may be too demanding when they call .30 a "modest" correlation in personality research. I do not, however, belabor that point, as I am sure they are right for some cases even if they are wrong here.

actually do. Descriptions are most useful when they permit comparison with the normative standard. For example, the most useful description of reflection–impulsivity compares the child to her own optimum rather than to other children (Baron et al., 1986). Such a description allows us to say how close a child is to her normative optimum.

If we find a gap between normative and descriptive accounts, we may then ask how we might close it. Statements that attempt to answer this question are *prescriptive*. In general, normative theories are not also prescriptive. For example, it does no good to tell people to take the optimum amount of time on every problem: If they try to figure out what the optimum is, they will use up more than the optimum just doing this figuring. People need something more like rules of thumb, rules that bring them closer to the optimum than they would be without the rules. These rules are prescriptive. Prescriptive rules are exactly those that people should try to follow.

Psychotherapy is a prescriptive discipline that tailors its advice to the person and the situation. (Arguably, it neglects the normative by not having a clear theory of its goals, as argued by Baron, Baron, Barber, & Nolen-Hoeksema, in press.) It is also possible to give people general advice, based on a knowledge of common discrepancies between normative and descriptive (Baron, 1985a, 1988b). For example, one common departure from the normative model is short-sightedness about the long-term future (Ainslie, 1975; Thaler & Shefrin, 1981), especially in children (Mischel, 1974, 1984). A variety of prescriptive mechanisms are available for dealing with this problem (Ainslie, 1986; Strotz, 1955).

Cantor and Kihlstrom's arguments for specificity (and against generality) are made at the descriptive level, and perhaps also at the prescriptive level. (They do not make this distinction, so their view on it is not completely clear.) Surely they are right at the descriptive level, putting my first quibble aside. At the prescriptive level, they are often right as well. The advice we give people ought to depend on their goals and abilities, which will vary from situation to situation. On the other hand, there may be certain kinds of prescriptive advice that counteract well-established biases, such as the neglect of the future. It may be helpful to teach all children to think more about the future than they are naturally inclined to do.

At the normative level, the situation changes radically. The most useful normative standards are the most general ones. Normative standards are not arrived at by empirical inquiry, but by philosophical reflection about our goals. If we have separate normative standards for different domains of life—e.g., self-interest versus morality, the present versus the future, work versus play—then we will also need some additional, general, standard to reconcile these when there is conflict. If possible, we should seek some general standards of rational conduct that can be applied throughout, and that can, if necessary, justify particular standards for particular problems. I have more to say about this later. For now, remember that I am speaking of a normative standard, not prescriptive advice. The normative standard is not the field manual for living; it is the justification of that manual.

The normative-descriptive distinction has implications for Cantor and Kihlstrom's claim that adaptation should be tested only in situations that are somewhat familiar. I do not want to reject this claim completely. Rather, I argue that its validity depends on the purpose of assessment. For the clinician's purpose, which is that of helping people achieve their goals in environments that are realistic for them, I accept the claim. The educator's (or parent's) purpose, however, may be something more like the maintenance and promulgation of certain standards of conduct or thought. For this purpose, the standards in question are normative, and it may be important to ask whether students (or children) understand the standards in their full generality, for that is the best test of understanding.

For example, we might have reason to be interested in whether a person understands the need to attend to future consequences in general, in government as well as in personal saving and investment. People may behave as if they understand this need in their own immediate lives only because they have learned by rote certain habits of thrift or self-restraint. The same people might vote for political candidates who care not a whit about the disappearance of ozone or tropical forests.

TOWARD A PRESCRIPTIVE THEORY OF PERSONALITY

Cantor and Kihlstrom accept the possibility of an evaluative theory of personality, a theory that has implications at least for particular people about what they should and should not try to do with their lives. The very idea that personality has something to do with social *intelligence* contains this implication, for intelligence is an evaluative concept. Cantor and Kihlstrom temper their moralizing with the implication that advice must be specific to the person and situation, but they moralize nonetheless. I applaud them for this. A theory of personality without implications for the advice we give to our clients, students, or children (or ourselves) is an empty theory indeed.

What I do from here on is to spell out a little more explicitly what a prescriptive theory of personality might look like. I suggest that there is in fact general advice that we can give to all people, for example, to children, about their personality and social intelligence. I further suggest that this advice cannot be separated from the more general standards that we have for each other and ourselves, standards that are loosely described by the old-fashioned but still useful word *character*.

Let us start with the idea of personal goals. So far, I have accepted the convenient fiction that these goals are givens, not to be evaluated, not to be the target of any helping interventions. I have assumed that people are doing well if they are achieving the goals *as they see them*. (Cantor and Kihlstrom do not seem to challenge this assumption.) One does not need to be a Freudian, however, to see that people's perceived goals might not be their real goals. Once we admit that people might not, in some sense, know their own goals, we must ask which goals are relevant to a prescriptive theory, the perceived goals or the real ones? The question becomes still more difficult when we ask what "real" goals are. Are they, to paraphrase Freud, the underlying causes of our perceived goals and behavior, our drives for sex, power, whatever? If so, should we try to satisfy these goals in their pure forms (as opposed to their sublimated forms)?

An alternative view, which I find better suited to the purposes of our theory, is that the goals we ought to try to satisfy are those that we would have on reflection (Baron, 1985a, ch. 2; Baron, 1985b; Rawls, 1971, ch. VII). If we satisfy these goals, we have no cause for regret or self-blame on the basis of some deeper understanding, no matter how things turn out. Of course, this is a normative theory, not a prescriptive one. A normal lifetime is not enough to complete the kind of reflection this definition requires, although we do have time to make some progress, especially if we are able to build on the wisdom of the past.

What kind of reflection is presupposed by such a view? How does one think about one's goals? Here is one possible answer. Goal formation may be seen as a kind of decision making. People may decide to try to be closer to God, to try to make a pile of money, or to try to be respected by people around them. If they decide these things, they acquire new personal goals for their lives. They will be happy when they see themselves as achieving these goals and unhappy when they see themselves as failing. These goals will become the bases for other decisions. If a woman believes that attending a certain church will bring her closer to God, she will decide to attend that church. In this way, these personal goals become the determinants of a person's "utilities," in the sense used in decision theory.

Goal formation is like decision making: It is a choice based on beliefs and other goals. For example, a personal goal of helping others (even at one's own expense) may be based on the belief that such altruism is rewarded in heaven. This dependence of goals on beliefs shows itself in our tenacious attachment to those beliefs that underlie our goals. If my personal goal of being altruistic is dependent on my belief in an afterlife, I will resist challenges to that belief, lest I be forced to see my life as purposeless.

Formation of personal goals is unlike other decision making in at least one important respect, and it is this respect that has prevented us from seeing the similarities. Personal goals are what Elster (1983) calls *essentially bi-products*. Creating a goal in oneself is like making oneself go to sleep; one can succeed only by trying to do something else (e.g., count sheep). One can decide to go to church and the decision can usually be carried out straightforwardly. It is not so easy, however, to simply decide to love God, one's job, or one's spouse (if one does not), even if one would like to love these objects. On a more mundane level, my son told me that he could not make himself want to practice a certain (difficult) piano piece. Because of the difficulty, people think of personal goals as things that happen to them rather than things they bring about themselves.[2]

It is also true, however, that goals, like sleep, may be influenced by our actions, so they may properly be the object of decisions. Pascal understood this when he proposed his famous wager (Elster, 1979). One cannot bring oneself to love the Christian God by directly willing to love Him, but one can increase the chance that this will happen by living as Christians live, by attending church, by associating with the faithful, and so on.

The adoption of goals is a problem in self-control. Self-control problems involve conflicts between immediate desires and the desires for our future (Ainslie, 1975, 1986) or our better judgment (Elster, 1985). The adoption of a goal to desire altruism, or exercise, may require actions that go against one's immediate desires. For example, one way to bring about new desires is to act as if one had them. By forcing oneself to exercise repeatedly, for example, the negative effects of exercise will decrease and the positive aftereffects increase (Solomon & Corbit, 1974), so that eventually one does not have to force oneself. (Similar effects may occur for altruism.)

A consequence of the fact that goals cannot be adopted by direct decisions is that we need to separate normative and prescriptive theories of goal adoption. Normatively, we may treat goal adoption as a simple decisions. The best goals for a person to have are those that would be chosen as if goals were easy to adopt. It is not helpful, however, to *try* to choose goals in this way. Therefore, the prescriptive advice we give or try to follow would be to do those things that tend to lead people to adopt the goals they would adopt on reflection and with full control.

To be sure, some of the things that people ought to do would probably include reflection itself. When asked about their plans, and the reasons for those plans, people ought to be able to give better answers than, ''That's just what I've always planned to do, I haven't thought about it.'' (Marcia, 1966, takes this kind of response as a sign of ''identity foreclosure.'') People ought to have a better understanding of the reasons behind their most important choices than they have of the reasons for their choice of a meal in a restaurant.

Still, reflection has its limits. It cannot help us choose the best goals without our having knowledge—or wisdom—of the type that usually comes too late to do any good. In the choice of goals, we must rely to some extent on the beliefs of others who are older and wiser. Psychological theories ought to reflect whatever wisdom they can. The fundamental criteria of social intelligence should be the *prescriptive* rules that bring people closest to the goals they would have on reflection. To determine what these goals are, however, we cannot simply ask people.

---

[2]For some, it may be just as well they see it this way, for the ultimate strength of their goals may be lessened by the belief that they created them.

By this view many attempts to assess personal goals are superficial. They assume that people's goals are given and known to them. Such assessments are useful if our goal is to help people achieve their current goals as they see them, but not if our goal is to help them achieve the goals they would have on reflection. For that purpose, we would need to enter into a longer dialogue with our subjects, in which we try to help them discover or construct their deeper goals through a process of reflection. Even this may be insufficient, because some of the relevant goals are those that persons will have later in their lives. It may be impossible for a young person to reflect enough to discover these goals. It may be better for an advice giver to make general predictions about a person's goals, based on knowledge of people like the advice recipient or even knowledge of people in general.

The traditional study of social intelligence seems to presuppose certain goals and ignore the possibility of others. There is little mention in the Cantor and Kihlstrom chapter, nor in the literature they review, of moral goals. The kinds of goals examined are those of getting ahead and being liked by others. People who live their lives according to moral goals, however, can be just as happy as those who seek success and popularity. Pursuit of moral goals can even lead to success and popularity. Sabini and Silver (1982) have shown how our everyday life is imbued with moral judgments, which presuppose moral goals. At least our social discourse presupposes such goals. Getting ahead and being liked are often bi-products of trying to do good or be good. The people we like and promote are those who appear to be genuinely unselfish, and the easiest way to appear to be unselfish is, quite possibly, to be unselfish.

Is it the business of personality theorists to say what goals people ought to have? We do this implicitly through our choice of topics for study. Why not do it explicitly, on the basis of some reflection about what goals people ought to have? Such an exercise must avoid two obstacles: that of being disrespectful of autonomy, on the one side, and that of being empty, on the other.

It is possible that something can be said that avoids both obstacles. In particular, people ought to have altruistic goals as well as selfish ones, and people ought to have goals for their whole future lives, not just the immediate future. By altruistic goals, I mean personal goals whose satisfaction depends on the satisfaction of the goals of others. Thus, I have an altruistic goal with respect to my son if I desire his happiness. (By this definition, I can still *enjoy* his happiness myself. The point is that this type of altruism is the kind we would want each other to have. By that criterion, an altruism based on empathy—taking pleasure in others' pleasures and suffering from their pains—is just as desirable as a principled altruism of the type favored by Kant.)

It would take too long to defend these claims fully here. But a few points can be made. First, these two criteria are related. If one should be concerned with others, it would be strange not to be concerned with one's own future as well (and vice versa—see Nagel, 1970; Parfit, 1984), for we may think of our future selves as somewhat different people, whose interests we have a special obligation to promote (mainly because we know these future people well).

Second, the pursuit of these two goals, prudence and morality, promotes happiness and prevents unhappiness. If one neglects one's future, one is likely to suffer later from decisions made now. If one knows that one is neglecting one's future, one has the additional burden of living with the dread of the consequences of one's folly. Moreover, concern with one's future permits the development of a life plan (Rawls, 1971) that includes the development of one's talents—a kind of long-term investment leading to legitimate self-esteem.

If one neglects others, one is likely to lose their respect. Admittedly, gaining the respect of others requires only that one be concerned with those whose respect one wants, who might not include, for example, those living in poverty on the other side of the world. Still, it is probably difficult to create in oneself the kind of moral motives that impress others as being real rather than manipulative and, at the same time, limit the scope of these motives to those one would want to manipulate.

Moreover, in helping people to shape their personalities, we must sometimes take the perspective of the educator (Baron, 1985a, ch. 2), asking not just what is good for the client before us, but what is good for everyone. It is good for everyone that everyone be concerned with everyone else, more than we now are on the average. Clinical psychologists are perhaps rightly less concerned with this perspective because their clients are often suffering, but a theory of social intelligence ought to inform other applications as well, such as education and child rearing. Even many clients in psychotherapy suffer in part because of the effects of their selfishness on the reactions of others to them.

In saying that people should pursue prudence and morality, we do not neglect their individual autonomy, for there are many ways to pursue these goals. Nor are we saying something that is empty, for many people do not pay enough attention to these goals. People tend to be myopic both in their concern for their futures (Ainslie, 1975, 1986; Mischel, 1974, 1984; Thaler & Shefrin, 1981) and in their concern for others (Baron, 1988b, chs. 18–20; Messick, 1985). On reflection, most people would want themselves and others to give more attention to their own futures and to the needs of others than they actually give. Selfishness and myopia are common biases of all people, and whatever prescriptive advice we can give to correct them is well given.

If this view is correct, a socially intelligent personality is one that lacks these biases. Socially intelligent people are fair to others, near or distant, and fair to their own futures. Within these broad goals of being prudent and morally good, there will be a great variety of specific goals characteristic of individuals. For children, we do not know what these specific goals will be. We should not, however, hold back from trying to shape their personalities so that they are generally prudent and caring, in a word, thoughtful. If we hold back—perhaps because of some kind of ideal of autonomy—we risk that the children grow up to be unhappy because they lack these very goals.

Of course, there is every good reason to have specific goals: To look out for one's future one does well to develop career-related interests. Those who do best at looking out for others may well be those who choose one primary way of doing so—a career of service, for example. When we learn what a person's individual goals are, we can assess more exactly how well he is achieving them.

There are many college students, probably some included in the sample studied by Cantor et al. (1987), who are doing well both in achievement and in personal relationships, yet who will live ultimately unhappy lives because their goals are too shallow. They pursue careers on the basis of ambience and style. By contrast, there are others who may not seem so successful at the moment, yet who are committed to doing something useful with their lives over the long haul. These are not people who set out to be happy, but people who set out to achieve some worthwhile goal in their work and to be caring in their personal lives. Happiness may be best achieved by trying to achieve something else.

What would we say of a person who was socially intelligent by these criteria? I think we would say that such a person has good character. From this viewpoint, good character is not a matter of sticking blindly to certain rules, such as never breaking a promise or telling a lie (Baron, 1986). It is, rather, a matter of developing dispositions of concern for others, such as trust, charity, and thoughtfulness, and dispositions that will help one in the future, such as some of those associated with being a good student, curiosity, diligence, and open-mindedness. By dispositions, I mean not just the goals, but the habits that result from having these goals for awhile and trying to learn how to achieve them. For example, people who truly care about others will develop a disposition not to break promises, and even when they must break a promise (say to avoid some greater harm), they will feel guilty (Hare, 1981).

What are the implications of this view for research? One is that part of the study of social intelligence and personality should concern itself with the formation of moral goals and goals for the future, and the dispositions that serve these goals. Much of this research is being done. There is a whole field concerned with the development of "prosocial" motives and the development of personal plans. I am suggesting only that we look at this research a little differently. We should study character in the way we now study intelligence, or biases in reasoning, in a way that is explicitly evaluative. I think this idea is just a small step further in the direction that Cantor and Kihlstrom have taken us.

REFERENCES

Ainslie, G. (1975). Specious reward: A behavioral theory of impulsiveness and impulse control. *Psychological Bulletin, 82,* 463–496.
Ainslie, G. (1986). Beyond microeconomics. Conflict among interests in a multiple self as a determinant of value. In J. Elster (Ed.), *The multiple self.* New York: Cambridge University Press.
Baron, J. (1985a). *Rationality and intelligence.* New York: Cambridge University Press.
Baron, J. (1985b). Rational plans, achievement, and education. In M. Frese & J. Sabini (Eds.),

Goal directed behavior: The concept of action in psychology. Hillsdale, NJ: Lawrence Erlbaum Associates.

Baron, J. (1986). Tradeoffs among reasons for action. *Journal for the Theory of Social Behavior, 16,* 173–195.

Baron, J. (1987). An hypothesis about the training of intelligence. In D. N. Perkins, J. Lochhead, & J. Bishop (Eds.), *Thinking: The second international conference.* Hillsdale, NJ: Lawrence Erlbaum Associates.

Baron, J. (1988a) Utility, exchange, and commensurability. (Invited paper.) *Journal of Thought, 23,* 111–131.

Baron, J. (in press b) Beliefs about thinking. In J. F. Voss, D. N. Perkins, & J. W. Segal (Eds.), *Informal reasoning and education.* Hillsdale, NJ: Lawrence Erlbaum Associates.

Baron, J. (1988b) *Thinking and deciding.* New York: Cambridge University Press.

Baron, J., Badgio, P., & Gaskins, I. W. (1986). Cognitive style and its improvement: A normative approach. In R. J. Sternberg (Ed.), *Advances in the psychology of human intelligence* (Vol. 3). Hillsdale, NJ: Lawrence Erlbaum Associates.

Baron, J., Baron, J(udith), Barber, J. P., & Nolen-Hoksema, S. (in press). Rational thinking as a goals of therapy. *Journal of Cognitive Psychotherapy* (special issue).

Cantor, N., Norem, J. K., Brower, A. M., Niedenthal, P. M., & Langston, C. A. (1987). Life tasks, self-concept ideals, and cognitive strategies in a life transition. *Journal of Personality and Social Psychology, 53,* 1178–1191.

Elster, J. (1979). *Ulysses and the Sirens: Studies in rationality and irrationality.* New York: Cambridge University Press.

Elster, J. (1983). *Sour grapes: studies of the subversion of rationality.* New York: Cambridge University Press.

Elster, J. (1985). Weakness of the will and the free-rider problem. *Economics and Philosophy, 1,* 231–265.

Hare, R. M. (1981). *Moral thinking: Its levels, method and point.* Oxford: Clarendon Press.

Marcia, J. E. (1966). Development and validation of ego identity status. *Journal of Personality and Social Psychology, 3,* 551–558.

Messick, D. M. (1985). Social interdependence and decision making. In G. Wright (Ed.), *Behavioral decision making.* New York: Plenum.

Mischel, W. (1974). Processes in delay of gratification. In L. Berkowitz (Ed.), *Advances in experimental social psychology* (Vol. 7). New York: Academic Press.

Mischel, W. (1984). Convergences and challenges in the search for consistency. *American Psychologist, 39,* 351–364.

Nagel, T. (1970). *The possibility of altruism.* Princeton, NJ: Princeton University Press.

Parfit, D. (1984). *Reasons and persons.* Oxford: Clarendon Press.

Rawls, J. (1971). *A theory of justice.* Cambridge, MA: Harvard University Press.

Sabini, J., & Silver, M. (1982). *Moralities of everyday life.* Oxford: Clarendon Press.

Solomon, R. L., & Corbit, J. D. (1974). An opponent-process theory of motivation. *Psychological Review, 81,* 119–145.

Sternberg, R. J. (1985). *Beyond IQ: A triarchic theory of human intelligence.* New York: Cambridge University Press.

Strotz, R. H. (1955).Myopia and inconsistency in dynamic utility maximization. *Review of Economic Studies, 23,* 165–180.

Thaler, R. H., & Shefrin, H. M. (1981). An economic theory of self-control. *Journal of Political Economy, 89,* 392–406.

3

Social Intelligence and the Construction of Meaning in Life

Roy F. Baumeister
Case Western Reserve University

Cantor and Kihlstrom (this volume) propose that social intelligence is concerned with how people perform life tasks. They focus on the strategies people use for setting up and achieving one's goals in life. Thus, social intelligence is intimately involved in the issues of life's meaning, for people use social intelligence in the service of the major life tasks. Life tasks are the ends, and social intelligence is the means.

But where do these tasks come from? Cantor and Kihlstrom rely on several standard sources for these answers. These sources include Klinger's (1975, 1977) insightful work that sought to reduce all issues of meaning in life to the simple matter of incentives. This is overly reductionistic. Another source is Plutchik's (1980) list of evolutionary (organismic) tasks: Establishing territory, getting food, mating, etc. These are what life is about, but they hardly depend on meaning, for they are the major life tasks even in species that have minimal or no language, culture, or other apparent usage of meaning. One may reduce human life to these basic biological tasks, but that too is overly reductionistic. Thus, work in a bureaucracy can be compared to a lower animal's quest for food in that both are means of obtaining food, but the comparison loses something. There are important differences between a corporate vice president and a wolf foraging in the wild. Many of these differences involve meaning. Modern human work is much more dependent on the social network of exchanging goods and services, and on the culture (a set of meanings that ties individuals, institutions, and behaviors together), than food-gathering. Few vice presidents do work that actually generates food that they themselves eat. Instead, people live in a world full of meanings, and their survival and success depend on how they use those meanings.

The purpose of this brief chapter is to outline a more thorough account of the notion of life task, one that encompasses how people construct meaning in their lives and how they use social intelligence to do so. Plutchik's list of tasks is a reasonable account of what living things must do to survive. Life alone, with or without meaning, brings those tasks. Meaning is a cognitive overlay on basic biological processes. In other words, meaning is superimposed; and meaning refines, complicates, and modifies the biological projects, often to the point where the biological origins become scarcely recognizable. Consider the vice president who commits suicide after a setback at work: The meanings involved in his work have led him to contradict all the basic biological reasons for working.

Human life consists of the basic biological tasks overlaid and altered through meaning, which is mediated by culture. Human life tasks are thus different from the simple biological life tasks, although the fundamental biological problems still remain to be handled in some way.

LEVELS OF MEANING

One important empirical key to understanding how meaning operates was furnished by Vallacher and Wegner's (1985, 1987) work on action identification. They note that any single action can be described in many different ways. Low-level descriptions of action are relatively devoid of meaning, such as referring to simple muscle movements. High-level descriptions involve long-term goals, symbolic meanings, broad and important contexts. Low-level thinking uses a very short-term time frame, whereas high levels tie the present and immediate circumstances to distal goals and enduring contexts, such as standards and values. If one extends Vallacher and Wegner's discussion of action to encompass experience, one has conceptual and empirical tools for studying the operation of meaning.

Movement between levels is psychologically important and consequential. Upward shifts entail moving to longer time frames, higher meanings, broader contexts. Low levels are means to high-level ends. Upward movements include insight, context finding, making attributions (e.g., inferring lasting entities from single events). Another important category of upward movement is evaluating, that is, comparing something to enduring standards. Upward movements add meaning to specific events. Upward movements interpret events by placing in context, inferring goals and causes at distant points in time, comparing against enduring standards, inferring stable dispositions. Downward movements remove meaning. They involve a shift to more immediate time frames. One may shift downward to find means of achieving broad goals, for (again) low levels are means to higher ends. Or one may shift downward to escape implications of high-level meanings, such as attributional implications that produce anxiety.

A critical function of social intelligence is to help the individual move between levels of meaning. Social intelligence enables the individual to move from the concrete and specific event to the broader interpretation, and they likewise help the individual translate broad high-level meanings into concrete actions and strategies.

Regarding upward movements in meaning, social intelligence enables the person to take concrete, specific, immediate events and interpret them, that is, subjectively endow them with meaning. There are two kinds of social stupidity: In one, the person is unable to see broader meanings in events, and in the other the person sees wrong meanings. Social intelligence means knowing how to make attributions about events, how to infer traits from specific actions, how to understand the causes for other people's actions. Social intelligence means knowing the standards. Psychologically, standards are a "given," a product of culture. A full theory of culture would tell us where standards come from and how they arise, but that is beyond our current concern. Culture furnishes standards and links them up with affective states. Standards include norms, expectations, qualifications, measures of competence and appropriateness. Social intelligence means knowing these and knowing how to compare specific events to them: Is this outfit stylish? Is this a fair salary? Is this the proper way to interact with a member of the opposite sex? Can I make jokes at a funeral? Should I be angry at what X just said to me? Social intelligence enables the individual to make these upward movements, endowing specifics with meaning as the cultures prescribes one ought.

Regarding downward movements in meaning, social intelligence enables the individual to translate broad values and distal goals into specific plans of action. So you want to become rich and famous, how do you go about that? So you want to fall in love, how do you go about it? Your work isn't proceeding smoothly, what needs to be altered? How repair a troubled relationship? To adjust well, you need to be able to elaborate distal goals into proximal ones (cf. Bandura & Schunk, 1981).

NEEDS FOR MEANING

Klinger suggested that all meaning in life can be reduced to one simple notion, that of incentives. Perhaps it's not that simple. This chapter seeks to replace that notion with a more complex version (from Baumeister, 1988). In this view, people have four basic interpretive needs, that is, four needs for meaning. People need for their lives to make sense in four basic ways.

There is nothing sacred about the number four in this context. The important thing is the total conceptual space they cover. These needs overlap somewhat, so they could conceivably be combined into three or perhaps even two distinct needs, and one might also subdivide them more precisely into six or seven needs. Again, what matters is that together they encompass the ways in which people need their lives to have meaning. People who have satisfactory answers to these four needs probably feel that their lives have meaning. People who are unable to satisfy these needs probably tend to feel that their lives lack meaning in some important sense.

Purpose

A first interpretive need is for purpose in life. Psychology has long known that human behavior is goal directed, and people want their lives to have this property as well. This is quite similar to Klinger's notion of incentives, although it may be desirable to refine his view and elaborate it somewhat differently from his original work.

Purposes can be subdivided into two types, corresponding to extrinsic and intrinsic motivations. Extrinsic goals refer to desired consequences of one's actions. Intrinsic goals refer to subjective states, typically satisfaction or some other positive affect, that are expected to accompany or result from one's actions.

To function as life purposes, these goals do not have to be realized in one's life, for they may remain indefinitely in the future. One can live one's life according to certain ambitions, certain sought-for achievements, certain ideas of fulfillment. Indeed, some goals have successfully given meaning to many lives without ever being realized in any of them. Failed revolutionary movements provide one example; another is rewards or fulfillment that are deferred until after death, such as Christian salvation. One reason such religious ideas are so effective at providing meaning to life is that they offer very compelling, attractive purposes that are immune from disconfirmation.

The need for purpose is a need to understand present and past events as moving toward some future event. It is a way of linking up events across time by using meaning. Such a way of understanding one's life also enables one to make present decisions by furnishing criteria, that is, purposes furnish the basis for making choices that will help one bring about the future desired states.

The tasks for social intelligence follow directly from the preceding analysis. Its first job may be to choose goals. Of course, not all purposes in life are chosen by the individual, for some are built in to the nature of life (as Plutchik's list shows) and others are ineluctably set by one's social and cultural context. As an example of the first, one has to find a stable source of food. As an example of the second, a medieval European had to live according to Christian ideals and models, within the specific place in the social order assigned to him or her by circumstances determined externally (esp. birth and family).

Still, in some cases choosing purposes is a first step. Pluralistic cultures such as our own offer the individual a wide assortment of mutually incompatible purposes, and one must choose from among them. Indeed, the adolescent identity crisis typically starts off with the struggle to select a set of personal values and goals from a broad set, and then one seeks to translate these basic abstract notions into a concrete ambition and a specific life plan (Baumeister, 1986).

The second task for social intelligence is to deduce proximal, low-level goals from the broad, high-level ones. To go from broad principles to personal ambitions and strivings requires knowledge of social opportunities, constraints, possibilities, and knowledge of how to go about achieving these goals, as well as knowledge of one's own capacities and limitations—thus, declarative knowledge, procedural knowledge, and self-knowledge.

The third and main function of social intelligence is to make choices and decisions that will lead toward the goals. This requires assessing the current situation to identify behaviors and circumstances that may be relevant to one's goals. Then one must evaluate the contingencies and probabilities from among the assorted options in the situation, in order to choose an optimal behavioral strategy. In other words, one has to determine which courses of action are most likely to lead to the desired outcomes.

Efficacy

A second interpretive need is for a sense of efficacy. Efficacy is essentially a feeling of control. People need to feel that they are making a difference, that in some way they are in control of important events happening in their lives. Although considerable research has established the importance of control per se in human motivation and behavior, the emphasis here is on efficacy (i.e., perceived or sensed control), for the need for meaning is the need *to believe* oneself to be capable of a certain degree of control. The need for efficacy can be satisfied without really having control, such as if the person merely has illusions of control (e.g., Langer, 1975; Taylor, 1983). Indeed, people show general tendencies to overestimate the degree of control they have. People like to have control, but if they do not have control they still want to believe that they have control. Thus, the crucial subjective motivation is to feel that one has control—to have a sense of efficacy.

Like purpose, control may be subdivided into two categories, primary and secondary control (Rothbaum, Weisz, & Snyder, 1982). Primary control means changing the environment to adapt it to one's own needs and wants. Secondary control means changing the self to adapt it to external circumstances and demands.

Social intelligence has a vital role in achieving a sense of efficacy. First, the actual achievement of objective (primary) control depends heavily on understanding. One can control the world better if one understands it properly, and this applies to the social world as well as the physical world. To be genuinely efficacious, one must understand other people and social institutions. One must also understand one's own resources and limitations.

Secondary control also depends on social intelligence. Indeed, one important form of secondary control is called interpretive control, that is, the feeling that one is more in control if one merely understands the environment, even if one is objectively unable to change it. Understanding the environment also permits one to predict what is going to happen, and even if one is unable to alter events one can at least prepare oneself for them (predictive control). Thus, accurately perceiving the environment and its contingencies is vital to both primary and secondary control.

As we have stressed, however, accurate perception of the environment is not the only means of achieving a sense of efficacy, for people derive self-efficacy partly from illusions of control. Social intelligence has important functions in the sustaining of such illusions. One has to find evidence, distort it to give the desired conclusions, and avoid risk of contact with any too-clearly disconfirming feedback.

Social intelligence may also resort to various illusions that have strategic value in promoting efficacy. Defensive pessimism, for example, entails convincing oneself that one's chances are slim, which causes some people to put forth maximum effort (Cantor & Kihlstrom, this volume). Thus, by imagining or exaggerating obstacles, one increases one's objective efficacy. Another strategy may be withdrawal of effort from domains one perceives as uncontrollable. Learned helplessness, although seemingly the quintessential expression of inefficacy, may be a strategy of avoiding further experiences of inefficacy (cf. Rothbaum et al., 1982).

Legitimation

The third interpretive need is for legitimation, that is, value and justification. People need to feel that their lives have some value, that what they do is right and good in some way. People whose actions are unjustifiable are vulnerable to guilt and anxiety. Legitimation is of course the domain of morality.

Legitimation, or justification, can be subdivided into its positive and negative aspects. The negative involves obeying rules that prohibit certain forms of behavior. Most moral rules can be expressed in negative terms, that is, prohibitions. Eight of the Ten Commandments, for example, are explicitly formulated in terms of what one should *not* do, and negation is implicit in the other two (keeping the sabbath means not doing work on it, and honoring mother and father can be understood as refraining from disrespect, disobedience, etc.). The prohibitions against adultery or theft, or having rival gods are hard to formulate in purely positive terms. This is not to say that all moral rules are always negative, but morality clearly and strongly leans toward the negative, prohibiting side.

There is, however, also a positive aspect of legitimation, and that involves the endowing of certain things with positive value. Moral rules tell us what actions are bad and wrong, but some social practices can also take on special, positive value. People are much more willing to suffer, to make sacrifices, and to exert themselves if some clear positive value is involved. Indeed, in a sense the positive nature of legitimation is more fundamental than the negative, for people are more willing to accept the restrictions of moral rules if there is some positive value served by doing so. Thus, moral systems are most compelling when linked to some powerful source of value, such as religion. Indeed, the gradual erosion of morality in modern life can be understood partly as a result of the decline of religion, which left morality as simply a set of rules without any compelling reason for people to follow those rules (cf. Bellah, Madsen, Sullivan, Swindler, & Tipton, 1985; MacIntyre, 1981).

Justification flows, almost like electricity, from one thing to another. But there has to be a generator, something that is accepted as a good for its own sake—something that can "export" justification without "importing" it from somewhere else. These sources of value can be called *value bases*. In the previous example, Christians followed the Ten Commandments and other elements of Christian morality because these rules were perceived to be God's will. God's will justified the moral rules. God's will, however, did not seem to need further justification; nobody asked, "Why should we care what God wants?" God's will thus functioned as a value base.

Each individual thus needs to have access to certain value bases. To understand right and wrong, good and bad, people need to accept certain things as inherently right and good, without needing to justify them further. These are the moral equivalents of first causes or first principles.

Value bases exist at very high levels of meaning. They are typically understood as transcending time or as being eternal, and so the temporal criterion for determining level of meaning marks them as extremely high. Thus, Christians could accept the death of their child as being part of God's will or plan, something that presumably involved the whole of human history. The immediate, specific event (the child's death) thus derived positive value from an extremely long-range, abstract, ineffable yet indisputable value base.

With legitimation, social intelligence again has several functions. It is necessary to learn about the main value bases and to learn the moral rules and prohibitions. Indeed, moral traits are typically perceived as being fairly stable and permanent (e.g., one single lie may define a person as a liar for years afterward). In small, closed societies, such as the European villages of past centuries, moral missteps could have disastrous long-term consequences for one's position in the community and for all of one's interpersonal relationships over the rest of one's life, so knowing the niceties of moral judgment was vital to social survival. In the transient, uniplex, and large communities of modern urban life, the importance of morality has declined somewhat, but it is still substantial.

Moral judgment clearly involves moving among levels of meaning, which was indicated earlier as a vital aspect of social intelligence. Specific, immediate actions are related to abstract, meaningful, enduring principles, and vice versa. One needs to anticipate possible meanings and moral implications when deciding how to act. After the fact, one may be called on to defend one's actions, and so one needs to be able to marshal justifications by appealing to high-level principles, even if these were not actually considered during the action.

An important arena for the operation of social intelligence with regard to justification, and one that has not yet received sufficient research attention in social psychology, is the interpersonal interplay of obligation, blame, and debt, perhaps especially in long-term intimate relationships. Partners work out a means of justifying certain actions, and when they step outside those guidelines they offend or hurt each other. These rules may be negotiated explicitly or they may be held implicitly as each person learned them in previous relationships.

The broader domain of attitudinal thinking is also relevant to this need for meaning, for many attitudes are essentially high-level evaluations of some entity as good or bad. Social intelligence may often operate to link high-level, general attitudes up with immediate, specific circumstances (cf. Fazio, Powell, & Herr, 1983).

Self-Worth

The fourth major interpretive need is for self-worth. People need for their lives to furnish them some means of believing that they are important, good, worthy people. The overlap with the other interpretive needs is apparent, for some people link feelings of self-worth to moral justifications, and others link self-worth to feelings of efficacy. But self-worth is a need in its own right. It is possible to feel efficacious or justified without having high self-esteem.

Bases for self-worth may be subdivided into individual and collective types. A collective basis for self-worth means belonging to some valued group or category, usually one that is regarded as superior to another group or category. In many past societies, for example, the primary reason for owning slaves was not any pragmatic or material benefit derived from the slaves' work but rather the esteem that derived from membership in the slave-owning class (Patterson, 1982). In our society, actors, physicians, and major-league professional athletes, even quite mediocre ones, derive self-worth simply by virtue of their membership in an esteemed category of persons.

An individual basis for self-worth focuses on comparisons of people within the same category. Many categories of identity and achievement contain competitive standards of measurement, and individuals may strive to outdo each other. Sometimes the standards may be absolute, but more often they are relative, which means the assessment of self-worth relies heavily on social comparison.

The maintenance of self-worth is an important function of social intelligence. One needs to ascertain the implicit rules and criteria and then ensure that oneself compares favorably with others. Choice of criteria of self-worth and choice of comparison others are two important tasks that social intelligence faces. Further, social intelligence must frequently assess particular situations for their relevance to one's high-level self-worth, including assessing the implications of possible outcomes. For example, to prevent potential loss of self-worth, it may be necessary to avoid certain arenas of performance (e.g., Baumeister & Tice, 1985), or to furnish oneself in advance with excuses for possible failure (Jones & Berglas, 1978). At other times, one engages in downward comparison (Taylor, 1983; Wills, 1981), which means finding someone worse off than oneself to enable one to feel superior or fortunate.Regarding collective self-worth strategies, one needs to cement one's membership in a valued group and sustain the impression of its superiority over other groups. Maintaining derogatory stereotypes of outgroups, for example, may be an important strategy of preserving self-worth.

It is important to recognize that illusions may be centrally important in the achievement and maintenance of self-worth. Social psychology has amply documented the statistical paradox that most people consider themselves above average. This inflation of subjective self-worth is achieved by distorted perception and recollection of feedback, by self-serving attributional patterns, by strategic choice of comparison others, and by other strategies. The need for meaning does not entail that one has actually to *be* superior to others; it requires only that one be able to *convince oneself* that one is superior to others. The latter is a much easier task than the former.

Conclusion

Many personality dynamics can be understood as the operation of social intelligence. This brief chapter has sought to elaborate the broad notion of "life tasks" and "incentives" into a more systematic and thorough account of the human quest for a meaningful life. People desire their lives to have purpose, they want their lives to furnish them with a sense of personal efficacy, they desire to feel their actions have value and are justifiable, and they need some basis for self-worth.

These four interpretive needs may be conceptualized as the generic tasks for social intelligence. Each of them requires the individual to process incoming information, to understand the social world, and to assess the self. Social intelligence's function of connecting high and low levels of meaning is vital to success at each of them.

These tasks do not begin anew each day. Rather, each day presents a new version of or variation on the same tasks that pervade the individual's entire life. At higher levels of meaning, one needs to sustain enduring answers to each of them. It is not surprising, therefore, that individuals may develop habitual and consistent means of using their social intelligence in the service of persistent solutions to each of the four needs. The stability and consistency of human personality can thus be understood as arising from the regular use of social intelligence in working out enduring solutions to these four interpretive needs.

REFERENCES

Bandura, A., & Schunk, D. H. (1981). Cultivating competence, self-efficacy, and intrinsic interest through proximal self-motivation. *Journal of Personality and Social Psychology*, 41, 586–598.

Baumeister, R. F. (1986). *Identity: Cultural change and the struggle for self*. New York: Oxford University Press.

Baumeister, R. F. (1988). *Meanings of life*. Book manuscript in preparation.

Baumeister, R. F., & Tice, D. M. (1985). Self-esteem and responses to success and failure: Subsequent performance and intrinsic motivation. *Journal of Personality*, 53, 450–467.

Bellah, R. N., Madsen, R., Sullivan, W., Swidler, A., & Tipton, S. (1985). *Habits of the heart*. Berkeley: University of California Press.

Fazio, R. H., Powell, M. C., & Herr, P. M. (1983). Toward a process model of the attitude-behavior relation: Accessing one's attitude upon mere observation of the attitude object. *Journal of Personality and Social Psychology*, 44, 723–735.

Jones, E. E., & Berglas, S. C. (1978). Control of attributions about the self through self-handicapping strategies. The appeal of alcohol and the role of underachievement. *Personality and Social Psychology Bulletin*, 4, 200–206.

Klinger, E. (1975). Consequences of commitment to and disengagement from incentives. *Psychological Review*, 82, 1–25.

Klinger, E. (1977). *Meaning and void: Inner experience and the incentives in people's lives*. Minneapolis: University of Minnesota Press.

Langer, E. (1975). The illusion of control. *Journal of Personality and Social Psychology*, 29,253–264.

MacIntyre, A. (1981). *After virtue: A study in moral theory*. Notre Dame, IN: University of Notre Dame Press.

Patterson, O. (1982). *Slavery and social death*. Cambridge, MA: Harvard University Press.

Plutchik, R. (1980). A general psychoevolutionary theory of emotion. in R. Plutchik & H. Kellerman (Eds.), *Emotion: Theory, research, and experience*. New York: Academic Press.

Rothbaum, F., Weisz, J. R., & Snyder, S. S. (1982). Changing the world and changing the self. A two-process model of perceived control. *Journal of Personality and Social Psychology*, 42, 5–37.

Taylor, S. E. (1983). Adjustment of threatening events: A theory of cognitive adaptation. *American Psychologist*, 38, 1161–1173.

Vallacher, R. R., & Wegner, D. M. (1985). *A theory of action identification*. Hillsdale, NJ: Lawrence Erlbaum Associates.

Vallacher, R. R., & Wegner, D. M. (1987). What do people think they're doing: Action identification and human behavior. *Psychological Review*, 94, 3–15.

Wills, T. A. (1981). Downward comparison principles in social psychology. *Psychological Bulletin*, 90, 245–271.

4 The Functions of Personality Theories

Randall S. Bergen
Carol S. Dweck
University of Illinois at Champaign/Urbana

Cantor and Kihlstrom's model of social intelligence is intuitively appealing and far reaching. It has both the time-tested strength of an expectancy-value framework, and the sophistication that the current social-cognitive approach provides. We believe that Cantor and Kihlstrom's model holds the promise of becoming a comprehensive theory of personality.

Because it is such a strong and enterprising effort, the social-intelligence model commands a sense of respect, and a sense that it should be evaluated against the highest of standards. Cantor and Kihlstrom's promising ideas challenged us to consider what the functions of an "ideal" theory of personality are. In our critique, we have tried to answer that question and then ask: To what extent does the social-intelligence model fulfill the functions that we have set forth? Where would we take this theory in the future if it were ours? The suggestions we make emerge from *our* goals for a model of personality. We recognize, of course, that Cantor and Kihlstrom may have had somewhat different goals when they cast the model.

In our view, then, an ideal model should: (1) Organize complex phenomena so that they may be readily identified and understood; (2) "explain" behavior—that is, give a reason and impetus for why behavior occurs; (3) provide constraints such that behavior may be predicted; and (4) provide heuristics for research. In other words, a comprehensive theory should say what is happening, why it is happening, what will happen next, and how we can discover more about basic phenomena. We argue that whereas the social-intelligence approach has the potential to fulfill each of these functions, it has not yet reached the level of specificity to do so at this time.

THE MODEL OF PERSONALITY

We have presented an overview of the social-intelligence model in Fig. 4.1. This figure will serve as a guide for our critique. Our depiction is not as complex as Cantor and Kihlstrom's model,[1] and, although the way we have broken down their theory is relatively faithful to their conceptualization, it does require some justification.

We have chosen to simplify their model for two reasons. First, the figure serves as a clear road map for our critique. We begin with a discussion about the structure of personality. We move to a discussion about personality dynamics (the motivational level). We then discuss the actualized level of personality.

Our second reason for making the simplifications is perhaps more significant. Typically, personality theorists postulate underlying processes to explain and predict the more overt manifestations of their basic phenomenon. Thus, we feel that an understanding of the most fundamental level of personality—the structural level—should help us explain and predict the next level—the motivational level. Specifying the nature of both the structural and motivational levels should explain and predict phenomena at the actualized level. A question that we discuss repeatedly in this critique is how does an understanding of one level of personality help us understand the next level?

Again, we use the figure as a guide for our critique. We begin our discussion by focusing on the "Structural Level."

The Structural Level

Cantor and Kihlstrom (this volume) clearly articulate that the structure of personality is "the social intelligence repertoire used in interpersonal problem-solving." (p. 17) This is their central construct, as well as their major contribution to the field of personality psychology. Because this construct is of central importance, we spend a fair amount of time evaluating it. Our evaluation focuses on three criteria that we believe a structure should meet. First, we believe that the structure should be sharply delineated; there should be no ambiguity about what

---

[1]The most obvious difference between our figure and their model is that we have not shown their construct of "context." Cantor and Kihlstrom argue that the structure of personality is greatly affected by context, defined as a person's unique social environment. The reader should understand that we are not ignoring its existence. We are assuming that the impact of the context on life tasks and problem-solving strategies is channeled through the cognitive structure of personality. In addition, we made a clear boundary between social intelligence and life tasks. Cantor and Kihlstrom do the same. The difference lies in our taking life tasks physically out of social intelligence in our figure. We do not mean to imply that they do not reside in the cognitive structure. We simply wish to highlight the importance of the motivational aspects of personality. Finally, we did not map all the possible interactions that could occur between levels. For example, we did not show that social intelligence and life tasks interact to influence life-task problem-solving strategies.

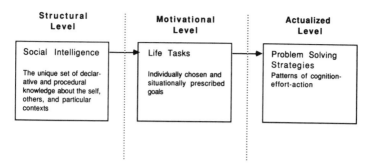

Structural Level	Motivational Level	Actualized Level
Social Intelligence The unique set of declarative and procedural knowledge about the self, others, and particular contexts	Life Tasks Individually chosen and situationally prescribed goals	Problem Solving Strategies Patterns of cognition-effort-action

FIG.. 4.1 A simplified version of the Social Intelligence Model of Personality.

is and is not part of the structure. This means that these central constructs should be precisely defined and consistently used. Second, we think the structure should simplify the phenomenon it is modelling, such that it provides the means to gain a stable and coherent understanding of what is being studied. Finally, the structure should help to explain and predict more overt aspects of personality. How does the personality structure set forth in the social-intelligence model conform to our desires for a personality structure?

Understanding Social Intelligence.   When the social intelligence repertoire is explicitly defined, the reader gets a fairly clear picture of what it is. The following paragraph from the beginning of Cantor and Kihlstrom's (1987) book defines it this way:

> From this view, the cognitive basis of personality can be conceptualized as the declarative and procedural knowledge that individuals bring to bear in interpreting events and making plans in everyday life situations. These concepts, personal memories, and interpretive rules are the cognitive structures of personality; together they constitute the expertise that guides an individual's approach to the problems of social life. *We refer to this knowledge repertoire as social intelligence.* (p. 2, our italics)

Thus, social intelligence appears to be the set of social knowledge used in inter and intrapersonal problem solving.

Formal definitions play a critical role in the formulation and presentation of a theory. However, their definition notwithstanding, it is important to understand the concept by examining how it is *used* by the authors throughout their writing. By examining how it is used in this chapter and in their book as a whole, the reader can get a different picture of the construct. We have identified two additional forms of social intelligence.

First, social intelligence is occasionally expressed not as what people *do* use, but simply as a set of knowledge that people possess and *can* use. Cantor and

Kihlstrom (1987) say that: "When the structures of personality are equated with the knowledge about people and events and oneself that individuals gather across the lifespan, there is necessarily and assumption of complexity and fluidity about personality" (p. 77). This statement occurs directly under the heading "Social Intelligence as Personality Structure." Thus, we are led to infer that social intelligence is not only what one does use, but also what one can use. Further, if social intelligence is information "gathered across the lifespan," it seemingly may consist not only of "expert" knowledge, but of *any* social knowledge.

A third form of social intelligence emerges when one tries to understand the construct through its assessment. Cantor and Kihlstrom (this volume) suggest that "general features of social-intelligence assessment" include uncovering "patterns of problem solving in social life contexts" and judging the "adaptiveness" of those patterns in relationship to a person's unique goals. Surprisingly, assessment of the structural level of personality does not center on describing *what* knowledge is used in solving life tasks, but rather it centers on *how* and how well that knowledge is used. If social intelligence is the manner in which knowledge is applied, then it becomes difficult to find features that distinguish between the social-intelligence repertoire and life-task problem-solving strategies (defined as "patterns of thoughts, feelings, and effort," which "involve the coordination of declarative and procedural knowledge," in order to achieve goals). Perhaps social intelligence is both expert knowledge and the application of the expertise. Indeed, near the end of their book, Cantor and Kihlstrom (1987) seem to have enlarged the meaning of the term *social intelligence* to include both knowledge and life-task problem-solving strategies: "Accordingly, we have emphasized declarative and procedural expertise, *strategies of action and self-regulation,* and mechanisms for effecting change in a social context, as central features of social intelligence" (p. 240, our italics).

It is not entirely clear whether social intelligence is what a person can use, what a person does use, how a person uses what he or she has, or some combination of the three. The divergence between the formal definition of social intelligence and the construct-in-use creates problems to be solved in understanding the model as a whole. Although each definition is plausible and defensible, each has different implications for the nature of personality, the structure of personality, the assessment of the structure, and, as we soon see, the prediction of behavior from personality structure.

Social Intelligence as a Simplifying Structure.   One of our goals for the construct of personality at the structural level is to have it provide a way of simplifying and organizing the phenomenon it is modelling. Models are valuable when they provide comfortable know-ledges on which our minds can rest a sense of understanding. This demands that the structure be as parsimonious as possible, given the nature of the subject matter. As noted earlier, Cantor and Kihlstrom believe that social intelligence is a very "complex" and "fluid" structure.

They argue forcefully that personality should not be boiled down into simplistic categories with which to label people. We see the inherent value of having a complex structure of personality, given that the phenomenon is quite complex. Nevertheless, we feel that the complexity of the social-intelligence model may inadvertently court confusion.

Whether social intelligence is defined as knowledge that is used, latent knowledge, or characteristic ways of applying knowledge, it constitutes a highly complex set of variables. Identifying the set of important variables, and then understanding their organization and inter-relationships will be a difficult job. As an example of how difficult it might be to understand an individual with the social-intelligence framework, let us say that we would like to use the model in the idiographic way it was intended—to understand one individual. We begin by looking for expert knowledge clusters (or by identifying knowledge, or by looking for patterns of knowledge application) within that person. Even if we identify as few as 10 important knowledge clusters or patterns, we would be challenged to understand this person, especially because the variables may well interact to produce particular behavior patterns in specific situations. Moreover, we may discover that the knowledge clusters we are using to understand the behavior are themselves not stable. Thus, we would be required not only to deal with large numbers of variables and their inter-relationships, but also to try to understand how unstable personality variables will change as a result of learning that takes place in an unstable environment. Therefore, we would welcome more explicit guidelines from Cantor and Kihlstrom for delimiting and organizing the variables at the structural level.

Social Intelligence as a Means of Understanding Motives and Behavior. We feel that structural-level variables should put constraints on behavior; any structure constrains movement to some degree. If structure limits movements, and we know the properties of a structure, we should be able to predict movement and understand the particular patterns of movement that we have identified. Thus, we would like to be able to use social intelligence to understand and predict the more overt phenomena—the life tasks and the problem-solving strategies. We suggest that there are two issues the authors should consider if at some point they address this question. The first relates to the definitional ambiguity that we have discussed earlier. The second relates to the complexity of the model.

First, if social intelligence is assessed by the specific strategies that become manifest at the problem-solving level, then it is measured by the very things we would like it to predict or cause. If we try to use the model in its present form for prediction, we run into a problem of circularity. On the other hand, if social intelligence *is* the set of strategies used in problem solving, there exists no circularity, but, if that is the case, then the question becomes, why is there a clear distinction made between social intelligence and life-task problem-solving strategies throughout most of the book and the chapter? We would like to see the structure assume the role of a structure, and we would like to see the more overt phenomena (such as the problem-solving strategies) be predicted by means of the structure.

Second, for the same reason that the social-intelligence model may pose difficulties for understanding the structure, it may pose problems when trying to predict the more overt levels of personality. Predictions made with complex sets of variables and their interactions prove very difficult. Thus, predicting behavior and motives from knowledge about multiple self-concepts, multiple person, place, and event concepts, and a large number of processing rules would probably require complicated algorithms, and understanding motives and behavior from these complex interactions may be even more difficult than prediction.

In conclusion, we reiterate that our goals for structural-level constructs are precision, parsimony, and predictive utility. We suggest that the formal definition of social intelligence and the assessment procedures used to understand it become more in agreement. We suggest that a clearer way of simplifying the complex set of variables be laid out so that understanding and prediction will be facilitated. We feel that the social-intelligence framework would be more powerful if it made strides in these areas.

The Motivational Level

The social-cognitivist tradition, exemplified by the social-intelligence framework, evolved from the social-learning tradition. Because of their historical roots in learning theory, Cantor and Kihlstrom may have some hesitation when delving into dynamic explanations of behavior and personality. They acknowledge the need to account for motivation in their personality system but do not go into great detail in specifying motivational processes and mechanisms. We see motives as central in importance in a personality theory, and, because of this, we have tried to make extensive comments about the role of motivation in the social-intelligence model. Again, these suggestions arise out of our own goals for a personality theory.

Our goals for motivational-level constructs are similar to our goals for structural-level constructs. First, we desire to know what gives rise to motives. Where do they originate? Second, we believe the model should organize the complex sets of motives into meaningful subunits. Finally, we suggest that a knowledge of a person's motives should lead to clear predictions about his or her thought and behavior patterns.

The Origin of Motives. In the writings on the social-intelligence model, we do not yet find any clear explanations of where motives come from. We have been told simply that they exist within the social-intelligence framework. Cantor and Kihlstrom (this volume) state:

We start by viewing emotions and motives as integrated within cognitive structures and processes of life-task problem-solving. For the present we simply wish to explicitly recognize these reciprocal relations between cognition and emotion: emotions are subject to cognitive construction and control, but cognitions are clearly influenced by emotional and motivational processes . . . it is virtually impossible to consider cognition and emotion separately when discussing life-task problem-solving. (p. 13)

These statements provide a relatively clear statement of their *assumptions* for motivations. We agree with most of their assumptions, but we believe that they need to be placed in a strong theoretical network that explains and justifies them. The model in its present form seems to be saying simply that life tasks (what we see as the fundamental motivational unit) are motivational constructs simply because they possess motivating qualities. Specifically, we would like to see Cantor and Kihlstrom eventually address some of the fundamental questions relating to motivation: How are motives linked to the cognitive structures and processes? When will they be linked? Why are they linked? They apparently intend to pursue answers to such questions (because they say "for the present . . . ""), and we are eager to see them do so.

Life-tasks as a Simplifying Construct.   Cantor and Kihlstrom note that life tasks constitute a very broad set: "Life-tasks vary from long-term, abstract goals to short-term, concrete ones" (p. 27). The construct is limited somewhat by the restrictions that life tasks must "possess motivational properties" and "offer goal states around which large portions of life must be organized." Even with those qualifiers, however, the set of possible life tasks seems to cover a range with outer boundaries marked by "leading a happy life" on the long-term, abstract end, to, perhaps, "maintaining a clean room" on the short-term, concrete end. The average person spends a great deal of time trying to be happy, and most people spend at least a moderate amount of their life dealing with simple domestic chores. Thus, life tasks probably constitute an exceedingly complex set of motives within any single individual. Earlier, we suggested that a complex model of personality was highly desirable *if* it broke the phenomenon into meaningful subunits that could be understood. We believe that the social-intelligence model should strive to bring greater coherence to the motivational-level complexity by (1) providing clearer guidelines for breaking down people's motives into more organized units, and (2) providing theory-based criteria for selecting appropriate life tasks to study.

The social-intelligence model, as it is formulated now, seems to imply that people's motives are loose bundles of life tasks. These bundles of goals seem to exist at various levels of abstraction and temporal duration without any clear subjective organization. Although we feel that life tasks, as goals, can provide a reasonable foundation for understanding motivation, we would like to see Cantor and Kihlstrom work toward a more explicit motivational framework. This, we believe, will provide a means of understanding the inter-relatedness among and between the various levels of life tasks.

In its present form, the complexity of the construct "life tasks" may present problems not only in understanding motivation, but also in the pragmatics of doing research. Cantor and Kihlstrom realize that the complexity of the life-task construct must be broken down to make it more manageable for researchers. They say: "effective research depends on selecting the appropriate size [of life-tasks] for analysis," (p. 27). They make reasonable suggestions for how to select the appropriate size, but, this selection process is not strongly grounded in their theory: "We are particularly interested in those life-tasks that confront us at particular epochs in the life course . . . these seem to provide an appropriate balance of characteristics for research purposes: they are relatively broad, relatively universal, relatively significant, relatively concrete, relatively enduring, relatively frequent in appearance" (p. 28).We are fearful that such general guidelines will not place the life-task construct securely in a nomological net (Cronbach & Meehl, 1955). We think a far stronger approach to researching these goals would be to develop a theoretical basis for selecting appropriate life tasks to study. We would like to see more explicit theory regarding the organization of life tasks, and more theory-based guidelines for how research on life tasks should be conducted.

Life Tasks as Predictors.   A guiding assumption in this critique has been that higher level personality constructs should lead to prediction of lower level behavioral variables. We believe that knowledge of an individual's life tasks, combined with knowledge of social intelligence, should ideally lead to some strong predictions about life-task problem-solving strategies and about behavior. Thus, we believe the social-intelligence model has the components necessary to make such explicit predictions, but the model, in its present form, does not yet allow us to do so.

We noted earlier that the number of variables needed to describe and understand the structure "social intelligence" was very large. When discussing life tasks, we noted that the set of life tasks would be enormous for any one individual. If the structure of personality is as fluid as has been suggested, and if there is no specified way of knowing what life tasks an individual may pursue at any given moment, then predicting trends in life task problem-solving strategies and behavior will be extremely difficult.

To conclude our section on the motivational level of personality, we suggest that a complete model of the motivational process should strive to explain where motives come from and how they direct behavior. We suggest that what is implicit in Cantor and Kihlstrom's writing on motivation be made much more explicit as they grapple with such issues as how motives are integrated into the personality structure, how motives are organized, and how motives can be used to explicitly predict phenomena at the actualized level.

The Actualized Level

Cantor and Kihlstrom have done an admirable job of specifying and using the constructs that make up what we call the *actualized level* of personality. We suggest that the actualized level in their model has two components—the life-task problem-solving strategies and actualized behaviors performed to accomplish the goals. We see that the origins of life-task problem-solving strategies are theoretically rooted in both an individual's life tasks and his or her unique set of social knowledge. We have also seen that problem-solving strategies (such as "defensive pessimism") can be effectively used to predict overt behaviors. Cantor's research program has demonstrated this clearly.

Our suggestions concerning this level are related to our previous ones. Cantor and Kihlstrom's model is highly elaborate and complex; yet it seems to us that the complexity does not lead us to a step-by-step understanding of the more overt phenomena of thought and behavior patterns. The model attempts to link life tasks and social intelligence to the problem-solving strategies, but the hypothesized links do not yet yield clear predictions. For example, the strategies "optimism" and "defensive pessimism," rather than being differentially predicted by underlying variables, seem to be rooted in the same motivational-level variables (academic achievement). We would like to understand how different personality and motivational processes cause people to behave in such different ways.

Our Model

To understand the suggestions that we have made regarding Cantor and Kihlstrom's model, it may help to see how the model we are working on deals with similar issues. As will be apparent, our model is similar to theirs in many of its guiding assumptions. However, we have begun our task by attempting to limit and delimit our domain to facilitate understanding and prediction. Although we have limited the domain of the model, we are working toward greater comprehensiveness and complexity. Thus, in our "Theories of Attributes" social-cognitive approach to personality (see Dweck & Leggett, 1988), we postulate a relatively simple structure that leads to clear predictions about people's motives and behavior patterns. Basically, we propose that (1) at the structural level, individuals identify valued attributes of themselves, others, and the world, and that they hold implicit theories about those attributes; (2) at the motivational level, individuals adopt particular goals with respect to those attributes, and that their choice of goals is guided by their implicit theories; and (3) at the actualized level, individuals display distinct and coherent patterns of cognition, affect, and behavior in their goal pursuit, and that these patterns are generated and organized by the goal they are pursuing (see Fig. 4.2).

Although individuals can be classified as holding a particular implicit theory, these theories are not seen as traits that propel the individual in a rigid way. Rather, they are seen as creating a *bias* toward a given goal choice that, in

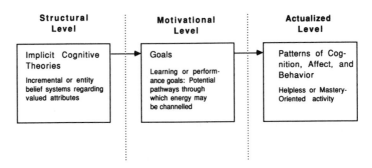

FIG. 4.2   The "Theories of Attributes" Model of Personality.

conjunction with the situational cues, guide the person's actual goal choice. The relative values placed on various attributes (e.g., one's "intelligence" vs. one's social skills) are seen as imparting relative value to goals. It is this value that provides the motive or energy for the pursuit of those goals.

The structure of personality in our model, then, is a set of beliefs (called theories) that individuals have about valued attributes. Specifically, we suggest that in any given domain in which we are living (e.g., the social or achievement domains), we may have one of two basic belief systems about ourselves or the world. We can either believe that we can change some aspect of ourselves or the world so that adaptation will be possible (called an "incremental theory"), or we can believe that we cannot alter some aspect of ourselves or the world to adapt (called an "entity theory"). For example, several studies (summarized in Dweck & Leggett, 1988) have now shown that different children tend to have different beliefs about the nature of intelligence. Some children believe that their level of intelligence may be increased through effort. Other children believe that intelligence is a fixed entity—that nothing they do will alter their set amount of "smartness." The central construct, then, is a theory—a set of beliefs about the nature of reality. Although we suggest that people adopt one of the two theories about any particular attribute, they may adopt the opposite theory about another attribute of themselves. For example, a person may believe that "intelligence" is a fixed attribute, while believing that "friendliness" is something he or she can alter through effort.

Dweck and her colleagues (Bandura & Dweck, 1985; Dweck & Bempechat, 1983; Dweck, Tenney, & Dinces, 1982; Elliott & Dweck, 1988; Leggett, 1985) have shown that identification of people's theories about particular attributes leads to reliable predictions about particular motives (goals) that the individuals have. In general, entity theories tend to bias the individual toward adopting "performance" goals and incremental theories tend to lead to "learning" goals; that is, if people believe some part of themselves is stable and unchangeable (a fixed "entity"), they will spend more time trying to prove that they do or do not possess the attribute (depending on whether it is negative or positive). If people believe some attribute of themselves is malleable (it can be changed in "incremental" units), they will spend more time learning to increase their abilities relating to that attribute. Thus, children who have entity theories of intelligence generally try to prove to themselves and others that they are smart. Alternatively, children who have incremental theories of intelligence generally try to increase their competency through learning.

Identification of performance or learning goals, combined with knowledge of one other variable (confidence levels) can lead to explicit and relatively accurate predictions about cognitive, affective, and behavioral patterns. Specifically, these variables predict whether a child will exhibit the maladaptive learned-helpless pattern (risk avoidance, as well as self-denigrating attributions, depressed mood, and lack of adaptive perseverance in the face of obstacles) or the more adaptive mastery-oriented pattern (challenge seeking, as well as greater task focus, positive affect, and strategic behavior in the face of failure; M. Bandura & Dweck, 1985; Elliott & Dweck, 1986). These patterns have been shown to have a profound influence on performance in both laboratory and real-world settings. Thus, the model has been shown to effectively predict cognitive, affective, and behavioral patterns by identification of motivational level constructs.

We do not believe that in reality only two theories are possible, that only two goals are possible, or that only two behavior patterns exist. Nevertheless, we have simplified the structure, the set of motives, and the important behavior patterns to allow for a clearer understanding of personality processes; that is, we have chosen to start with simplicity and slowly to advance toward greater complexity. Cantor and Kihlstrom have begun with greater complexity than we have, but we would not be surprised if the two models, with their many similarities and their affinities of approach, met somewhere in the middle.

Conclusion

In our introduction we suggested that the social-intelligence model was an intuitively appealing and compelling one. We wish to underscore that here. Cantor and Kihlstrom desire to capture the "flexibility and discriminative nature of the human experience" through the construct of social intelligence. Our agenda in this critique was to try to build on this effort, but we feel that their effort has already laid the groundwork for a significant advance in understanding personality.

REFERENCES

Bandura, M. & Dweck, C. S. (1985). *Self-conceptions and motivation: The relationship of conceptions of intelligence and achievement goals to patterns of cognition, affect, and behavior.* Manuscript submitted for publication.

Cantor, N., & Kihlstrom, J. F. (1987). *Personality and social intelligence,* Englewood Cliffs, NJ: Prentice-Hall.

Cronbach, L. J., & Meehl, P. E. (1955). Construct validity in psychological tests. *Psychological Bulletin, 52,* 281–302.

Dweck, C. S., & Bempechat, J. (1983). Children's theories of intelligence. In S. Paris, G. Olsen, & H. Stevenson (Eds.), *Learning and motivation in the classroom* (pp. 239–256). Hillsdale, NJ: Lawrence Erlbaum Associates.

Dweck, C. S., & Leggett, E. L. (1988). A social-cognitive approach to motivation and personality. *Psychological Review, 95,* 256–273.

Dweck, C. S., Tenney, Y., & Dinces, N. (1982). *Implicit theories of intelligence as determinants of achievement goal choice.* Unpublished data.

Elliott, E. S., & Dweck, C. S. (1988). Goals: An approach to motivation and achievement. *Journal of Personality and Social Psychology, 54,* 5–12.

Leggett, E. L. (1985, March). *Children's entity and incremental theories of intelligence: Relationships to achievement behavior.* Paper presented at the annual meeting of the Eastern Psychological Association. Boston.

5
Social Intelligence and Personality: Some Unanswered Questions and Unresolved Issues

Charles S. Carver
University of Miami

Michael F. Scheier
Carnegie-Mellon University

In many ways, we are sympathetic to the line of argument that Cantor and Kihlstrom present in their target chapter, and with the general approach to understanding behavior that is reflected more broadly in their work. We find congenial the emphasis that they place on such concepts as hierarchical organizations of goals and strategies, monitoring of feedback concerning the consequences of one's actions, and so on. We do, however, have some questions and concerns to raise regarding their chapter and some of its themes.

IS SOCIAL INTELLIGENCE PER SE ADEQUATE AS A MODEL OF PERSONALITY?

In their chapter Cantor and Kihlstrom (this volume) treat the concept of social intelligence as roughly equivalent to the concept of personality. In proposing their conceptualization as a theory of personality, they seem to be suggesting that the theory deals adequately with the issues addressed by other approaches to personality. Does it?

Is Social Intelligence a Broad Enough Construct?

Cantor and Kihlstrom's use of the term social intelligence follows from common-sense use of the term intelligence, rather than from technical use. Thus social intelligence, as Cantor and Kihlstrom use the term, is not an aptitude (i.e., a presumed underlying capacity) but rather a current condition of relative expertise in some domain of social activity. It is the mental content (including its elaboration, structure, and manner of deployment) that enables the person to engage in commerce with the social environment. To put it differently, it is the current knowledge and current level of skill that a person brings to bear on some social phenomenon.

Social intelligence as a concept clearly covers a lot of ground with respect to the human experience. But just as clearly it does not cover everything that is important to personality. As an example, it does not address the existence of temperamental differences between people that seem to be biologically based—differences such as activity level, emotional reactivity, and even the extent to which the person desires to be with other people (e.g., Buss & Plomin, 1984). These are broad-scale variables that influence people's behavior in widely varying contexts and play a major role in making people different from each other. As such, they seem intrinsically a part of personality, although they have little or nothing to do with social intelligence. To say that variables such as these fall outside the purview of one's theory is fully acceptable. To imply that they are irrelevant to personality is not. Too often Cantor and Kihlstrom seem to imply that social intelligence is *all* of personality.

Does This Approach Address the Important Issues of Personality?

There is another aspect of Cantor and Kihlstrom's theoretical stance that poses a greater challenge to its adequacy as a model of personality. This is the position they take regarding the conceptualization and assessment of individual differences.

We would hold that personality theories should address two different issues. One of these issues is how to construe what Allport (1961) termed the *dynamic organization of systems within the person,* or what we have more prosaically called *intrapersonal functioning* (Carver & Scheier, 1988). This organization of systems creates a sense of continuity within the person across time and circumstances, even as the person acts in very different ways from context to context. A focus on this issue is the strength of the approach taken by Cantor and Kihlstrom.

The other issue that should be addressed is individual differences. A viable approach to personality should suggest a basis for the existence of individual differences, and some strategies for measuring individual differences. The model offered by Cantor and Kihlstrom suggests that there will be a tremendous range of differences, based on the usual social-learning processes; that is, variations in social intelligence derive from individualized life experiences.

The model takes a very negative stance, however, on the matter of measurement. According to the view expressed in the target chapter, the attempt to measure important differences between people is futile and misguided. The important differences between people occur at such a micro level, and are so interwoven with differences in context, that meaningful assessment is next to impossible. "If the assessment of practical intelligence requires systematic in vivo sampling, all hope of comparative ranking vanishes (this, of course, is just as things should be from our perspective)" (see p. 9).

Cantor and Kihlstrom seem to take this stance on assessment on the basis of two other convictions, which we address separately a little later in our commentary. For now, our point is that when Cantor and Kihlstrom take this stance, they deny the importance or relevance (or resolvability) of one of the two major issues that define personality psychology. We doubt that many personality psychologists would be very happy about doing this, and we doubt that doing this is really necessary.

Is This a Theory of Personality, or Only a Theory of Success?

There is another sense in which Cantor and Kihlstrom's approach fails to address the full range of issues that should be addressed by a theory of personality. The problem in this case derives from the fact that social intelligence is such a positively valued quality.[1] Intelligence is reflected in successful attainment of one's goals, flexibility in one's transactions, and sensitivity to feedback concerning one's behavior. One can attain a given goal in diverse ways (as the research on academic optimists and defensive pessimists demonstrates). But behavior is intelligent only inasmuch as it facilitates flexibility and goal attainment. The Cantor and Kihlstrom theoretical analysis of personality, then, focuses almost entirely on the adaptive and functional.

This also is true of the research that Cantor and Kihlstrom use to illustrate the theory's viability (the project on college students' adaptation to the college experience). In describing this work, the emphasis throughout is on the idea that many strategies are functional and useful for goal attainment. This emphasis is fitting, because Cantor and her colleagues are studying *only people whose behavior is "intelligent"*—i.e., people who are *successful* at attaining their goals. The academic optimists in this research are people who have been successful in the past and who expect to be successful in the future. The defensive pessimists—by operational definition—are people who express a sense of worry and pessimism about being successful in the future, but who have been successful in the past.

What the research illustrates is that these two categories of successful people have different routes to success. But let's not forget the fact that they are, by and large, successful. People who have not been successful in the past are simply not part of the study.

---

[1]We are unable to understand the basis for Cantor and Kihlstrom's assertion that the social-cognitive approach is nonevaluative. Bandura's construct of personal efficacy is highly evaluative: efficacy is good, an absence of efficacy is bad. Similarly, in Cantor and Kihlstrom's model of personality flexible adaptation is good, rigid automaticity is bad.

The fact that this research focuses selectively on people whose behavior is highly intelligent raises a serious question about the generality of the conceptual analysis. Rather than being a comprehensive approach to personality, the social-intelligence approach might be viewed as being a psychology of successful people. The fact that other people may fail to adapt and fail to attain their goals is largely disregarded.

In our view, then, this theory of social intelligence would benefit from also having a theory of social inadequacy. As it stands, the emphasis is on the fact that there are many strategies to attain desired goals. We are left knowing little about the ways in which goal attainment is disrupted or short-circuited. A theory of personality should have implications for understanding difficulties in self-management, as well as for success.[2]

To summarize the points made in this section, the social-intelligence model addresses some of the questions and issues of personality psychology, but not all of them. Cantor and Kihlstrom's analysis captures part of the domain of personality, but perhaps not as much of it as they imply.

IS IT NEW? IS IT DIFFERENT?

A second response to the position taken by Cantor and Kihlstrom is that it is not as new or different as it might seem to be. Cantor and Kihlstrom's examination of previous theoretical traditions focuses narrowly on cognitive conceptions of personality, rather than more broadly on discussions of how people negotiate the flow of their life's experiences. By doing so, they have underestimated the similarity between certain of their central themes and themes stressed for some time by others, albeit in literatures that some might regard as outside mainstream personality psychology. To illustrate this point, we touch briefly on two of those literatures.

Processes of Stress and Coping

One theory that appears closely related in several ways to Cantor and Kihlstrom's theoretical analysis is the model of psychological stress that was proposed quite some time ago by Lazarus (1966) and refined over the years by Lazarus and his colleagues (e.g., Lazarus & Folkman, 1984). Lazarus analyzes stress in terms of two kinds of appraisals that occur while people are engaged in transactions with their surrounding environments (both social and nonsocial), and the ways in which these appraisals lead people to adopt various strategies of coping.

---

[2]Interested readers are referred to Carver and Scheier (1983) for a discussion of problems in self-regulation that seems not very incompatible with the general line of reasoning used by Cantor and Kihlstrom.

Each of these appraisal processes is a complex event with multiple causes and consequences. The first appraisal is the interpretation of a situation in terms of its potential threat or challenge to the person. Lazarus has always argued that this appraisal is influenced by how the person approaches the world, as well as what the world presents to the person. More concretely, the person's idiosyncratic organization of knowledge influences the extent to which a given event appears threatening. This assertion in the Lazarus model is very similar to the viewpoint that Cantor and Kihlstrom present in broader terns in their chapter; that is, people's construal of any event depends partly on the event as it exists and partly on the knowledge structures that the people bring to the event.

The second appraisal postulated by Lazarus involves determining how to respond to the perceived threat. By treating this appraisal process as conceptually distinct from the first one, Lazarus is distinguishing between two aspects of the person's knowledge: knowledge used in perceiving a threat, and knowledge used in determining how to respond to the threat. This distinction is, of course, reminiscent of the distinction that Cantor and Kihlstrom stress in the target chapter between declarative (interpretive) and procedural knowledge.

Just as perception of threat is influenced by individualized organizations of prior knowledge, so are decisions about how to respond to the threat. The person implicitly sorts through the strategies that come to mind and evaluates the usefulness of each. The strategies that come to mind are different for different people, and the perceived usefulness of any given strategy will also vary from person to person. Again, this viewpoint is very similar to assumptions made by Cantor and Kihlstrom regarding the manner in which procedural knowledge is organized, and the idiosyncratic nature of people's strategies for social problem solving.

Once a coping strategy has been selected (in the Lazarus model), it is put into action in the person's behavior. In recent years Lazarus and his colleagues have distinguished between two large classes of coping strategies. What they term problem-focused coping is the attempt to eliminate the stressor or modify it in some way so as to diminish the threat that it poses. Problem-focused coping typically means taking direct action. What is termed emotion-focused coping is the attempt to deal in some way with the distress emotions that are elicited by the stressor. Presumably the reduction in distress permits the person to cope more effectively with the stressor itself. Thus, the two classes of coping responses are easily viewed as alternative strategies that can be used to attain the same end (successful coping).

It is interesting how similar these strategies are to the two sets of strategies employed by the subjects in the research on academic adjustment among college students conducted by Cantor and her colleagues. The academic optimists in that research are problem-focused copers, taking direct action to deal with academic stressors. The subjects who express a defensively pessimistic orientation to their academic outcomes are more emotion-focused copers. That is, Cantor and

Kihlstrom characterize these latter people as having more concern about the anxiety that they experience in association with academically evaluative events, and as spending more of their efforts in dealing with this anxiety.

As a final similarity between viewpoints, Lazarus has long argued that coping is best viewed as a dynamic process that shifts in nature across stages of a stressful transaction and varies greatly from situation to situation. He does not see it as useful to treat coping style as a dispositional characteristic (e.g., Folkman & Lazarus, 1980). This orientation is very similar to the position taken by Cantor and Kihlstrom regarding personality as it is expressed in social intelligence. That is, they argue that social intelligence is specific to contexts and varies in its expression from moment to moment.

Structure of Self-Regulation

A second literature with similarities to the position expressed by Cantor and Kihlstrom—a literature to which we have contributed—focuses on themes in the self-regulation of action (e.g., Carver, 1979; Carver & Scheier, 1981, 1983; Scheier & Carver, 1988; see also Kanfer & Busemeyer, 1982; Kirschenbaum, 1985). Many of the processes that are reflected in the Lazarus model of stress are also assumed in our own work. Though our own interest has not focused on social cognition per se, we have repeatedly emphasized the idea that act-specifying information (procedural knowledge) is linked in memory to information used in perception and construal. We have also stressed the theme that human behavior is directed toward goals at various levels of abstraction, and that behavior is guided by information feedback in a self-reflective process of assessing the consequences of prior acts. These concepts have provided a way for us to talk about both functional and dysfunctional qualities in people's self-regulation (Carver & Scheier, 1983, 1986a, b).

Though there are obvious differences between overt action (which is the focus of our writing) and problem solving (Cantor and Kihlstrom's focus), there are also similarities. It should be apparent that in complex human behavior, movement toward goals (and movement toward multiple goals simultaneously) is partly a matter of solving problems. That is, the person who knows what the next action ought to be is considerably closer to goal attainment than is the person who has no idea what act should come next. A focus on problem-solving strategies as a major aspect of social intelligence seems eminently compatible with a view of behavior as reflecting a process of feedback control. Indeed, the two focuses seem mutually supportive: Problem solving provides one way of specifying behavioral output for feedback systems, and feedback systems provide a way to account for the fact that problem-solving activities result in systematically regulated overt behavior.

Another theme that we have emphasized in our work is that encountering difficulties results in a divergence of responses as a function of other variables.

For example, knowing that a stimulus creates moderately intense anxiety in a person does not, in itself, permit prediction of the person's behavior. One must also know how the person is disposed to respond to the sense of fearfulness: with renewed effort, or with disengagement from effort (Carver, Blaney, & Scheier, 1979). Toward the end of their chapter Cantor and Kihlstrom make much the same point: Knowing that a person frames a particular task in a negative light provides less insight into the person's subsequent behavior than does knowing what kind of strategy is thereby evoked.

A final theme that we have used conceptually, though not studied empirically, is the notion of hierarchical organization among the goals and strategies that define the self and permit the carrying out of actions (see also Vallacher & Wegner, 1987). A very similar theme emerges at several points in the target chapter, where Cantor and Kihlstrom note that there is a hierarchy of declarative and procedural qualities, with regard both to objects in the social world and to the self. Indeed, the principle of hierarchical organization is appearing with increasing frequency these days in widely divergent places, ranging from discussions of the nature of control of physical movement (Rosenbaum, 1985, 1987) to discussions of the organization of the nervous system (Baron, 1987).

To summarize the point made in this section, the model presented in the target chapter has important similarities to other theories, similarities that have not been fully recognized. Though this might be regarded as a criticism of the target chapter, this point can also be viewed in a more positive light. That is, the similarity among theories suggests a convergence on the idea that certain principles are fundamental. This convergence provides grounds for greater confidence in the importance of these principles.

WHAT ARE THE IMPLICATIONS FOR ASSESSMENT?

The title of Cantor and Kihlstrom's chapter is "Social intelligence and cognitive assessments of personality." Although measurement issues do come up throughout the chapter, the chapter does not really represent a strong statement on the process of assessment. In two respects, however, the model they present appears to have implications for assessment.

How Much Should the Idiographic Be Emphasized?

The first of these implications follows from the fact that one of Cantor and Kihlstrom's major themes is the importance of viewing people as unique psychological entities. They repeatedly emphasize that life's experiences are individualized. Accordingly, to capture the richness of real, meaningful individual differences, assessment must be idiographic. On occasion Cantor and Kihlstrom even appear to press for a totally idiographic approach to interpreting and understanding behavior. This is one of two broad themes that leads them to their negative stance regarding the assessment of individual differences.

It is difficult for us to understand why Cantor and Kihlstrom emphasize the idiographic so strongly here. Once the point has been made, they proceed to disregard the idea almost entirely whenever they turn to research (which of course was also true of Allport, from whom the emphasis on the idiographic derives). Throughout the chapter, research illustrations are drawn from the work done by Cantor and her associates studying academic optimists and defensive pessimists. The subjects of this research project have been classified into two nomothetic categories, differing from each other in the degree to which they express concern and pessimism about their academic outcomes.

The research strategy that lies behind this project (and presumably others pertaining to social intelligence) involves deciding what social intelligence means in some particular context (in this case, the context of academic achievement), and then examining some strategies by which people express their intelligence. Note, however, that Cantor and her colleagues are not studying all possible strategies of approaching achievement tasks. They are studying two relatively coherent and intelligible, largely adaptive strategies for managing these tasks. Without imposing these (or some other) categorical boundaries on what strategies are being studied, what would be the point of the research? Imposing these criteria, however, makes assessment in the research nomothetic rather than idiographic.

Nor is this the only reason for skepticism about the idiographic theme. While placing their work in historical context, Cantor and Kihlstrom say that social-cognitive theorists "avoid the ranking of individuals on continuous dimensions and other classificatory exercises" (see p. 7), implying that such theorists instead hold an idiographic view. But this statement certainly can't be accurate. Surely it is meaningful to compare the efficacy expectancies that two people hold for any given task, and surely Bandura would not shrink from making such comparisons.

Cantor and Kihlstrom also suggest in at least two places that restricting one's constructs to specific domains precludes comparisons between persons (see pp. 7, 11). We see no basis for that assertion. If we choose to assess test anxiety instead of overall anxiety, does that mean we can no longer compare people with each other? If we assess math-test anxiety instead of general test anxiety, can we no longer compare people? What if we assess anxiety that is specific to multiple-choice math tests? It doesn't seem obvious why any of these restrictions should preclude comparisons between persons.

The Idiographic Approach: A Different View. Our view is that the idiographic perspective is an idealization that is useful for some purposes but not for others. As a philosophical notion, the idea that each person sees and responds to the world in a unique way is appealing and probably correct. For a theorist trying to trace the logic underlying a process, it is sensible and useful to think through specific unique cases. For a researcher, however, a purely idiographic position is less useful. Even when idiographic techniques are used successfully (e.g., Higgins, King, & Mavin, 1982), they are used in combination with category labels, or some other nomothetic technique, rather than alone.

Cantor and Kihlstrom appear to be well aware of the usefulness of the idiographic approach to trace processes in people's behavior. For example, their description of the students who use a "social-constraint" strategy for handling social interaction provides a wealth of process information concerning how these individuals live their social lives. It is not apparent, however, why we would suffer any loss as theorists or as observers of behavior *if we were to label these people as being high in social anxiety or shyness*—the nomothetic constructs upon which Cantor and Kihlstrom's description converges. Indeed, there may well be something to gain from applying such constructs (which exist at a higher level of abstraction than does the behavioral description). Once one realizes that these people are socially anxious, that label suggests other behavioral qualities to look for. The idiographic process description provided by Cantor and Kihlstrom adds refinement to the more descriptive nomothetic approach, but it does not render the latter irrelevant or obsolete.

Extrapolations From Cantor and Kihlstrom

To accept Cantor and Kihlstrom's emphasis on the ideographic would make it impossible to do research in the usual way (because in their view people cannot be ranked or compared). Nor does their emphasis seem especially helpful with regard to clinical assessment. On the other hand, if one were to disregard the emphasis on the idiographic, other aspects of the theoretical perspective adopted by Cantor and Kihlstrom suggest novel focuses for assessment of personality, though these are not particularly emphasized in the target chapter.

For example, Cantor and Kihlstrom place a major emphasis on the need to understand a person's goals and life tasks (cf. Emmons, 1986; Markus & Nurius, 1986). It should be plain from this viewpoint on human behavior that people can be assessed in terms of the goals that occupy them, and the nature of the hierarchical organizations among those goals. Knowing what goals are salient to a person, and what strategies the person sees as steps toward attaining those goals, may be more informative than knowing other aspects of what the person is "like."

This general approach to thinking about behavior also suggests other novel qualities to assess (cf. Carver & Scheier, 1988, pp. 492–493). It might be useful to know, for example, whether the person habitually thinks mostly about relatively high-level goals, or instead thinks mostly about low-level goals (cf. Vallacher & Wegner, 1987). It might also be useful for some purposes to obtain information about other "process" aspects of self-regulation, including the degree to which people habitually focus attention on themselves (or on various aspects of themselves), for purposes of monitoring their actions.

In the view we are suggesting, personality assessment would have several components. One component would involve assessing meaningful biases in certain kinds of self-regulatory process tendencies (e.g., degree of self observation, typical level of abstraction of one's goals). Another component would involve assessing the nature of the goals that occupy people's minds, and the organizations that a given person imposes on his or her array of goals and strategies. A third component is the more typical assessment of the content of people's behavior—what they say, think, feel, and do—in various domains.

LEVELS OF GENERALITY: ARE ONLY DOMAIN-SPECIFIC CONSTRUCTS USEFUL?

Another major theme in Cantor and Kihlstrom's chapter is that the only way to understand personality (social intelligence) is to fine-tune the assessment of personality to specific domains and even to specific situations. The theme that highly situation- or domain-specific assessment is preferable to the assessment of broader dispositions is not an altogether new one. For example, as Cantor and Kihlstrom note, Bandura believes that the sense of self-efficacy is a meaningful construct only when it is assessed with respect to very restricted domains of behavior. Similarly, there is evidence that general personality and attitude measures tend not to be strong predictors of specific actions (e.g., Mischel, 1968). Currently, then, there is an emphasis in all of personality psychology on the notion that social knowledge and self-knowledge are compartmentalized and should be assessed accordingly.

We wonder, however, if this point is not being overstated at this stage of investigation. In our view, there remains a question about the extent to which social intelligence, and dispositions more generally, are compartmentalized. There thus remains a question about whether measures that are highly focused are inevitably to be preferred over those that are broader.

Generalized Expectancies for Good Versus Bad Outcomes

Consider an illustration of this issue, taken from our own work. We have recently developed a measure of optimism (Scheier & Carver, 1985), which we define in terms of generalized expectancies for good versus bad outcomes in one's life. This construct is explicitly broad-scope, rather than being situation- or domain-specific. We see the distillation of people's expectations as potentially a useful predictor of a wide range of distinct qualities in people's actions and experience.

Our tentative view places generalized optimism at the top of a pyramid of expectancies (or perhaps at the core of an onion). We believe that people hold very global expectancies about their future in general, that they hold more domain-specific expectancies concerning outcomes in various classes of events with which they are familiar, and that they also hold situation-specific expectancies concerning outcomes in various restricted and specific situations that fall within any given event class.

Which of these expectancies is most useful in predicting behavior? Two possibilities seem reasonable to us. One is that the best prediction may come from the expectancy that best matches the criterion variable in level of specificity. That is, a specific expectancy would best predict a specific criterion (which would be relatively compatible with Cantor and Kihlstrom's position), and a general expectancy would best predict a broader criterion (a possibility that Cantor and Kihlstrom did not consider). Alternatively, the best prediction may come from assessing multiple expectancies. That is, it may be that expectancies at several levels of abstraction influence the person's orientation to even very specific acts.

As an illustration of these possibilities, imagine a college student who is moderately pessimistic in general, who also has relatively unfavorable expectancies concerning academic outcomes as a class, but who feels relatively confident about the experience of multiple-choice exams in particular. Presumably, if you wanted to predict a general outcome of some kind, for example, success at coping with life during a difficult period in the school year, you might do better by using the student's general orientation to life as a predictor than you would do by using expectancies about either academic outcomes or multiple-choice exams. If you wanted to predict the student's academic performance (integrated across several courses), you might do best by using the student's expectancies concerning academic outcomes. If you wanted to predict the student's performance on a specific multiple-choice exam, you might do best by using the specific expectancy.

On the other hand, it is not altogether clear that you wouldn't be best off thinking about the student's behavior in even the specific case as being influenced by "layers" of expectancies. Even as the student enters the exam room, his or her generalized sense of pessimism (which derives in part from domains of life that are irrelevant to the exam) may be coloring how the situation is construed (cf. Blaney, 1986; Clark, Milberg, & Ross, 1983). The academic domain-relevant doubts may be at work simultaneously, as well as the confidence that comes from knowing that at least the exam is multiple choice instead of essay.[3]

---

[3]Indeed, the level of abstraction at which the student is focusing on the exam may also influence how the various expectancies influence behavior. If the student focuses on the fact that the exam is multiple choice, the student may be disproportionately confident. If he instead focuses on higher level qualities of the experience—the fact that the exam is just one more in a series of manifestations of his life's karma—he may be disproportionately pessimistic. This point illustrates the importance of the theme of hierarchical organization, while also supporting Cantor and Kihlstrom's general position that personal construal is important in determining behavior.

We are certainly not the first to suggest the possibility that behavior is best predicted by an expectancy whose level of specificity matches that of the behavior itself, or by a combination of expectancies of varying specificity (see Lefcourt, 1976; Rotter, 1954). But these possibilities have not yet received careful research attention. In our view it is premature to abandon the possibilities prior to testing them.

What If There is No Prior Experience?

We thus far have considered situations in which people, by implication at least, have had previous experiences in the behavioral domain that they are entering. This is not always the case, however. Sometimes people have no prior experience to draw on and consequently have no real basis for knowing what to expect or what to do. In entering situations such as this, people must use mental structures that don't quite fit the situation. Two possibilities seem likely. One is that people will use mental structures from domains that are similar in some way to the new situation, generalizing from one domain to the other. The second possibility is that people will bring more global or generalized orientations to bear on the new situation.

As a concrete illustration of how a generalized orientation might be used when the person has had no prior experience, consider the following study, which focused on the experiences of men about to undergo coronary artery bypass surgery for the first time (Scheier, Matthews, Owens, Magovern, Lefebvre, Abbott, & Carver, 1988). Levels of generalized outcome expectancies (dispositional optimism) were assessed in these men on the day prior to surgery. Six to 8 days postoperatively the men were asked to report specific expectancies about when important aspects of their lives would return to normal. For example, the men were asked to estimate how long (in weeks) they thought it would take them to return to work on a full-time basis, to resume active sexual relations, to return to any recreational activities they might have had, and so on. Six months postoperatively the men were reinterviewed to determine how long it had actually taken for these events to occur.

Two aspects of the data are of interest in this context, concerning the role of specific versus generalized expectancies as predictors of normalization of life activities. First, when asked to indicate how long it would take for their lives to normalize, many of the men had difficulty in generating these specific expectancies. For example, when asked how long in weeks it would take them to return to work, many of the men simply replied "I'll go back as soon as I can," or "Whenever I feel well enough." When asked to be more precise about how many weeks would be required, the men often became evasive, saying that they couldn't be more precise because they just didn't know what to expect. These anecdotal accounts provide support for the notion that people who have no prior experience with an event have no basis from which to generate specific expectations.

The second interesting aspect of the findings concerns the relative predictive power of generalized expectancies versus specific expectancies in predicting actual normalization of life activities across the various domains. In the majority of cases, specific expectancies (among men able to generate them) predicted the corresponding specific outcome better than did general optimism. For example, specific expectancies for resumption of sexual relations correlated with actual resumption of sexual relations more strongly than did optimism. This finding, of course, is perfectly consistent with the "matching" analysis described earlier and with the analysis offered by Cantor and Kihlstrom.

In other life domains, however, generalized optimism predicted actual rate of recovery almost as well as did specific expectancies, and in certain life domains optimism predicted better than did specific expectancies. For example, optimism was a significant predictor of return to vigorous physical exercise whereas specific expectancies for returning to vigorous physical exercise were not. In brief, whereas specific expectancies may have held a predictive edge in some of the domains sampled, the advantage tended to be slight and in some cases the advantage even reversed.

Contrary to what may be the prevailing view, these findings suggest that global optimism as a generalized personality quality may well play an important role in responses to situations with which people are unfamiliar. By extrapolation, the findings suggest that other general personality qualities may be more important than Cantor and Kihlstrom have credited them with being, particularly when a person is in unfamiliar circumstances.

LEVELS OF GENERALITY: FURTHER QUESTIONS

The preceding section was devoted to the empirical question of whether situation-specific constructs (and more particularly, situational expectancies) should inevitably be better predictors of behavior than would more general orientations. This is not, however, the only question that arises when considering Cantor and Kihlstrom's position on the level of generality issue. Two additional questions are addressed in the following sections.

What is a Domain?

Thus far we have addressed the issue of domain-specific assessment just as Cantor and Kihlstrom presented it, as an in-principle issue. In some measure, however, Cantor and Kihlstrom's position on the issue reflects the same disjunction between exhortation and operationalization as characterizes their position on the issue of idiographic assessment. In principle, they speak of domain- and context-specific assessment. In practice, however, they define "domains" quite broadly.

The two domains addressed in the research that Cantor and Kihlstrom discuss are achievement and social interaction. Those are rather broad domains. For college students (the subjects of the research), the two taken together cover a good deal of the territory of life. Indeed, if one were to substitute "work" for achievement and "relationships" for social interaction, the two together would cover a lot of the territory of life for anyone.

In a sense, then, the emphasis on specificity in the target chapter is a bit misleading. There apparently is a *middle level* of specificity that is intuitively meaningful to the theorists when they change hats and become researchers. Cantor and Kihlstrom's view in the researcher role is certainly narrower than the view holding that personality exerts a constant and unvarying influence on all behavior, regardless of its content (which, of course, almost no one believes). But their view when in the researcher role is also considerably less fine grained than one would expect from the theoretical stance they take.

Personality Can Be Manifest in Many Ways: Behavior is Multiply Determined

There is another issue that deserves some attention here, which stems from the fact that behavioral tendencies displayed by a person in one domain do not always generalize to conceptually similar domains. There seem to be two ways to construe this failure of behavior to generalize, one of which employs broad personality constructs and one of which does not. Because Cantor and Kihlstrom address only one of these possibilities, it would seem useful to examine both of them.

Consider, as a working example, the disposition of sensation seeking (e.g., Zuckerman, 1979). Being relatively high in sensation seeking might cause a person to engage in such activities as sky diving, scuba diving, sports car racing, wind surfing, or dozens of other possibilities. Yet two people who are high in sensation seeking may differ greatly in what they actually do. One person may manifest sensation seeking primarily via water sports, for example, whereas the other may display the same disposition primarily by racing a sports car on weekends.

A view of personality that assumes the existence of relatively general dispositions would account for this difference between the two people by saying that any action tendency is the product of multiple influences, with the personality disposition being just one of them. As a result, the same underlying disposition is manifest overtly in different ways in different people. The first person may engage in water sports because he is a naturally good swimmer, tans easily, and lives near the ocean; he doesn't race cars because he doesn't like the noise and grease. The second person, in contrast, is not a skilled athlete (he can't swim at all) but he has extremely good reflexes and peripheral vision, which are very well suited to racing, and his brother is a mechanic. Thus, for each person there are influences (whether dispositional or contextual) causing him to express the disposition of sensation seeking in his own idiosyncratic way.

As we have portrayed them here, both of these people are high in sensation seeking, but the tendency is expressed in different ways, modulated by other variables. From the view that Cantor and Kihlstrom advocate in their target chapter, on the other hand, personality must be understood in specific contexts, rather than more generally. In their view, the first person would be high in water-sport participation (or water-sport sensation seeking), whereas the second person is high in motor-sport participation (or motor-sport sensation seeking).

It is hard to be sure which of these construals is more useful conceptually, and we leave it to readers to mull over the possibilities. We suggest, however, that each view is likely to have some empirical merit. A measure of generalized sensation seeking should predict both action tendencies (engaging in water sports and motor racing) at a moderate level (i.e., diminished by the unassessed influence of other variables). Measures of specific sensation seeking should better predict the act classes to which they are targeted, but more poorly predict alternative acts. If one wants to predict a specific action, one should probably use a specific measure (cf. Heberlein & Black, 1976; Weigel, Vernon, & Tognacci, 1974). If one wants to predict a broader range of actions (or perhaps an index reflecting that range), one should probably use a general measure (cf. Weigel & Newman, 1976).

CONCLUDING COMMENT

As has been reflected in the substance of the preceding sections, we are somewhat skeptical of the merit of certain of the themes that Cantor and Kihlstrom emphasized in their target chapter, particularly their emphasis on the idiographic. We also prefer that closure not be reached prematurely on empirical questions such as the relative value of general versus specific constructs. On the other hand, our various concerns and criticisms should not be read as suggesting wholesale rejection of the point of view that Cantor and Kihlstrom have taken. As we said in our opening paragraph and elsewhere in this chapter, our own view on personality shares several themes with theirs. We find commendable their effort to produce a comprehensive view of personality. Accordingly, we offer our comments in the spirit of collaboration (in the broadest sense), and in the desire to see further theoretical development and integration.

ACKNOWLEDGMENTS

Preparation of this commentary was facilitated by NSF grants BNS87-17783 and BNS87-06271.

REFERENCES

Allport, G. W. (1961). *Pattern and growth in personality*. New York: Holt, Rinehart, & Winston.

Baron, R. J. (1987). *The cerebral computer: An introduction to the computational structure of the human brain*. Hillsdale, NJ: Lawrence Erlbaum Associates.

Blaney, P. H. (1986). Affect and memory: A review. *Psychological Bulletin, 99,* 229–246.

Buss, A. H., & Plomin, R. (1984). *Temperament: Early developing personality traits*. Hillsdale, NJ: Lawrence Erlbaum Associates.

Carver, C. S. (1979). A cybernetic model of self-attention processes. *Journal of Personality and Social Psychology, 37,* 1251–1281.

Carver, C. S., Blaney, P. H., & Scheier, M. F. (1979). Focus of attention, chronic expectancy, and responses to a feared stimulus. *Journal of Personality and Social Psychology, 37,* 1186–1195.

Carver, C. S., & Scheier, M. F. (1981). *Attention and self-regulation: A control-theory approach to human behavior*. New York: Springer-Verlag.

Carver, C. S., & Scheier, M. F. (1983). A control-theory model of normal behavior, and implications for problems in self-management. In P. C. Kendall (Ed.), *Advances in cognitive-behavioral research and therapy* (Vol. 2, pp. 127–194). New York: Academic Press.

Carver, C. S., & Scheier, M. F. (1986a). Functional and dysfunctional responses to anxiety: The interaction between expectancies and self-focused attention. In R. Schwarzer (Ed.), *Self-related cognitions in anxiety and motivation* (pp. 111–141). Hillsdale, NJ: Lawrence Erlbaum Associates.

Carver, C. S., & Scheier, M. F. (1986b). Analyzing shyness: A specific application of broader self-regulatory principles. In W. H. Jones, J. M. Cheek, & S. R. Briggs (Eds.), *Shyness: Perspectives on research and treatment* (pp. 173–185). New York: Plenum.

Carver, C. S., & Scheier, M. F. (1988). *Perspectives on personality*. Needham Heights, MA: Allyn & Bacon.

Clark, M. S., Milberg, S., & Ross, J. (1983). Arousal cues arousal-related material in memory: Implications for understanding effects of mood on memory. *Journal of Verbal Learning and Verbal Behavior, 22,* 633–649.

Emmons, R. A. (1986). Personal strivings: An approach to personality and well-being. *Journal of Personality and Social Psychology, 51,* 1058–1068.

Folkman, S., & Lazarus, R. S. (1980). An analysis of coping in a middle-aged community sample. *Journal of Health and Social Behavior, 21,* 219–239.

Heberlein, T. A., & Black, J. S. (1976). Attitudinal specificity and the prediction of behavior in a field setting. *Journal of Personality and Social Psychology, 33,* 474–479.

Higgins, E. T., King, G. A., & Mavin, G. H. (1982). Individual construct accessibility and subjective impressions and recall. *Journal of Personality and Social Psychology, 43,* 35–47.

Kanfer, F. H., & Busemeyer, J. R. (1982). The use of problem-solving and decision-making in behavior therapy. *Clinical Psychology Review, 2,* 239–266.

Kirschenbaum, D. S. (1985). Proximity and specificity of planning: A position paper. *Cognitive Therapy and Research, 9,* 489–506.

Klinger, E. (1975). Consequences of commitment to and disengagement from incentives. *Psychological Review, 82,* 1–25.

Lazarus, R. S. (1966). *Psychological stress and the coping process*. New York: McGraw-Hill.

Lazarus, R. S., & Folkman, S. (1984). *Stress, appraisal, and coping*. New York: Springer.

Lefcourt, H. M. (1976). *Locus of control: Current trends in theory and research*. Hillsdale, NJ: Lawrence Erlbaum Associates.

Markus, H., & Nurius, P. (1986). Possible selves. *American Psychologist, 41,* 954–969.

Mischel, W. (1986). *Personality and assessment*. New York: Wiley.

Rosenbaum, D. A. (1985). Motor programming: A review and scheduling theory. In H. Heuer, U.

Kleinbeck, & K.-M. Schmidt (Eds.), *Motor behavior: Programming, control, and acquisition.* Heidelberg: Springer-Verlag.

Rosenbaum, D. A. (1987). Hierarchical organization of motor programs. In S. P. Wise (Ed.), *Higher brain functions: Recent explorations of the brain's emergent properties.* New York: Wiley.

Rotter, J. B. (1954). *Social learning and clinical psychology.* New York: Prentice-Hall.

Scheier, M. F., & Carver, C. S. (1985). Optimism, coping, and health: Assessment and implications of generalized outcome expectancies. *Health Psychology, 4,* 219–247.

Scheier, M. F., & Carver, C. S. (1988). A model of behavioral self-regulation: Translating intention into action. In L. Berkowitz (Ed.), *Advances in experimental social psychology* (Vol. 21). New York: Academic Press.

Scheier, M. F., Matthews, K. A., Owens, J., Magovern, G. J., Sr., Lefebvre, R. C., Abbott, R. A., & Carver, C. S. (1988). *Dispositional optimism and recovery from coronary artery bypass surgery: The beneficial effects on physical and psychological well-being.* Manuscript submitted for publication.

Vallacher, R. R., & Wegner, D. M. (1987). Action identification theory: The representation and control of behavior. *Psychological Review, 94,* 3–15.

Weigel, R. H., & Newman, L. S. (1976). Increasing attitude-behavior correspondence by broadening the scope of the behavioral measure. *Journal of Personality and Social Psychology, 33,* 793–802.

Weigel, R. H., Vernon, D. T. A., & Tognacci, L. N. (1974). Specificity of the attitude as a determinant of attitude-behavior congruence. *Journal of Personality and Social Psychology, 30,* 724–728.

Zuckerman, M. (1979). *Sensation seeking: Beyond the optimal level of arousal.* Hillsdale, NJ: Lawrence Erlbaum Associates.

6 On the Personalization of Motivation

Robert A. Emmons
Laura A. King
University of California, Davis

Cantor and Kihlstrom (this volume) present a persuasive and sophisticated treatise arguing for the reconceptualization of personality and motivation in terms of social intelligence. Within this perspective, personality is best identified with the strategies that individuals use in confronting developmental tasks that organize and define their purposeful action at various periods in the life course. Although compelling, this reconceptualization is not without its difficulties. For instance, the assumption is made that all individuals are preoccupied with the same life tasks—that undergraduate subjects all share equal interest in social and academic challenges. Also, Cantor and Kihlstrom tread rather gingerly on the fine line between nomothetic and idiographic research. To our minds, they stress the nomothetic when they ought to stress the idiographic (e.g., in the definitions of the life tasks themselves), and they emphasize idiographic characteristics when they might opt for more nomothetic dimensions (e.g., individual construal styles within the life tasks). Through an examination of specific instances in which, by our standards, the social-intelligence approach goes awry, we hope to reveal the general biases that underly Cantor and Kihlstrom's conceptualization of personality. No doubt along the way we will reveal many of our own biases as well.

In this reply, we discuss four specific areas neglected by Cantor and Kihlstrom. We list these points here and then expound on each separately. First, their approach lacks a formal assessment model and is unconcerned with traditional psychometric principles. Second, they fail to address conflict and complexity, two important relational properties of goals. Third, they unfortunately dismiss the literature on motive dispositions—an area that is compatible with and could offer significant contributions to their framework. The last major point to be made here is that Cantor and Kihlstrom fail to address the relationships that may exist between the idiographic goal units (one of which is the "life task") that have recently been proposed. We examine these four main points through the rest of this reply. Our central thesis is that the social-intelligence conceptualization of personality could be even more powerful through the incorporation of these concerns.

THE NEGLECT OF RELIABILITY AND VALIDITY

The first problem to be addressed is the absence of measurement concerns in the chapter. Despite its title, "Social intelligence and cognitive *assessments* of personality," a formal assessment model is not advanced. This neglect for measurement issues has long been the Achilles heel of the cognitive-social-learning perspective. For example, in the cognitive-social-learning person-variable approach (Mischel, 1973, 1981), one searches in vain for a means of assessing these person variables (i.e., encoding strategies, expectancies, self-regulatory systems and plans, competencies, subjective values), and discussions of reliability and validity in the measurement of these. To the detriment of the social-intelligence approach to personality, Cantor and Kihlstrom do not break from this mold. They are steadfast in their desire to avoid "the ranking of individuals on continuous dimensions and other classificatory exercises" (p. 7). Through the social-intelligence approach, "all hope of comparative ranking vanishes" (p. 9). Whereas an emphasis on individualized, dynamic phenomena as well as the flexibility and discriminativeness that such an emphasis entails are commendable, the lack of concern for measurement principles is not.

Traditionally, such concerns have been the province of the nomothetic individual-difference approach to personality, which has sought to identify a person's standing on relevant dimensions and to use this information to predict relevant criterion behaviors. Perhaps because the study of personality has relied on correlational work using potentially fallible measures of complex psychological phenomena, personality psychology has been uniquely concerned with the validity and reliability of its instruments. In proposing to take on the topic of personality with the social-intelligence perspective, Cantor and Kihlstrom must offer concepts commensurate with this traditional wisdom. Other fields of psychology have looked to personality for a sophisticated assessment technology and are likely to be disappointed by what they find in the social-intelligence paradigm.

An emphasis on idiographic, context-specific assessment does not give one license to ignore fundamental measurement properties of reliability and validity. It might be argued that traditional psychometric concerns are less applicable to the idiographic perspective that Cantor and Kihlstrom advance. Indeed, the most obvious methods of assessing reliability (e.g., test–retest reliability) or validity (e.g., concurrent measures) may not be suited to idiographic research that emphasizes, as the social intelligence quite admirably does, the changing nature of its subject matter. This fact does not preclude any concern for reliability or validity, however. It merely calls for more innovative approaches to these psychometric principles. Various other idiographic approaches to motivation, such as personal goals (Wadsworth & Ford, 1983), current concerns (Klinger, 1987), and personal strivings (Emmons, in press) have demonstrated the feasibility of incorporating psychometric principles into the assessment of these constructs. Some examples of the reliability and validity assessment procedures utilized by other researchers may provide illustrations of how these concerns may be addressed without compromising the idiographic, dynamic nature of the elements being measured.

In his work on current concerns, Klinger (1987) acknowledges the unique problem of assessing the reliability of a measure of a changing construct. Conventional methods do not account for the changes in measurement that occur as a function of the instability of the construct under investigation rather than as a function of the unreliability of the measure itself. To tackle this problem for his Interview Questionnaire (IntQ) measure of current concerns, Klinger had subjects complete the questionnaire twice, once at the beginning and once at the end of a 2-month period. Rather than relying on a correlation of measures at time 1 and time 2 as an indicator of the dependability of the IntQ, Klinger asked subjects to compare the two sets of responses and identify the current concerns from time 2 that related to the concerns at time 1. In examining concerns from time 1 that did not correspond with any concerns mentioned at time 2, subjects were asked why the concern was no longer mentioned, whether this was due to forgetting or to the subject attaining the goal and moving on to other concerns. In this way, the instability in scores that was due to error and that which was due to the dynamic nature of the current concern construct was determined. To address the issue of validity, subjects completed daily diaries to assess the extent to which current concerns related to behaviors. In this manner, it could be shown that the current concerns measured in the IntQ actually drove behaviors.

In a similar vein, Wadsworth and Ford (1983) assessed individuals' goal hierarchies by obtaining lists of personal goals, taping interviews, and obtaining behavioral measures from their subjects. Wadsworth and Ford employed a difficult and complex procedure for coding interviews and goal hierarchies, stressing the idiographic nature of their endeavor throughout. Issues of reliability and validity, however, remained an important concern. Coders categorized the goals with regard to their time frame as well as the life domain to which the goal was relevant. These coders also assessed the means–end connections between subjects' activities and goals. Interrater reliability was a key measure in their study. In addition, to assess the construct validity of their measures of goals, Wadsworth and Ford made predictions about the extent to which two different groups of subjects (undergraduates vs. blue-collar workers) would differ in the number of long-term goals listed. Their measure of goal hierarchies proved valid by this hypothesized criterion. A study of life tasks might use this kind of measure as a means of demonstrating that different (age- and life-experience) groups do have life tasks that are appreciably different in content but which play the same basic organizing, motivating role across these lives and life stages.

As another innovative measure of validity, Wadsworth and Ford invited a subset of subjects to examine the goal hierarchy assessments prepared for them. These subjects then provided their reactions as to the accuracy of the goal scheme. This validity assessment proved to be an interesting experience for experimenters and subjects alike. Some subjects were surprised to find that their activity patterns were not really in sync with their own personally valued goals. One can see how such an assessment would also be valuable to individuals engaged in a variety of life tasks. Other forms of reliability assessment, more familiar to traditional approaches, are also possible. For example, split-half reliability coefficients can and should be calculated for such life-task characteristics as difficulty, enjoyment, threat, etc., across all life tasks listed by subjects.

The Failure to Consider Goal Conflict and Complexity

The second problem in the social-intelligence perspective is the lack of attention to two relational properties of goals that have considerable effects on cognition, affect, and behavior: conflict and complexity. Although they give attention to the common strategy selection dynamics that occur *within* both of the two major life tasks, Cantor and Kihlstrom neglect to consider the important characteristics of the relationships that may exist *between* the two life tasks and among subgoals within each life task. One potential characteristic of these relationships is conflict. Conflict refers to the situation in which an individual has two or more goals whose accomplishment would interfere with the accomplishment of the others. For instance, an individual may wish to spend time with a boyfriend or girlfriend and at the same time excel in all his or her classes. The conflict that could occur here between a social goal and an academic goal is obvious. Conflict describes the relationship between two goals when the accomplishment of one would have a harmful effect on one's pursuit of the other. Ambivalence is a form of conflict. An individual may be said to be ambivalent about the achievement of a goal to the extent that the accomplishment of the goal would bring them both happiness and unhappiness. An example of a social goal about which a subject in a recent study (Emmons & King, 1988) reported feeling ambivalent is "express my feelings to others." Inasmuch as human life is innately complex and varied, some amount of conflict and ambivalence may be inevitable.

In their chapter, Cantor and Kihlstrom seem to work under the implicit assumption that social and academic life tasks peacefully coexist with equal relevance and force in individual lives. To some, this may sound like a plausible ideal but for many individuals it paints an idealistic portrait that is far removed from their own experiences. In terms of the amount of time that can be committed to each, parental and peer pressure for achievement in each, and personal appraisals of the impact of failures or successes in each, social and academic tasks are clearly nonorthogonal. Indeed, and unfortunately, these concerns are likely to collide, on many occasions to the detriment of individual well-being. Cantor and Kihlstrom maintain that the life tasks of their undergraduate subjects fall into a variety of categories, including making friends, managing time, establishing future goals, getting good grades, and being independent. Conflict is likely to occur within and between these domains (e.g., between making friends and getting good grades).

In our studies of personal strivings, we have found that conflict within striving systems is related to increased rumination about and inhibition of action toward conflicting goals, as well as a number of psychological and physical complaints (Emmons & King, 1988). Conflict between and within life tasks could also be an important predictor of psychological and physical well-being, as well as the day-to-day successes of individual strategies for life-task achievement. It might be that individuals are more prone to use particular strategies when they are experiencing conflict between life tasks. These conflict-driven choices might figure significantly into the success or failure of certain strategies. Cantor and Kihlstrom do hint at the potential importance of negotiating conflict to social intelligence when they state, "Intelligent action is reflected in selecting a preferred strategy that *does not jeopardize other personal goals* (p. 16 emphasis added)." Intelligence should permit one to resolve conflict and integrate potentially conflicting interests. Certainly, the life-task approach provides a promising framework in which to address these issues.

Along these same lines, and more optimistically, goals or tasks may have a positive influence on each other; that is, the accomplishment of one goal or task may actually contribute to the achievement of another goal or task. Instrumentality refers to this kind of harmonious relationship between one's goals. Instrumentality has been found to be related to high life satisfaction (Emmons, 1986). In ignoring the nuances of the vertical structure between tasks or strategies, the social-intelligence perspective cannot detect the existence of this kind of relationship either.

A second important attribute of the relationship between tasks and among the subgoals within tasks that is given only brief mention by Cantor and Kihlstrom is complexity. The flexibility component of social intelligence is identified with complexity in their chapter. Complexity refers to a system that is characterized by a high degree of differentiation among constituent parts and the integration of these varied parts into a coherent whole. Complexity may be applied to a goal system that contains a number of differentiated goal units that are hierarchically integrated. Like conflict and instrumentality, complexity in goal systems has also been linked to other aspects of experience. For instance, in our work on personal strivings we have found that individuals with highly differentiated goals tend to experience more extreme affect (Emmons & King, 1989).

Aside from the important connection between flexibility and complexity, how might the concept of complexity be applied to life tasks? Whereas most previous work on complexity (e.g., Emmons & King, in press; Linville, 1985) has focused on differentiation, the life-task framework might be useful in assessing the degree of integration of goals. Examining the extent to which differentiated strivings or specific goal units overlap across more broadly defined life tasks may provide a measure of the amount of integration present in an individual's goal structure. As in the case of conflict and instrumentality, the complexity of one's goal structure may play an important role in the selection of strategies and the ultimate success of those strategies.

The Dismissal of the Motive Disposition Literature

The life-task approach has been offered as an alternative to traditional views on personality and motivation. These traditional approaches have found it useful to conceptualize motivation in terms of broad classes of incentives that concern individuals and toward which they strive in their everyday behavior. There is considerable consensus that the three major motives, nAchievement, nAffiliation–nIntimacy, and nPower provide useful representation of the human motivational system, and considerable literatures have developed around each of these motives (McAdams, 1985; McClelland, 1985). A brief definition of each of these motives should suggest the possible connections between the motives and the life-task approach. Need for achievement can be characterized as an interest in excelling, in competing with a standard of excellence. It involves the expense of energy in the pursuit of a goal. Need for affiliation concerns establishing and maintaining interpersonal relationships. It is characterized by a desire to win friends and gain approval and acceptance. Need for intimacy, although similar to nAffiliation, concerns a deeper commitment with another person. Intimacy motivation involves the desire to help others, a concern for experiencing a warm, close communicative exchange with another person. Power motivation involves the drive to have impact on the environment. It may be characterized as a need to dominate, manipulate, and control. Research on the behavioral correlates of these motives has provided provocative results. The potential connections between these motives and life tasks are fairly obvious. An analogy could easily be drawn between the concepts of nAffiliation/Intimacy and the social-life tasks. In addition, nAchievement corresponds to academic life tasks. In some sense, the social-intelligence perspective has before it the formidable task of demonstrating that it offers us something over and above these motive dispositions.

Cantor and Kihlstrom unfortunately dismiss the literature on motive dispositions—an area that could offer at least three significant contributions to their framework. First, an examination of individual differences in underlying motivation could provide a means by which their perspective could be tied into a more inclusive hierarchy. It seems unwise to divorce a personalized goal approach from a hierarchy rooted in deeper dynamic motivational forces. Cognitive structures cannot simply drive themselves. Something must invigorate them and excite them to action. Within the present social-intelligence framework, life tasks stand alone as a driving force in behavior. Placing life tasks within the context of motivation in general would define their scope, allow the life-task research to feed into a body of literature, and make sensible the individual differences that are found in approaches to these tasks.

This need to make sense of individual differences within life tasks is the second area in which the motive disposition approach could contribute to the social-intelligence paradigm. An inclusion of the subjects' predominant needs in an analysis of life-task strategy efficiency could account for individual differences in value and commitment to different types of life tasks. Put simply, some individuals are going to be more interested than others in the successful completion of certain life tasks as a function of their underlying motives. For instance, an individual who is high on nAchievement might find it perfectly acceptable to sacrifice social-task performance in favor of his or her academic goals. Thus, he or she might utilize more efficient strategies in the academic life domain. Also, such an individual might not be as experienced in the social domain and may find that their academic strategies do not generalize to the realm of interpersonal relationships. Because social and academic (or, more broadly, interpersonal and achievement) interests do, to some extent, compete for our time and energy, our underlying needs and values will serve as a determinant of the choices we make—not only in terms of which strategies we choose but also in terms of whether or not we choose to act on a given situation at all. Thus, use of the need concepts provides a motivational backdrop for Cantor and Kihlstrom's situation-specific intelligence, or expertise.

Finally, the inclusion of motive disposition information could provide a means by which to track individuals through their life tasks and strategic choices throughout the life-span. For, although the tasks change in a somewhat normative fashion, the individual motives would be likely to remain somewhat stable providing landmarks for those interested in studying individuals throughout their lives (McAdams, 1988). Motive dispositions would lend a sense of what is continuous and persistent alongside the changing and developing individual life-task trajectory. The ways in which these enduring life interests are translated into life-task strategy choices and the "goodness of fit" between individual motives and life tasks could provide fascinating information about what is stable and what is changing in human life.

We have begun to place personal strivings into just such a larger framework, by categorizing the idiographic strivings in terms of the broader underlying motives they suggest. Table 6.1 includes examples of the strivings that have been

TABLE 6.1
Striving Content Categories

Motive	Example
Achievement	"Work toward higher athletic
Affiliation	capabilities"
Intimacy	"Be friendly with others so they will
Power	like me"
Personal Growth and	"Help my friends and let them know I
Health	care"
Self-Presentation	"Force men to be intimate in
	relationships"
	"Maintain an optimistic outlook"
	"Always appear intelligent"

placed in the various motive categories. We conceptualize the individual strivings as existing in the service of the underlying motives. We are using these
motive systems to characterize types of conflict (e.g., intimacy vs. achievement)
and ambivalence (e.g., about intimacy). The data in Table 6.2 are representative
of the kind of interplay that can exist between idiographic and more abstract
concepts, with regard to sex differences on certain motives. Using the motives to
categorize strivings, we were able to determine that indeed the sexes do differ in
their concern with certain goals, and these differences are somewhat consistent
with the literature on sex differences in motivation (McAdams, in press; Stewart
& Chester, 1982).

This approach allows for a more fine-grained analysis of how the motive
dispositions are translated into everyday goal concerns in people's lives. Within
the social-life task category, the more task-oriented form of interpersonal relation
and the more communal form of relating are unfortunately lumped together. The
method of categorizing strivings into motive concerns enables us to distinguish
between affiliation and intimacy motivation, and the differential impact that
these have on the person's goal strivings, in a manner that is not achieved by

TABLE 6.2
Sex Differences in Striving Content

	Males	Females		
	$(N = 28)$	$(N = 60)$	t	p
Achievement	3.07	2.55	1.24	n.s.
Affiliation/Intimacy	4.04	5.09	1.78	.10
Power	2.61	1.26	2.37	.001
Personal Growth	2.96	3.59	1.60	n.s.
Self-Presentation	2.10	1.31	2.04	.02

examining the amorphous category of "social-life tasks." Whereas it is reasonable to study motivation either at the level of the motive disposition or at the idiographic personal-striving level, having information on *both* levels allows for movement between these levels of analysis. Thus, we may describe the individual in his or her particularity and just as easily look at people as they fall relative to each other on various motive dimensions. Indeed, to understand the individual more fully, we must have information about both the deeper enduring forces and the ways in which these are manifested in the transient "everydayness" of life. The life-task approach seems incomplete in its emphasis solely on the latter and dismissal of the former.

The Relationships Among the Various Idiographic Units

The fourth and final point we wish to make with regard to the social-intelligence approach to personality concerns the importance of integrating life tasks and the other goal-oriented constructs that have been developed recently. The proliferation of these units is a sign of the creative good health of the field; however, the fact that there are so many potentially overlapping concepts for the organization of everyday action begs for the imaginative minds who developed them to give some thought to their ultimate integration. We find it regrettable that Cantor and Kihlstrom make no effort to integrate the life-task construct with the other constructs in their conceptualization of personality as social intelligence.

Researchers and theorists who share an interest in the concerns of daily human life have presented life tasks, personal strivings, current concerns, personal projects, and personal goals as constructs that are useful in this endeavor. Are these constructs really different and do we have room for all of them in our field of study? There are some similarities between these constructs to be sure. All are means of organizing the natural stream of behavior. All seek to make significant contributions to psychology through the study of mundane human activity. Note, however, that there are some definite differences between these goal constructs. For instance, life tasks are more normative than personal strivings, and strivings are more enduring than current concerns. Tasks represent problems to be solved, whereas the other concepts need not. One way to integrate life tasks, personal strivings, current concerns, personal projects, and personal goals may be through a hierarchy of abstraction (Emmons, 1987; Vallacher & Wegner, 1985). Such an arrangement is possible, but, as might be expected from the preceding discussion, such a hierarchy would lack foundation without an explicit tie into the concepts of motives or other higher-level motivational unit.

Another important concern is whether or not these constructs can be used together. Previously, we have suggested a way in which personal strivings and life tasks might be used together to examine integration and complexity. The use of two or more of these concepts within single studies is certainly something to be encouraged. Comparisons of the kinds of phenomena they each predict (or fail to predict) would begin to clarify the roles that each of these constructs can play in the study of personality.

CONCLUSIONS

Before concluding this reply to Cantor and Kihlstrom, we have some last points that deserve mention. Cantor and Kihlstrom have presented an engaging case for taking the preferred strategies of life-task resolution as the basic subject matter for personality. Traditionally, such a social-cognitive point of view has been seen as incommensurate with traditional trait and motivational perspectives, and, in fact, was developed as a reaction against traditional dispositional models. Our view is that instead of forcing an incommensurability, the two perspectives could profit by paying greater attention to one another. The commonalities are greater than proponents from either side may wish to acknowledge. For instance, the description of individuals who "frequently consider the possibility of social failure, evaluate specific social life tasks as very difficult and stressful, and feel inhibited in initiating actions in social situations" (p. 38) sounds remarkably similar to what personality psychologists have been calling "social anxiety" all along (Briggs, 1985). In addition, it has been found that defensive pessimism is moderately correlated across social and academic tasks, indicating perhaps a generalized tendency.

At the same time, trait adherents would do well to address how the dispositions of the person are reflected in their everyday actions (Buss & Craik, 1983), for failure to do so risks burying the person in trait labels. Those who advocate the usefulness of traits may shy away from the human capacity to change. Cantor and Kihlstrom seem to struggle to avoid admitting that there are stable aspects of the human personality. Obviously, there are aspects that remain the same and aspects that change, and to ignore one or the other contributes only to our continued confusion.

The life-task approach could profit by taking a more historical or developmental perspective, by dealing with distal in addition to proximate influences on social behavior (Kenrick, Montello, & McFarlane, 1985). Anchoring life tasks within an evolutionary framework would be a step in this direction. Buss (1986), a staunch trait proponent, argues that individual differences manifest themselves in the strategies that people adopt to deal with universal and species-typical tasks. He speculates that these strategies may also be life-stage specific, a perspective that is highly congruous with the social-intelligence approach.

A last minor point that deserves reflection concerns the extent to which social-life tasks can really be considered "tasks." Tasks are normally thought of as difficult or arduous work, to be endured rather than enjoyed. The use of the term task itself connotes something very different from our usual conceptualization of interpersonal relationships. In adopting the perspective that social activities are tasks, Cantor and Kihlstrom impose a competitive, achievement orientation to a realm that is, presumably, neither competitive nor achievement related. How likely is it that individuals engaged in social activities view these activities through achievement-colored glasses? This is not to say that there are not occasions when concerns over intimacy could be construed as problems to be solved. Certainly at times our relationships can become problematic. Nevertheless, for most of the people most of the time, portraying interpersonal relationships as work to be done misrepresents the psychological meaning of close human encounters. Subjects in the life-task study found their social-life tasks to be less threatening and less difficult than their academic tasks, suggesting that these "tasks" are viewed much differently from academic tasks.

Cantor and Kihlstrom conclude by stating that "the field knows too little about what personality does" (p. 47) (dynamics) implying that we have been too concerned with finding out what personality is (structure). As personality psychologists, however, we are all concerned with both the *structures* and *processes* that underlie affective, cognitive, and behavioral coherences. The time has come to stop "adding apples and oranges" (Hogan, 1982) and expand the linkages between what people do, what they are like, and how they got that way.

REFERENCES

Briggs, S. (1985). A trait account of social shyness. In P. Shaver (Ed.), *Review of personality and social psychology* (Vol. 6, pp. 35–64). Beverly Hills, CA: Sage.

Buss, D. M. (1986). Can social science be anchored in evolutionary biology? Four problems and a strategic solution. *Revue Europeene Des Sciences Sociales, 24*, 41–50.

Buss, D. M., & Craik, K. H. (1983). The act frequency approach to personality. *Psychological Review, 90*, 105–126.

Emmons, R. A. (1986). Personal strivings: An approach to personality and subjective well-being. *Journal of Personality and Social Psychology, 51*, 1058–1068.

Emmons, R. A. (1987, August). *The current status of the motive concept.* Paper presented as part of a symposium entitled "Fifty Years of Personality Psychology" (K. Craik & R. Hogan, Chairs.) at the 95th Annual Convention of the American Psychological Association,New York.

Emmons, R. A. (in press). The personal striving approach to personality. In L. Pervin (Ed.), *Goal concepts in personality and social psychology.* Hillsdale, NJ: Lawrence Erlbaum Associates.

Emmons, R. A., & King, L. A. (1988). Personal striving conflict: Immediate and long-term implications for psychological and physical well-being. *Journal of Personality and Social Psychology, 54*, 1040–1048.

Emmons, R. A., & King, L. A. (1989). Personal striving complexity and affective reactivity. *Journal of Personality and Social Psychology.*

Hogan, R. (1982). On adding apples and oranges in personality psychology. *Contemporary Psychology, 27*, 851–852.

Kenrick, D. T., Montello, D. R., & MacFarlane, S. (1985). Personality: Social learning, social cognition, or sociobiology? In R. Hogan & W. Jones (Eds.), *Perspectives in personality* (Vol. 1, pp. 201–234). Greenwich, CT: JAI Press.

Klinger, E. (1987). The Interview Questionnaire: Reliability and validity of a mixed idiographic–

nomothetic measure of motivation. In J. N. Butcher & C. D. Spielberger (Eds.), *Advances in personality assessment* (Vol. 6, pp. 31–48). Hillsdale, NJ: Lawrence Erlbaum Associates.

Linville, P. W. (1985). Self-complexity and affective extremity: Don't put all of your eggs in one cognitive basket. *Social Cognition, 3,* 94–121.

McAdams, D. P. (1985). *Power, intimacy, and the life story.* Homewood, IL: The Dorsey Press.

McAdams, D. P. (1988). Biography, narratives, and lives: An introduction to this special issue. *Journal of Personality.*

McAdams, D. P. (in press). Personal needs and personal relationships. In S. Duck (Ed.), *Handbook of research on personal relationships.* New York: Wiley.

McClelland, D. C. (1985). *Human motivation.* Glenview, IL: Scott, Foresman.

Mischel, W. (1973). Toward a cognitive social learning reconceptualization of personality. *Psychological Review, 80,* 252–283.

Mischel, W. (1981). A cognitive-social learning approach to assessment. In T. V. Merluzzi, C. R. Glass, & M. Genest (Eds.), *Cognitive assessment* (pp. 479–502). New York: Guilford Press.

Stewart, A. J., & Chester, N. L. (1982). Sex differences in human social motives: Achievement, affiliation, and power. In A. J. Stewart (Ed.), *Motivation and society.* San Francisco: Jossey-Bass.

Vallacher, R. R., & Wegner, D. M. (1985). *A theory of action identification.* Hillsdale, NJ: Lawrence Erlbaum Associates.

Wadsworth, M., & Ford, D. H. (1983). Assessment of personal goal hierarchies. *Journal of Counseling Psychology, 30,* 514–526.

7

Goal Orientation as Psychological Linchpin: A Commentary on Cantor and Kihlstrom's "Social Intelligence and Cognitive Assessments of Personality"

Eric Klinger
University of Minnesota

Cantor and Kihlstrom have managed a significant conceptual achievement that is likely to influence the agenda for research on social intelligence and personality for some time to come. There are a number of facets to this achievement. Their richly elaborated treatise, in fact, has a somewhat breathless quality about it, resulting in part from the large number of conceptual domains and behavioral phenomena whose linkages need to be mentioned intelligibly in a limited space. This chapter focuses on one critically important subset of these: The interweaving of cognitive and motivational factors that enter into the production of personologically and socially meaningful behavior.

The attempt to link cognition and motivation is not, of course, new. Before the authors mentioned by Cantor and Kihlstrom there was Kurt Lewin (e.g., 1928) and before Lewin there was Narziss Ach (1910), to name only two of the pioneers who, besides Sigmund Freud, tried to systematize the relationships. One thing that the treatise by Cantor and Kihlstrom makes clear is the greater degree of differentiation in constructs and the increasing sharpness of empirical dissection in this area in recent years.

This is perhaps nowhere plainer than in the array of constructs available for discussing motivational and volitional factors. Although these may at first glance seem to be cavalier renamings of similar concepts, they actually fill quite separate conceptual niches. From the 1930s to the 1960s, psychologists who wrote about motivation cast their discourse largely in terms of drives and needs, although incentives, goals, covert anticipatory goal responses, wishes, and intentions also played a role. To these have now been added current concerns, personal projects, personal strivings, and current life tasks.

It may be helpful to highlight the differences among these. A current concern (e.g., Klinger, 1975, 1977, 1987) is an underlying state that persists from the beginning to the end of a pursuit after a goal. It is specific to the particular goal in potentiating responses to the cues associated with the pursuit of the goal. A personal project (Palys & Little, 1983) is defined not as an underlying state but as a set of related acts over time—presumably the observable behavior that corresponds to a concern. Cantor and Kihlstrom's concept of life task focuses on the goal (problem) on which the individual is working. The concept refers to goals that are nontrivial and rooted in both developmental stages and sociocultural contexts. In this it is akin to Havighurst's (1953) concept of developmental tasks but is culturally less nearly universal. A personal striving (Emmons, 1986, 1989) refers to a class of goals that is characteristic for a particular person.

All these concepts, in contrast to constructs such as drive and need, are defined idiographically. Each does a special job. Concerns do not refer directly to overt behavior or even conscious thought but do denote a continuing dispositional state. Personal projects are defined in terms of related acts but do not label the state underlying them. Both are defined in terms of particular goals. Life tasks constitute a subset of those goals. None of these concepts describes broad characteristics of a personality; that job is performed by the concept of personal striving.

From this analysis, it is apparent that motivational influences on cognition may be *consistent with* personal projects and strivings but would be *mediated by* current concerns (or, conceivably, by drives or needs, but for evidence on their limitations see Klinger, 1971).

How does motivation in these kinds of terms influence cognition? Cantor and Kihlstrom suggest that individual goals or life tasks influence choices of cognitive strategies and outcomes. Indeed, the work of Cantor and Norem and their associates on cognitive strategies such as illusory-glow optimism and defensive pessimism (Cantor, Norem, Niedenthal, Langston, & Brower, 1987; Norem & Cantor, 1986) represents a major gain growing out of this approach. Their work is supported by growing evidence from a number of other vantage points (e.g., Harkness, DeBono, & Borgida, 1985; Heckhausen & Gollwitzer, in press; Kunda, 1987; Srull & Wyer, 1986). The formulation by Cantor and Kihlstrom suggests further that a part of the motivating force arises out of the emotions or anticipated emotions associated with various goals, such as the anxiety engendered by failure.

Thus, anticipated emotion seems to play a guiding role in the selection of cognitions. This is an important point, and it raises the question of just what might be the nature of the linkage among motivational factors such as life tasks, emotion, and cognition. The nature of these linkages is not fully developed in

Cantor and Kihlstrom's treatise. However, a growing data base is gradually making possible a closer specification of these linkages, and it suggests a degree of integration even closer than Cantor and Kihlstrom's treatise already implies. There is reason to believe that emotion mediates at least a part of the relationship between motivation and cognition, and, furthermore, that emotional processes are integrated into the very microstructure of cognition.

Cues related to an individual's current concerns attract the person's attention, are more likely than other cues to be recalled, and find their way into the person's thoughts (Klinger, 1978; Klinger, Barta, & Maxeiner, 1980). That this process is automatic rather than voluntary is indicated by the fact that such cues also exert an above-average influence on the content of dreams during sleep (Hoelscher, Klinger, & Barta, 1981); that is, when concern-related words are presented to a sleeping individual, they are much more likely to be incorporated into the dream, perhaps even diverting the direction of the dream, than is true of words less closely associated with current concerns.

This automatic quality with which concern-related cues affect cognition has been shown in other contexts with waking subjects as well. Young (1988a, 1988b) asked subjects to engage in a lexical decision task, pressing buttons as quickly as possible according to whether a letter string in the center of a monitor screen constituted a word or not. They were asked to ignore apparently irrelevant, computer-program-related words to the left of the target stimulus. When Young embedded an occasional concern-related word amidst the others to the left, reaction time to target words was increased. Reaction time was longer for important concerns than for less important concerns.

Aside from studies based on the concept of concern, however, a number of other investigations have shown that presenting certain other kinds of information, even apparently outside of consciousness, can influence various phases of concurrent, presumably involuntary cognitive processing. This information may be construed as self-referent (e.g., Bargh, 1982) or as emotionally tinged (e.g., Nielsen & Sarason, 1981). Are these all different paths into cognitive processing, or are they all related in some way?

The common denominator appears to be affect; that is, concern-related, self-referent, and, obviously, emotionally tinged words are all rated as emotionally more evocative than other words. There is good reason to believe that the self-reference effect is due to emotional arousal (Bock, 1988; Bock & Klinger, 1986). Furthermore, although both the current-concern relatedness and the emotional-arousal potential of a word predict recall, these effects are not independent of each other. When the two kinds of effect are examined head to head, it turns out that, at least for words that are processed semantically, words that are concern related but emotionally not very arousing are recalled no better than words that are neither; whereas words that are emotionally arousing but not closely associated with a current concern are recalled as well as words that are both (Bock & Klinger, 1986; Klinger, Bock, & Bowi, 1988; Klinger, in press).

Thus, insofar as concern relatedness and emotional evocativeness can be separated, it is emotional evocativeness of cues that appears to play the pivotal role in influencing recall.

These various findings are based on investigations in which the emotional-arousal potential of words was estimated through subjective ratings. What can we say about their construct validity? Findings by Schneider (1987, and private communication) not only extend the preceding relationships but also tie the results to a somewhat broader nomological net. Using a choice-reaction-time task, he placed target stimuli above or below the site of a fixation point on a monitor screen. The site of the fixation point was either empty or occupied by a distractor stimulus (a word, nonword letter string, or number). The presence of distractor stimuli slowed reaction time, especially when the distractor was an emotionally arousing word. This finding provides additional support to the findings already described; but beyond this there was an additional key finding: The slowing of reaction time was particularly pronounced in those subjects who scored high in affective intensity as measured by the Affect Intensity Measure (Larsen & Diener, 1987). This result provides consistency across conceptual and methodological domains, extending from self-rated emotional evocativeness of stimulus words to a psychometric trait measure of emotional responsiveness. It therefore shores up the validity of the inferences that may be drawn from the various investigations.

These results, taken together, point in a particular direction. Current concerns—and hence also life tasks—influence cognitive processing because the concern state predisposes the individual to react with emotional arousal to many cues associated with the corresponding goal pursuit. The emotional arousal, in turn, provides a kind of priority tag for cognitive processing. It is therefore the emotional response to a cue that provides the direct influence on cognition.

One corollary of this position is that, although most emotionally arousing cues are also concern related, those that are not but nevertheless retain their emotional charge, for instance through a residual conditioned effect, will grab attention as effectively as if they were concern related. This principle would explain some of the phenomena associated with post-traumatic stress syndrome: Cues strongly associated with powerful emotions as a result of trauma re-evoke those emotions and associated memorial images long after the concern with the trauma has ceased to be current. Those cues may reside in the person's own thought stream as well as in the external environment and hence may disrupt ongoing processing with distressing images or, during sleep, produce anxiety dreams.

The effects of emotions on cognition described thus far are by no means the only kinds that have been reported. For example, existing moods appear to affect long-term recall of life experiences (Lewinsohn & Rosenbaum, 1987; Snyder & White, 1982) and shorter term word recall (Ingram, Kendall, Smith, Donnel, & Ronan, 1987) as well as predictions of how subjects would experience future emotionally arousing situations (Branscombe & Diener, 1987). Whether these kinds of effects employ some of the same mechanisms as those described previously it is still too early to say. What has become obvious is that emotion, or at least something closely related to emotion, is intimately tied to cognition. The evidence that links emotion to cognition indicates that the effects occur at a number of phases of cognitive processing. The concern-related words that distracted Young's subjects, for instance, very probably operated at a preattentive phase of processing. The better recall of emotionally arousing words as compared with less arousing words by Bock and Klinger's subjects required either an encoding or a retrieval role for emotion. The effects of mood on recall clearly indicate a retrieval role. The effects on judgments, predictions, and thought content require either additional roles for emotion in cognition or a carrying forward of the effects exerted at prior processing steps. It appears, then, that emotional arousal infiltrates the microstructure of cognition to direct its processing.

This notion raises many intriguing questions. How do emotions come to play such a role? One normally thinks of emotional reactions as rather slow-decay phenomena that last at least minutes and often much longer. How can they possibly play the pinpoint kinds of roles required to steer cognitive processing toward emotionally arousing cues? At this microstructural level of effect, "emotional arousal" can in general obviously not mean long-duration or marked swings in emotion. Whatever the effects that are related to emotional arousal, they must operate at low-emotional amplitude and quickly. There are reasons to doubt that the effects are purely associative. How then account for them?

We may begin by recalling that what we think of as emotions are probably facets of complex organismic states, states that may change their character with duration and amplitude. It is conceivable that there are central emotional microreactions too slight to register in peripheral physiology or even in consciousness but that nevertheless account for the effects we have observed. Furthermore, at least some emotions are routinely accompanied by at least rudimentary behavioral scripts for orientation and motor action. These accompanying reaction tendencies may exert their own directional effect on cognitive processing. If all this is so on some occasions, it raises an intriguing further question: Do these emotional microreactions perhaps play a role in all cognitive processes, so that there is always a substantial integration of emotional and cognitive-processing steps?

There are still further important questions regarding the implications of these findings. For example, if emotional reactions mediate the effects of motivation on cognition, then they are in a position to influence the priority a person places on various goals. Insofar as emotional reactions can be shifted through the many means that have been demonstrated in the literature on emotion, this position suggests a possible source of irrationality (or, less judgmentally, of inconsistency) in the effective priority that people place on their goals at a given moment in time.

Let us return now to one of Cantor and Kihlstrom's central theses, their tenet that intelligence is legitimately assessable only with reference to the individual's goals. This point takes on special force in light of the aforementioned data and considerations. Insofar as intelligence refers to something cognitive, it cannot be disentangled from emotion or motivation, because these suffuse the entire process, phase by phase. Cognitive processes not only operate in the service of goals; they are also steered and in some ways limited by the emotional reactivity instated with those goals.

To put this more concretely, let us consider the situation of a person engaged in a task in connection with which someone holds a priori standards for judging the quality of the person's performance. The existence of a quality standard is presumably necessary if we are to speak of intelligence, even though the standard may be very different from conventional ones.

In such a situation, intelligent behavior depends among other things on selecting optimal items and features for cognitive processing, on processing speed, and on selecting optimal actions in response. Anything that biases processing toward suboptimal material, that potentiates suboptimal actions, or that slows processing down erodes the quality of the person's response. But as we have seen, attentional speed and direction depend on the individual's current concerns and, probably even more directly, on the associated tendency to react to particular cues with emotional arousal. These factors also seem to codetermine memory storage and retrieval, and individual concerns have been shown repeatedly to be associated with the cues individuals select to think or dream about. Insofar as the actor's concerns and emotional reactivity are not fully consonant with the objectives assumed by the person who applies the standards, the actor is likely to be distracted from the most productive cues, to misjudge contextual cues, to have more difficulty retrieving the most useful stored information, and to launch more often into suboptimal lines of thought. Thus, the apparent quality of performance suffers and the actor will be judged to have performed less intelligently. This is just as Cantor and Kihlstrom, without spelling out the intervening links, have argued happens when judgments of intelligence fail to take into account the actor's major life goals.

REFERENCES

Ach, N. (1910). *Über den Willensakt und das Temperament.* Leipzig: Van Quelle & Meyer.
Bargh, J. A. (1982). Attention and automaticity in the processing of self-relevant information. *Journal of Personality and Social Psychology, 43,* 425–436.
Bock, M. (1988). Self and memory. In K. Fiedler & J. Forgas (Eds.), *Affect, cognition, and social behavior.* Toronto: Hogrefe.
Bock, M., & Klinger, E. (1986). Interaction of emotion and cognition in word recall. *Psychological Research, 48,* 99–106.
Branscombe, N. R., & Diener, E. (1987). *Consequences of priming emotions: Contrast and assimilation effects.* Paper presented at the annual meeting of the American Psychological Association, New York.

Cantor, N., Norem, J. K., Niedenthal, P. M., Langston, C. A., & Brower, A. M. (1987). Life tasks, self-concept ideals, and cognitive strategies in a life transition. *Journal of Personality and Social Psychology, 53*, 1178–1191.

Emmons, R. A. (1986). Personal strivings: An approach to personality and subjective well-being. *Journal of Personality and Social Psychology, 51*, 1058–1068.

Emmons, R. A. (1989). The personal striving approach to personality. In L. A. Pervin (Ed.), *Goal concepts in personality and social cognition*. Hillsdale, NJ: Lawrence Erlbaum Associates.

Harkness, A. R., DeBono, K. G., & Borgida, E. (1985) Personal involvement and strategies for making contingency judgments: A stake in the dating game makes a difference. *Journal of Personality and Social Psychology, 49*, 22–32.

Havighurst, R. J. (1953). *Human development and education*. New York: Longmans, Green.

Heckhausen, H., & Gollwitzer, P. (in press). Thought contents and cognitive functioning in motivational versus volitional states of mind. *Motivation and Emotion*.

Hoelscher, T. J., Klinger, E., & Barta, S. G. (1981). Incorporation of concern- and nonconcern-related stimuli into dream content. *Journal of Abnormal Psychology, 90*, 88–91.

Ingram, R. E., Kendall, P. C., Smith, T. W., Donnell, C., & Ronan, K. (1987). Cognitive specificity in emotional distress. *Journal of Personality and Social Psychology, 53*, 734–742.

Klinger, E. (1971). *Structure and functions of fantasy*. New York: Wiley.

Klinger, E. (1975). Consequences of commitment to and disengagement from incentives. *Psychological Review, 82*, 1–25.

Klinger, E. (1977). *Meaning and void: Inner experience and the incentives in people's lives*. Minneapolis: University of Minnesota Press.

Klinger, E. (1978). Modes of normal conscious flow. In K. S. Pope & J. L. Singer (Eds.), *The stream of consciousness: Scientific investigations into the flow of human experience* (pp. 225–258). New York: Plenum.

Klinger, E. (1987). Current concerns and disengagement from incentives. In F. Halisch & J. Kuhl (Eds.), *Motivation, intention and volition* (pp. 337–347). Berlin: Springer.

Klinger, E. (in press). Emotional mediation of motivational influences on cognitive processes. In F. Halisch & J. van den Bercken (Eds.), *International perspectives on achievement and task motivation*. Nisse, Netherlands: Swets & Zeitlinger.

Klinger, E., Barta, S. G., & Maxeiner, M. E. (1980). Motivational correlates of thought content frequency and commitment. *Journal of Personality and Social Psychology, 39*, 1222–1237.

Klinger, E., Bock, M., & Bowi, U. (1988). *Emotional mediation of motivational factors in word recall*. Unpublished manuscript.

Kunda, Z. (1987). Motivated inference: Self-serving generation and evaluation of causal theories. *Journal of Personality and Social Psychology, 53*, 636–647.

Larsen, R., & Diener, E. (1987). Affect intensity as an individual difference characteristic. *Journal of Research in Personality, 21*, 1–39.

Lewin, K. (1928). Wille, Vorsatz und Bedürfnis. *Psychologische Forschung, 7*, 330–385.

Lewinsohn, P. M., & Rosenbaum, M. (1987). Recall of parental behavior by acute depressives, remitted depressives, and nondepressives. *Journal of Personality and Social Psychology, 52*, 611–619.

Nielsen, S. L., & Sarason, I. G. (1981). Emotion, personality, and selective attention. *Journal of Personality and Social Psychology, 41*, 945–960.

Norem, J. K., & Cantor, N. (1986). Defensive pessimism: "Harnessing" anxiety as motivation. *Journal of Personality and Social Psychology, 51*, 1208–1217.

Palys, T. S., & Little, B. R. (1983). Perceived life satisfaction and the organization of personal project systems. *Journal of Personality and Social Psychology, 44*, 1221–1230.

Schneider, W. (1987). *Ablenkung und Handlungskontrolle: Eine 'kognitiv-motivationale Perspektive'* (Distraction and action control: a "cognitive-motivational perspective"). Diploma thesis, University of Bielefeld, West Germany.

Snyder, M., & White, P. (1982). Moods and memories: Elation, depression, and the remembering of the events of one's life. *Journal of Personality, 50,* 149–167.

Srull, T. K., & Wyer, R. S., Jr. (1986). The role of chronic and temporary goals in social information processing. In R. M. Sorrentino & E. T. Higgins (Eds.), *Handbook of motivation and cognition* (pp. 503–549). New York: Guilford.

Young, J. (1988a). *The role of selective attention in the attitude–behavior relationship.* Doctoral dissertation, University of Minnesota.

Young, J. (1988b). *Looking for consistency: Goal-directed attention in the attitude-behavior relation.* Article submitted for publication.

8 Production Systems and Social Problem Solving: Specificity, Flexibility, and Expertise

Patricia W. Linville
Yale University

Leslie F. Clark
Memphis State University

In their provocative chapter on social intelligence, Cantor and Kihlstrom (this volume) argue that social problem-solving strategies tend to be fine tuned to meet goals in specific life tasks. They argue that social intelligence is characterized by flexibility, expertise, and sensitivity to the specific context. This perspective leads them to focus on the specialized strategies that people bring to bear on different life tasks. The following quotations illustrate their approach:

> Social intelligence is multi-faceted, domain- and task-specific, and reformulated in each significant life task. (p. 1)

> Understanding social intelligence, then, requires some characterization of the expertise that people bring to bear in solving life problems, the contexts that render certain problems more important that others, and the pragmatic considerations that define the goals to be achieved in an intelligent solution. (p. 10)

> The intelligent person is one who can employ social knowledge flexibly and adaptively to meet personal goals and create good feeling. (p. 13)

> . . . adaptive behavior has all the qualities of intelligent action. It is purposive, flexibly attuned to the individual's goals, not rigidly stereotyped or indiscriminate. (p. 8)

> Rigid and overgeneralized reliance on a single strategy as a solution to diverse life-task problems constitutes a failure of intelligent action, in our opinion. (p. 36)

Cantor and Kihlstrom's approach is novel in the personality literature because of its emphasis on domain- and task-specific personal strategies. We believe that their emphasis on specificity makes good sense from a cognitive perspective.

In this chapter, we focus on Cantor and Kihlstrom's assertions that social intelligence is characterized by specificity, flexibility, and expertise. Specifically, we address the question: What kind of cognitive system would favor personal problem-solving or coping procedures that are domain specific, flexible in application, and based on individual expertise? We suggest that it is useful to view personal problem-solving rules using the *production system* representation that is widely used to model problem-solving processes in artificial intelligence (AI) and cognitive psychology. We begin by describing the learning mechanisms in a production system. Then we consider whether these learning mechanisms create procedures that are domain specific, flexible in their application, and based on expertise. Our discussion relies in part on the cognitive literature on problem solving, skill acquisition, and expertise. Our focus is on social problem-solving and coping procedures within this production system framework.

Our analysis suggests first that production system learning mechanisms do lead to task-specific coping skills. Second, our analysis indicates that although these coping skills will be flexible in some respects, they will not be flexible in others. Specifically, production-system learning mechanisms lead to rules that are inflexible in their application. Thus, greater coping expertise is likely to result in less flexible application of coping rules according to production system models. Third, our analysis leads us to question whether expertise has the same benefits in social problem solving and coping contexts as it does in more traditional problem-solving domains. The learning conditions that lead to expertise effects in traditional problem-solving domains often are not present in social problem-solving and coping contexts. Finally, throughout our discussion of these issues, we hope to illustrate how a production system architecture can add to our understanding of social problem solving, stress processes, and coping behavior.

PRODUCTION SYSTEMS

Personal problem-solving procedures and coping skills fit naturally into a production framework. Production systems are used widely in AI and cognitive psychology. Examples include the problem-solving work of Newell and Simon (1972; Newell, 1988), most expert systems, psychological models of human memory (e.g., Anderson, 1983, 1987), and induction systems (Holland, Holyoke, Nisbett, & Thagard, 1986). In these rule-based systems, cognitive processing occurs as the result of the firing of productions. A production is a condition–action (if–then) pair that specifies that if a certain state or situation is represented in working memory, then a particular mental or physical action should occur. Productions constitute procedural knowledge, or how to do things. Whereas this often suggests motor skills such as dialing a number or driving a car, research has focused on cognitive skills such as problem solving, language, computer programming, induction, and inference. Consider a few simple production rules related to these cognitive skills:

- If the goal is to generate the plural of a noun, Then say "noun" + "s."
- If the goal is to prove that two triangles are congruent, Then try the side–angle–side method.
- If the goal is to find the log of variable Y, Then write Y = ALOG10(X).
- If the object barks, Then infer that it is dog.
- If the person is wearing work clothes and a hard hat, Then infer that the person is a construction worker.

Consider a few simple production rules that relate to social problem solving.

- If the goal is to make up with someone, Then say "I'm sorry."
- If I fail a test and did not study, Then infer that the cause was lack of effort.
- If the goal is to avoid feeling embarrassed socially, Then attend to the behavior of others and only behave as they behave.
- If my husband criticizes me, Then infer that I am worthless.
- If I get negative feedback at work, Then seek out a supportive friend.

ACT* Theory

We focus on Anderson's ACT* theory because it is a unified cognitive theory that has combined precision with scope of application (covering findings in skill acquisition, language, priming, fact retrieval). Recently the ACT* framework has been applied to social inference (Smith, 1984) and personality and psychotherapy (Nasby & Kihlstrom, 1985).

The basic architecture of ACT* (Anderson, 1983, 1987) includes a long-term *declarative memory* to represent facts, and a long-term *procedural memory* encoded in productions. Declarative knowledge takes the form of a network with basic cognitive units as nodes linked together by associations. The ACT* architecture is activation-based; nodes in declarative LTM each have a degree of activation or strength, and activation spreads automatically from currently active knowledge to associated knowledge in LTM. *Working memory* is that part of LTM that is highly activated.

The *production system* is a set of rules that guide cognitive behavior. A cognitive task may be thought of as a sequence of cognitive actions evoked by patterns of knowledge. Productions reflect this by representing each step of cognition as a condition–action pair. Thus the sequence of productions that apply in problem solving reflect the cognitive steps taken in solving the problem. Each production has the form of a rule with a *condition* (or "if" statement) that specifies when the rule applies and an *action* (or "then" statement) that specifies what should be done when the rule applies. In ACT*, the condition specifies a pattern of knowledge that must match the contents of working memory for the production to apply; and when the production applies, the action specifies information to be deposited into working memory (e.g., adding new structure such as an inference to memory, activating existing structure, setting subgoals, or causing external behavior). Working memory acts as the communicative link between declarative and procedural knowledge in the following manner: Declarative facts enter working memory from the external environment or by spreading activation through LTM; and productions match only to the facts in working memory.

There is a hierarchical *goal structure* in memory, with only a single goal active in working memory at a time. A production can specify a goal as part of its condition, requiring that the goal be active for the production to apply. In this way, a production fires to achieve a current goal. Each production also has a *strength*, reflecting the frequency with which it has been successfully applied in the past. When several productions have their conditions matched at the same time to data in working memory, only one production can apply during any cycle. ACT* has several *conflict resolution principles* used in deciding which production to apply. Preference is given to a production that (1) best matches the current situation (i.e., whose condition most completely matches the current contents of working memory), (2) has a history of being successful (i.e., greater strength), (3) specifies the most complete description of the current problem (i.e., has a more specific condition pattern), and (4) has greater relevance to the current goal.

In summary, the *application of a production* involves a matching and an execution process. The general activity of a production system involves a cycle of matching knowledge in working memory against productions to determine which productions have their conditions satisfied, selecting a production to apply, then executing a production by depositing the actions of the production into working memory. The new contents of working memory then match to productions, beginning a new cycle.

Example: Application of a Coping Production.   Before discussing how people learn new productions, consider a simple example of the application of a production rule for a coping problem. We assume that well-practiced coping behavior involves selecting productions whose conditions match information currently active in working memory, then executing the actions of those selected productions. Features of a current problem, as well as the current goal, are represented in working memory. If the conditions of a production embodying the coping rule match the contents of working memory, the production fires, adding information to working memory (e.g., an attribution, appraisal of potential harm, expectation, emotional inference, self-evaluation, or specific coping behavior).

For example, a student might have the following production (in nontechnical notation and compact form):

IF   the goal is to set an expectation about a future outcome
and the outcome is self-relevant
and the outcome involves an academic event
and the outcome is important
THEN set a high expectation

Suppose that a student with this production has an important midterm in one week. If this knowledge plus the goal of setting an expectation regarding the exam are currently active in working memory, then the conditions of the production will be satisfied and the production will apply,[1] adding the expectation to working memory.[2] Thus the student will set a high expectation regarding the outcome of his or her midterm. The ACT* theory does not argue that people have productions in this form in their heads, only that people's thought processes follow such rules.

Example: Productions of a Defensive Pessimist.   To give a slightly more complex example, consider a set of productions representing the strategy of defensive pessimism in the achievement realm. As described in Cantor and Kihlstrom (this volume), defensive pessimists set unrealistically low expectations for a future outcome, despite a history of success. Rather than being debilitating, their negative expectations actually help them to use their anxiety to motivate themselves through effort and planning toward successful performance. It is noteworthy that the strategy appears to be domain specific, that is, those defensively pessimistic about achievement outcomes will not necessarily be pessimistic about social outcomes. The following productions suggest one possible set of cognitive steps representing this strategy.[3]

IF   the goal is to avoid failure
and the event is academic
and the outcome is important

---

[1]This particular production may not apply if the conditions of other productions better match the current contents of working memory.

[2]Most tasks, even simple ones, actually involve a set of many productions. Productions in the current chapter are thus compact versions. For example, rather than simply depositing a high expectation into working memory, the production would deposit into working memory the subgoals relevant to setting the expectation, which would then match and execute these other appropriate productions.

[3]The defensive pessimism strategy involves a complex relationship between expectations, anxiety, and performance and thus may actually take various specific forms (see Cantor, Norem, Niedenthal, Langston, & Brower, 1987; Showers & Cantor, 1985). Thus the specific set of productions suggested here is one of many possible representations and is provided as one illustration.

THEN set as subgoals:
1) to generate ways in which a bad outcome could occur
2) to set an expectation

This production will then evoke a set of productions to guide the process of generating potential paths to bad outcomes (the mental simulation process).[4] Together, the goal of setting an expectation coupled with knowledge of ways in which things can go wrong will then evoke:

IF   the goal is to set an expectation
      and there are multiple ways in which a bad outcome could occur
THEN set a low expectation
      and set a subgoal to find a strategy to improve performance

IF   the goal is to find a strategy for improving performance
      and the expectation for outcome is low
THEN set as subgoals
      1) to increase effort on the task
      2) to devise strategies for preventing each potential source of a bad
         outcome

Continuing in this fashion, additional productions would be evoked to generate strategies for preventing each of these anticipated paths to failure, and other productions to increase effort.

PROCEDURAL LEARNING MECHANISMS IN ACT*: DOMAIN-GENERAL TO DOMAIN-SPECIFIC RULES

In this section, we review the learning mechanisms in ACT*. Our goal is to see whether these learning mechanisms will tend to lead to the formation of domain-specific rules. If cognitive problem-solving skill is best characterized in terms of rules that are geared to particular problem tasks, then this would lend support to the idea that social problem-solving rules also develop into task-specific rules. This would be consistent with Cantor and Kihlstrom's major point that social intelligence involves strategies that are geared to meet the goals of specific life tasks.

It is important to note that the phrase "domain specific" has a different connotation in the problem-solving literature than in social research. In social research, the term domain is often used to refer to various roles or aspects of life—e. g., social, work, family. In problem solving, a domain is a task; for

---

[4]Mental simulation of the paths to failure is a very complex process, and we do not attempt to model these processes here. It probably involves the application of general problem-solving productions to declarative knowledge about the task, though an expert might proceduralize the process.

example, solving problems in physics or mathematics. But some tasks cut across many aspects of life. For example, productions for solving arithmetic problems can be used in a variety of contexts including solving physics problems, designing a bridge, making investment decisions, balancing a checkbook, and baking a cake. So as we use the term, *domain-specific productions are task specific* but are not necessarily limited to one aspect of life. In many cases, however, specific tasks map onto specific aspects of life. In these cases, the two meanings of the term are the same.

In AI, there has been a shift from building intelligent programs that rely on general problem-solving techniques emphasizing heuristic search for *any* problem (e.g., the General Problem Solver, GPS, used in the work of Newell & Simon, 1972) to knowledge-based programs that utilize highly organized domain-specific knowledge (e.g., Larkin's, 1981, ABLE programs for physics problems). Research on the acquisition of complex cognitive skills also strongly demonstrates how domain and expertise differences are dependent on experience with specific task domains (see Anderson, 1987; and Chi, Glaser, & Farr, 1988). First, problem-solving processes change from one task domain to another (e.g., expert problem solving in physics involves reasoning forward to the solution, whereas problem solving in computer programming involves reasoning backward from the solution). Second, problem-solving processes change qualitatively as experience increases in a task domain (e.g., experts in physics use a working-forward strategy, whereas novices use a working-backward strategy).[5] Thus domain and expertise differences are based on specialized strategies and representations of knowledge about the relevant domain. As we see later, the learning mechanisms in production systems (e.g., knowledge compilation and strengthening) demonstrate how such domain and expertise differences in problem solving are based on specific task-domain experience.

Interpretive Stage

How do we develop rules to handle a specific problem? ACT* assumes that we cannot directly add a new production to memory in the way that we can simply encode a new declarative fact. Rather, all knowledge starts out in declarative form and can be built through use or practice into procedural rules (productions). Thus we learn procedural skills only by performing them.

In learning a new skill or solving a new problem, we initially encode all information in declarative form (e.g., facts about a particular task domain includ-

---

[5]The strategy of the expert is to work from the variables given in the problems, successively applying equations that they can solve from the given information. The strategy of the novice, however, is to begin with an equation incorporating the unknown of the problem; when it contains a variable that is not given, then select another equation to solve for it, and so forth (Chi, Glaser, & Rees, 1982).

ing features of the task, instructions, text materials, past attempts to solve problems, successful and unsuccessful examples). For this knowledge to be converted into behavior, general problem-solving procedures must apply to task-specific declarative knowledge, interpreting it to guide behavior toward a solution. Thus, *people initially solve problems in a new task domain by applying general problem-solving productions to specific declarative knowledge.* These general procedures have no domain-specific knowledge, but they interpret facts about a domain to generate domain-appropriate solutions. Common general problem-solving procedures include analogy, means–ends analysis, trial-and-error search, working backward, and decomposing a problem into an ordered set of subproblems.

For example, working backward involves reasoning from the final desired state or outcome backward to the current state. A general working-backward production might look like the following:

IF   the goal is to accomplish X
        and if conditions C1, C2, . . . , Cn lead to X
THEN   set as subgoals to accomplish C1, C2, . . . , Cn

By applying this general rule recursively, we can work backward to create a chain of steps from our final goal back to our current state. A backward inference rule is a useful search heuristic in problems such as geometry proofs: IF the goal is to prove two triangles congruent, THEN set as subgoals to prove two corresponding sides and their included angle congruent (Anderson, 1983). Working backward is also a useful search heuristic in a coping problem such as how to feel less lonely. For example: I could feel less lonely if I had more friends. I could develop more friendships if I tried harder to meet other people and if I made myself more appealing to other people. I could make myself more appealing to others if I smiled more and complained less. And so forth.

These domain-general methods are flexible in that they can apply to a wide range of tasks, contexts, or problems; but they are called weak because they make no reference to domain features useful in specific problems. These domain-general productions will apply as long as appropriate knowledge of the task is encoded in declarative knowledge to be used by these general methods. The form of declarative knowledge about a task domain determines which general method is used, e.g., analogy may be used in finding a solution if declarative knowledge mainly takes the form of examples.

Interpreting knowledge in declarative form has the benefit of flexibility in that knowledge can easily enter the system and can be used in multiple ways. But the interpretive process is slow and can make heavy demands on working-memory capacity. The process is slow because relevant declarative knowledge is being retrieved from LTM, and the individual steps in the productions interpreting the knowledge are small in order to maintain their general applicability. The demands on working memory are heavy because the general problem-solving productions apply only to knowledge represented in working memory.

Knowledge Compilation Stage

When task-specific declarative knowledge is repeatedly used in the same way to solve a problem or perform a task, the learning mechanisms in ACT* create new productions that directly apply the knowledge without this interpretive step. These new productions for performing a task-specific skill are more efficient, saving time and working-memory capacity. This type of learning, shifting from the interpretive application of declarative knowledge to the direct application of procedures, is called *knowledge compilation.*

The knowledge compilation process is the basic mechanism for learning new productions. In solving a problem by interpreting declarative knowledge, a hierarchical problem solution is generated by productions. The knowledge compilation process converts the trace of the problem-solving episode into new productions that incorporate the solution process. By repeatedly performing a task, the specific declarative knowledge that is interpreted by general problem-solving productions is gradually built into domain-specific productions that perform the behavior directly and automatically. In this way, *domain-general productions are converted into domain-specific ones.* And the next time one encounters a similar problem, the new productions can produce a solution more efficiently— without exploring many solution paths, and without retrieving into working memory the declarative facts used to produce the solution. For instance, it is more efficient to apply a compiled attribution rule than to extract it from an example being held in working memory. With a compiled rule, one goes directly from the problem features to the solution steps.

Knowledge compilation consists of two mechanisms that work together to create new productions—proceduralization and composition. *Proceduralization* operates by building into new productions the problem-specific declarative knowledge that was previously held in working memory for interpretation. Because these new productions contain the task-specific problem solution, this eliminates the need for retrieving and holding task-specific knowledge in working memory. *Composition* operates by collapsing the conditions and the actions of a sequence of productions used in a problem-solving episode, creating a single new production that has the same effect as the sequence. The goal structure of a problem is critical here. Only those parts of the original solution that belong together because they share a common goal can be collapsed together. Proceduralization and composition do not replace the declarative knowledge or old productions; rather, they simply add new productions.

Knowledge compilation results in a speed-up in performance, a drop-out of verbal rehearsal of relevant declarative knowledge, and an increased ability to perform a proceduralized task simultaneously with a second task that makes working-memory demands. The composition of multiple steps into a single production, as well as becoming more judicious in choosing solution paths, result in the speed-up. Proceduralization of knowledge eliminates the need to hold and rehearse information in working memory, resulting in the disappearance of both verbalizations and declarative interference effects. This shift from conscious to automatic processing of a rule is a gradual one occurring with practice. Newly compiled productions are weak and may require multiple creations to gain sufficient strength. A gradual creation of task-specific procedures is advantageous. Productions control behavior rather directly, and a gradual compilation process allows opportunity to detect unwanted consequences of productions and to correct them before a sequence of actions become automatic.

A Coping Example of Knowledge Compilation.   One interesting application of ACT* is to coping behavior. Applied to coping, ACT* implies that we initially bring weak, general problem-solving procedures to new coping situations, and we gradually compile domain-specific coping procedures. All coping-related knowledge is initially represented declaratively. In the early interpretive stage of acquiring a coping rule, general problem-solving productions provide useful search heuristics in the process of interpreting relevant domain-specific declarative knowledge. Although a variety of general problem-solving productions are potentially applicable to coping problems, we suggest that reasoning by analogy is frequently used to develop new coping procedures. With this approach, we may apply a strategy that we found successful in a similar problem, or one that we observed someone else use successfully in a similar problem.

We illustrate the knowledge compilation process with an example of a coping solution developed by analogy. Analogy is usually implemented by the operation of a sequence of general productions (see Anderson, 1983, Chapter 5, for an example), but the following is a simplified, nontechnical, compact version of the analogy process in a single production:

IF   the goal is to cope with a problem
      and there is an example of a successful coping solution to a similar
      problem
THEN   map that template to the current problem.

The current problem is encoded declaratively in working memory, and a search is generated for an appropriate example that has some of the same features as the current problem. If a relevant example is found, then these general analogy productions will extract knowledge from the example to solve the current problem. In the interpretive stage, an example of a similar coping solution is retrieved into working memory, and it is mapped onto the new problem by a sequence of general analogy productions. This process involves mapping individual elements of the example to their corresponding elements in the new problem, in order to generate a problem solution. Knowledge compilation mechanisms then convert the result of this initial analogy process into a new production rule that specifies the new coping solution without referencing the example. Compiling an analogy into new specialized productions allows more efficient problem solving for future similar problems because it eliminates the need to search for and hold the example in working memory.

Consider the following example: Suppose that you want to decrease your feelings of anxiety about the test you are about to take. Thinking about decreasing anxiety may activate in LTM the example of a time when thinking about yourself sitting by the lake at your summer cabin decreased your anxiety at the dentist. Both your current problem and the past example are now represented declaratively in working memory. The following is a *domain-general production* similar to those created in ACT*:

IF   the goal is to manage ⟨emotion1⟩ in response to ⟨stress1⟩
       and ⟨behavior⟩ manages ⟨emotion1⟩ in response to ⟨stress2⟩
THEN do ⟨behavior⟩ in response to ⟨stress1⟩

Terms in angle brackets represent variables that can be set to different values in different contexts. By mapping on corresponding elements[6], this general production can guide behavior in the current situation, retrieving into working memory the lake scene by analogy. This is the *interpretive process*. The actual firing of the general production depends on the example being held in working memory and being matched to the production. *Knowledge compilation* eliminates this requirement by then building the result of this analogy process into a new *domain-specific production:*

IF   the goal is to manage feelings of anxiety
       and the stress causing the anxiety is academic test-taking
THEN retrieve scene of the lake.

Proceduralization eliminates the need to reference the declarative source of knowledge in the future—in this case, the example that thinking about the lake scene lowered your anxiety at the dentist. It does this here by replacing the variables in the general production with the knowledge that they matched in the example (resulting in a task-specific goal and action), and by deleting the condition of the general production that references the declarative knowledge. This declarative knowledge of the link between imaging the lake scene and lowering anxiety is built into the new production and will now be applied directly. In the future, it will be more efficient to apply a compiled relaxation rule than to extract it from an example of a dental experience being held in working memory. With

---

[6]The production applies with the following variable bindings: anxiety ⟨emotion1⟩; academic test-taking ⟨stress1⟩; dental-work ⟨stress2⟩; thinking about yourself sitting by the lake at your summer cabin ⟨behavior⟩.

the compiled rule, one goes directly from the problem features (desire to lower academic anxiety) to the solution steps (image the lake scene).

The transition from the former production to the latter one illustrates the transition from domain-general to domain-specific productions. In this manner, particular coping and social problem-solving skills develop with practice into productions that apply efficiently and automatically.

Generalization and Discrimination

Generalization and discrimination processes search for problem features that are predictive of the success of a particular method of problem solving.[7] *Generalization* makes productions apply in a broader range of circumstances by using pairs of more specific productions to create more general ones. Suppose a person has the following two productions:

IF   the goal is to infer John's emotion
and John experiences a negative outcome
and the outcome occurred at the office
THEN infer that John is angry

IF   the goal is to infer Mary's emotion
and Mary experiences a negative outcome
and the outcome occurred at a social gathering
THEN infer that Mary is angry

The generalization mechanism would attempt to create a broader rule that applies to both circumstances as well as related ones:

IF   the goal is to infer ⟨Person X's⟩ emotion
and ⟨Person X⟩ experiences a negative outcome
THEN infer that ⟨Person X⟩ is angry

The process of *discrimination* handles overgeneral productions that need restricting. For example, this last production might apply whether the negative event was the fault of the actor or another, causing errors of inference in some cases. By looking for a feature that was present in a successful instance and not

---

[7]In his recent work, Anderson (1987) has changed his view of these mechanisms. Rather than being separate, independent tuning mechanisms that apply to compiled productions, the learning effects of generalization and discrimination are now thought to be the consequence of knowledge-compilation processes, relying on analogy processes. This means that these inductive processes may be in conscious awareness and subject to strategic influence rather than being automatic.

present in an unsuccessful instance, the discrimination mechanism can create more specific productions that avoid errors. For example:

IF   the goal is to infer ⟨Person X's⟩ emotion
and ⟨Person X⟩ experiences a negative outcome
and the outcome was caused by ⟨Person Y⟩
THEN infer that ⟨Person X⟩ feels angry

IF   the goal is to infer ⟨Person X's⟩ emotion
and ⟨Person X⟩ experiences a negative outcome
and the outcome was caused by ⟨Person X⟩
THEN infer that ⟨Person X⟩ feels regret

Thus rules may be generalized by deleting restrictive clauses or by replacing variables with constants. Likewise, a rule may be discriminated by adding clauses or replacing a variable with a specific constant.

Because the revision or addition of new productions does not eliminate older productions, multiple productions relevant to the same topic often exist at varying levels of specificity. Recall in our earlier discussion of conflict resolution principles that preference is given to productions that provide a more complete description of the current situation. That is, when two productions match the same data, preference is given to the production with the more specific condition. For example:

IF   I feel angry
THEN let my feelings out by yelling

IF   I feel angry
and I am at work
THEN count to 10, take a deep breath, and suppress my anger

The first production gives the general rule for dealing with anger, whereas the second is more specific, giving the exception for the domain of work. The second, more specific rule may have developed after experiencing disastrous consequences when applying the more general one at work. The specificity principle allows the domain-exception rule to take preference over the general rule. Specificity in rule selection is relevant to our current question of whether social problem-solving and coping rules tend to be domain specific.

Strengthening

A separate, automatic learning mechanism that enables learning to continue beyond the point at which a skill is compiled into domain-specific productions is *strengthening*. Each production has a strength associated with it, and the strengthening mechanism increases the strength of the production with every successful application of the production, increasing its chance of being applied in the future.

Summary of Learning Mechanisms and Domain Specificity

In summary, production systems are consistent with the development of domain-specific rules. Productions develop for specific use through problem solving on specific tasks, and they are further tuned for successful use in that particular task domain. This emphasis on task-specific productions acquired through practice with a task is not idiosyncratic to ACT*, but common to learning mechanisms in other rule-based cognitive systems, e.g., the chunking mechanism in SOAR (Newell, 1988). For example, in SOAR data is initially interpreted in performing a task, leading to chunks that then implement the task directly. This focus on specificity is also consistent with the cognitive literature. Newell (1988) recently noted that the acquisition of skill exhibits many regularities, including the fact that skill learning is highly specific.

Cross-Domain Effects

Whereas the bulk of the Cantor and Kihlstrom chapter speaks of the domain specificity of day-to-day coping strategies (e.g., particular strategies for the academic or social domain), note that traumatic stressors often affect individuals *across* domains. Coping with a traumatic stress has a pervasive impact on the individual in several respects. First, traumatic stressors can interfere with an individual's functioning across domains. For example, emotional (depression, anxiety), cognitive (ruminations, lack of concentration), and physiological (insomnia, lowered immunological functioning) reactions to the stressor disrupt an individual's functioning across many domains. Second, the process of adjusting to a trauma can result in major self-concept changes across life domains. Existing self-concepts may be redefined or deleted (e.g., death of a spouse or child); new self-concepts added (cancer patient, invalid, victim) (e.g., Taylor, Wood, & Lichtman, 1983); and self-concepts associated with the relevant domain modified (death of a spouse affects friendships, loss of a job affects one's marriage, divorce affects relationships with one's children) (e.g., Linville, 1987). Third, the way one copes with a traumatic stressor can affect feelings of self-efficacy and competence beyond the domain related to the stressor. For example, people dealing with trauma often report that the stress provided them with a learning experience and resulted in a change in their life priorities (see Taylor, 1983). Fourth, the restructuring process that occurs in response to traumatic events may radically change major goal structures, and it may reorder one's priorities across self-domains (losing a child may result in one's work becoming more important). To the extent that Cantor and Kihlstrom are correct in suggesting that one's self is defined by the strategies that one employs, adaptation to a major life trauma could ultimately lead to self-concept changes *across* domains.

Are these observations consistent with a production system framework? Can a production system account for coping responses that cut across traditional life domains—e.g., resetting one's priorities across domains? The answer appears to be yes. First, proceduralized productions are task specific (e.g., setting priorities) but not necessarily limited to a single domain of the self (e.g., parent, friend, scholar). For example, one could have proceduralized productions for setting life priorities, a task that by definition cuts across many self-domains (e.g., balancing the demands of being a good mother and a good scholar). Second, if proceduralized knowledge fails to produce acceptable outcomes in a crisis, one can resort to general problem-solving productions, like reasoning by analogy, that allow one to generate new strategies for dealing with a new task that cuts across life domains. To the degree that one interprets two life tasks similarly, then the underlying structure of the productions developed is also likely to be similar.

A related question is: How might the learning mechanisms of a production system account for similarities in coping strategies in different life tasks or domains? Because reasoning by analogy is one of the major ways that people generate solutions to a new task, it is quite likely that there will be similarities in the solutions that people generate for similar tasks in different parts of their life. For example, one may use the structure of a solution to an interpersonal conflict in one domain as an analogue for the structure of the solution to an interpersonal conflict in another domain. If the underlying structure of the tasks is perceived to be similar, then the analogy is likely to be more complete. Of course, an analogy is only an approximation—the elements of the two problems may not be identical, and each task has specialized knowledge. In addition, elements of several different examples may be used in generating a new solution. Therefore, the new compiled productions may be similar to the old ones but fine tuned to the new situation. Because of the fundamental role of analogy in problem solving, it is not surprising to see similar strategies in different life domains that have similar underlying structures. However, analogies tend to be formed "close to home" (using sources within the same domain or a similar task), so it is unlikely that we would see pervasive consistency across a wide range of domains.

FLEXIBILITY OF RULE APPLICATION

As suggested by our opening quotes, Cantor and Kihlstrom view problem-solving flexibility as a key component of social intelligence. In their model, expertise and flexibility appear to be linked in that expertise provides the knowledge base for this flexibility. But with increasing practice and proceduralization of knowledge that are characteristic of expertise, do we develop greater flexibility in our coping skills? From the perspective of our current framework, the answer depends on the notion of flexibility.

One notion of flexibility is whether behavior is tuned to variations in situations and tasks (e.g., many specialized rules). Cantor and Kihlstrom's model, entailing intricate, fine-tuned strategies that enable people to deal with specific requirements of different life tasks, is quite consistent with this notion of flexibility. And as we have argued, the current production-system theory supports the idea that social problem-solving rules develop a domain-specific character. But are problem-solving rules flexible beyond their domain-specific character?

A second notion of flexibility involves the ability to adapt quickly to changing situations or changing demands within a specific context. Unlike the rules of chess or programming, the goals and situational demands on a person often change in the midst of coping with divorce or job loss. Assuming that one has developed a set of coping productions early in the process, how fast and easily can one adjust to such changes? And how easily can a set of coping productions developed in the midst of solving an achievement problem transfer to solving an interpersonal problem? In this sense, proceduralized knowledge is not so flexible. In fact, the very learning mechanisms that build domain-specific problem-solving rules also limit their flexibility of application.

Frensch and Sternberg (1988) report an expertise-flexibility tradeoff among bridge players. Expert bridge players were slower to adjust to rule modifications in the game than were novices, presumably because experts rely on proceduralized strategies. It is interesting that experts were more affected by deep structural changes in the game, whereas novices were more affected by surface changes. Thus, problem-solvers appear to be less flexible when their rules have been proceduralized, and when the task modifications are incompatible with the structure of their knowledge representation.

A production system architecture offers flexibility in that individual productions are relatively small units, permitting them to be added or deleted without great disruption to the system and recombined in multiple possible ways. But compiled knowledge that develops with increasing practice and expertise is not flexible in application. In ACT*, expertise is reflected in part in a shift from general interpretive procedures applied to declarative facts about the task to procedures that contain the compiled task-domain knowledge. Proceduralized coping rules are advantageous in that they are more efficient, are performed much faster, and are less demanding on working-memory capacity. Consistent with this shift from controlled to automatic processing, however, is the tendency for proceduralized rules to be less consciously accessible, less flexibly applied, and less easily revised compared to problem solving by interpreting knowledge in declarative form.

When knowledge shifts from the interpretive use of declarative knowledge to proceduralized rules, there is a gain in efficiency but a loss in flexibility of application. In ACT*, declarative knowledge has flexibility in that it is stored in an unanalyzed form, with no commitment to how it will be used. This allows information to be stored easily and to be used for many purposes. But stored in this way, information is less easily converted into behavior. In contrast, productions compiled from task-specific declarative knowledge may only be used for those specific tasks. For example, one can apply an optimistic expectation setting rule but cannot use the same production to retrieve an example of optimistic behavior, define optimism, or infer possible consequences of optimism.

These differences in declarative versus proceduralized knowledge have consequences for the transfer of expertise between skills (see Anderson, 1987). Productions underlying different uses of the *same* declarative knowledge may be very different. So the same declarative knowledge about yourself in the achievement domain may be compiled into different productions for different uses (e.g., productions to generate an appraisal of a stressful event may not overlap with productions to evaluate an appraisal given by others). Research shows that almost no transfer occurs when the same knowledge is used in different ways (e.g., evaluating versus generating a geometry proof). This is because the productions to implement the two skills are fundamentally different even though they are based on the same abstract declarative knowledge. However, positive transfer does occur across tasks if the knowledge is used in the same way (e.g., transfer between learning text editors that have the same underlying structure). This is because the productions are the same for both tasks. Thus positive transfer will occur between skills to the extent that the skills involve the same productions (Anderson, 1987). Thus the current production-system theory would seem to predict little positive transfer of coping skills from one major stressor to another, nor from one particular problem to another within the same stressful life event, unless they have sufficiently similar structures to lead to overlap of productions. In summary, production system learning mechanisms suggest how we develop task-specific coping rules, but they also suggest that highly practiced coping skills will lose certain aspects of flexibility in their application.

EXPERTISE: APPLYING THE EXPERT-NOVICE LITERATURE

Cantor and Kihlstrom refer to expertise as one of the three key factors in social intelligence. For Cantor and Kihlstrom, expertise entails the repertoire of knowledge used in solutions to specific life tasks, including elaborate, well-organized declarative knowledge, and an extensive source of automatic procedures. A production system framework is compatible with the notion that an individual's goals, experiences, rules, and representation of current life tasks all guide responses to specific social problem-solving tasks.

Implicit in Cantor and Kihlstrom's formulation is the assumption that expertise in the social domain has the same advantages that it does in cognitive problem-solving domains. Thus, it is tempting to assume that expert–novice differences in the social domain will parallel expert–novice differences in traditional problem-solving tasks. This is intuitively appealing, but the analogy between expertise in social problem solving and expertise in traditional cognitive tasks should be approached with caution.

We know many of the characteristics of expert problem solvers in knowledge-lean domains (e.g., Tower of Hanoi task) as well as in knowledge-rich domains (e.g., physics, computer programming). Whereas the specifics depend on the task domain, experts generally have better and more complete representations of the task domain, allowing them to more quickly and completely encode new information. They also have a richer repertoire of strategies and appropriate mechanisms for accessing and applying these strategies. These strategies and the appropriate organization of knowledge allow experts to perform faster and to generate better solutions (See Chi, Glaser, Farr, 1988; Chi, Glaser, & Rees, 1982; VanLehn, 1988, for reviews.)

It is tempting to use this literature, for example, drawing on representation and strategy differences between experts and novices in cognitive skills, as a template for understanding individual differences in social skills. But how well can these models and their findings be applied to social problem-solving or coping expertise? Examination of expertise in decision making suggests caution. First, studies of medical, psychiatric, economic, parole, and academic admission decisions reveal that experts generally use the same types of strategies and display the same types of biases as nonexperts. Second, experts' performance often is no better than that of nonexperts and almost never as good as that of even the simplest statistical models (Dawes, Meehl, & Faust, 1988; Johnson, 1988).

Differences in the development of traditional cognitive skills compared to coping skills raise additional concerns in applying the expert–novice framework. The first set of issues centers around differences in the character of the tasks. In physics or computer programming, for example, a learner is usually provided with a task environment that is stable; facts relevant to a correct solution (instructions, correct examples, defined functions or theorems, "legal operators" in production-system terminology); feedback; and a final solution state. In forming coping rules, on the other hand, the environment is constantly changing; the problem space is ill-defined; examples and legal operators are often unknown; and the final desired solution state may be ill-defined. These distinctions do not lead us to question whether the cognitive representations and processes underlying social problem solving and coping differ from those underlying more traditional problem-solving tasks studied by cognitive psychologists. Rather, we question whether expertise in social problem-solving and coping contexts has the same advantages that it does in more traditional problem-solving domains. The learning conditions that lead experts to perform better in traditional problem-solving domains often are not present in social problem-solving and coping contexts. Thus so-called "social problem-solving experts" may perform no better than novices on many social problem-solving (Dawes, Meehl, & Faust, 1988) or coping tasks.

A second, related set of issues centers around the questions: What does coping expertise mean? Who would we expect a priori to be "experts" in coping? What would our performance criteria be? For example, with practice, one may actually become a more expert workaholic, or one may develop more automatic, efficient, faster inferences tied to feelings of worthlessness and depression. Cantor and Kihlstrom have provided interesting answers to some of these issues, but it remains to be seen whether the methods and findings in the cognitive expertise literature generalize to the social problem-solving and coping area.

CONCLUSION

As the summary of ACT*'s learning mechanisms suggests, referring to coping and social behavior as sets of productions that define the steps in problem solving is not a superficial notational change. Rather, it brings with it an entire set of structural and process assumptions. This framework has several important implications regarding issues of specificity, flexibility, and expertise. First, it suggests that social problem-solving and coping skills are based on domain-specific knowledge. Coping skills develop through practice, by performing them. The very structure of their productions reflects the specifics of the problem task and context. This is supportive of Cantor and Kihlstrom's argument that social problem-solving strategies are fine tuned to meet goals in specific life tasks. However, as we noted earlier, to the extent that people rely on the domain-general strategy of reasoning by analogy, they may form similar productions across tasks whose evoking conditions are interpreted as having similar structures. Thus, some cross-task similarities will occur.

Second, a production system framework suggests caution in assuming that expertise in a social domain will necessarily lead to flexible problem-solving or coping behavior. By definition, expertise involves highly proceduralized knowledge. With greater expertise, social problem-solving or coping skills develop with practice into compiled rules that lose certain aspects of flexibility but gain speed and efficiency in their application.

Third, we suggest caution in assuming that expert–novice differences in the social domain will parallel expert–novice differences in traditional cognitive problem-solving tasks. Because coping problems are often ill-defined, their task environment constantly changing, and feedback often delayed or ambiguous, we have no assurance that experts (i.e., those with lots of practice) will actually have more efficacious coping behaviors. Thus, expertise in the social domain may not have all of the same advantages that it does in cognitive problem-solving domains.

Finally, the production system framework discussed here offers a promising approach to understanding social problem-solving and coping behavior. Representing coping skills as production sets not only highlights the task-specific nature of such skills and the learning mechanisms responsible for their development; it also highlights the multiple units of cognition composing a coping skill. The stress and coping area often focuses on the outcome of coping processes, whereas the current framework forces our attention to the rich cognitive microstructure underlying coping skill. How useful will this be? One path is to develop computer-simulation models of the production systems underlying coping behavior. The interesting work of Cantor, Kihlstrom, and their colleagues provides a rich source of task-specific social problem-solving and coping strategies for such modeling endeavors. The usefulness of the production system approach to social problem solving and coping will be judged in terms of its success in explaining the development, application, and revision of strategies to deal with both the daily stresses as well as the major traumas of life.

REFERENCES

Anderson, J. R. (1983). The *architecture of cognition*. Cambridge, MA: Harvard University Press.

Anderson, J. R. (1987). Skill acquisition: Compilation of weak-method problem solutions. *Psychological Review, 94*, 192–210.

Cantor, N., Norem, J. K., Niedenthal, P. M., Langston, C. A., & Brower, A. M. (1987). Life tasks, self-concept ideals, and cognitive strategies in a life transition. *Journal of Personality and Social Psychology, 53*, 1178–1191.

Chi, M. T. H., Glaser, R., & Farr, M. (Eds.). (1988). *The nature of expertise*. Hillsdale, NJ: Lawrence Erlbaum Associates.

Chi, M. T. H., Glaser, R., & Rees, E. (1982). Expertise in problem solving. In R. J. Sternberg (Ed.), *Advances in the psychology of human intelligence* (Vol. 1, pp. 7–75). Hillsdale, NJ: Lawrence Erlbaum Associates.

Dawes, R. M., Meehl, P. E., & Faust, D. (1988). *Clinical versus statistical prediction*. Unpublished manuscript, Carnegie Mellon University.

Frensch, P. A., & Sternberg, R. J. (1988). *Expertise and flexibility: The costs of expertise*. Unpublished paper, Yale University.

Holland, J. H., Holyoke, K. J., Nisbett, R. E., & Thagard, P. R. (1986). *Induction: Processes of inference, learning, and discovery*. Cambridge, MA: MIT Press.

Johnson, E. J. (1988). Expertise and decision under uncertainty: Performance and process. In M. T. H. Chi, R. Glaser, & Farr, M. (Eds.), *The nature of expertise*. Cambridge, MA: MIT Press.

Larkin, J. H. (1981). Enriching formal knowledge: A model for learning to solve textbook physics problems. In J. R. Anderson (Ed.), *Cognitive skills and their acquisition* (pp. 311–334). Hillsdale, NJ: Lawrence Erlbaum Associates.

Linville, P. W. (1987). Self-complexity as a cognitive buffer against stress-related depression and illness. *Journal of Personality and Social Psychology, 52*, 663–676.

Nasby, W., & Kihlstrom, J. F. (1985). Cognitive assessment of personality and psychopathology. In R. E. Ingram (Ed.), *Information-processing approaches to psychopathology and clinical psychology* (pp. 217–239). New York: Academic Press.

Newell, A. (1988). *Unified theories of cognition. The 1987 William James Lectures*, Carnegie Mellon Univeristy.

Newell, A., & Simon, H. A. (1972). *Human problem solving*. Englewood Cliffs, NJ: Prentice-Hall.

Showers, C., & Cantor, N. (1985). *Defensive pessimism: The positive side of negative thinking.* Unpublished paper. University of Michigan.

Smith, E. R. (1984). Model of social inference processes. *Psychological Review, 91*, 392–413.

Taylor, S. E. (1983). Adjustment to threatening events: A theory of cognitive adaptation. *American Psychologist, 38*, 1161–1173.

Taylor, S. E., Wood, J. V., & Lichtman, R. R. (1983). It could be worse: Selective evaluation as a response to victimization. *Journal of Social Issues, 39*, 19–40.

VanLehn, K. (1988). Problem solving and cognitive skill acquisition. In M. Posner (Ed.), *The foundation of cognitive science*.

9 Psychodynamic-Systems Reflections on a Social-Intelligence Model of Personality

Lawrence A. Pervin
Rutgers University

The social-intelligence model of personality developed by Cantor and Kihlstrom represents a very significant contribution to the field. What particularly impresses me about this work is the importance of the phenomena considered, the sophistication with which these phenomena are considered, and the variety of research methods utilized. Such an ambitious endeavor is a fresh light in the field and invites us to consider what I believe are some of the most difficult issues that face those attempting to develop a comprehensive model of personality.

In this chapter, then, I would like to consider such issues as the domain-specific model of personality, skills and motives as units of personality, the role of unconscious schema in personality functioning, and why people find it so difficult to change aspects of their functioning. I bring to this consideration a psychodynamic-systems model, utilizing clinical illustrations, because I believe that it is this model that most invites attention to the issues before us. The authors indicate their interest in clinical phenomena, though from a cognitive perspective, so the utilization of some clinical illustrations hopefully serves to highlight these issues and contrasts between alternative models of personality.

THE DOMAIN-SPECIFIC MODEL OF PERSONALITY

In their introduction the authors (Cantor & Kihlstrom, this volume) suggest that social intelligence is multifaceted, domain specific, and task specific. I agree that intelligence, as well as personality, is multifaceted. I would like to consider, however, the implications of considering it to be domain specific as well. Earlier (Pervin, 1986), I have considered four models of personality in relation to the person-consistency issue. At one extreme is the view of the person as made up of responses associated with stimuli in the environment, either in terms of operants or stimulus–response connections. Such a view suggests considerable stimulus control of behavior, little central organization, and the potential for almost unlimited behavioral variation according to the exigencies or contingencies of the environment. At the other extreme, we have the psychoanalytic view of character, which suggests that the stamp of personality is present in every piece of behavior, that is, that all behavior is governed by essentially the same dynamic forces. This view suggests considerable internal control of behavior, central organization, and consistency of behavior, at least in latent (genotypic) form if not in manifest (phenotypic) form.

Few psychologists today would hold to either extreme, though proponents of each model can still be found. Most psychologists recognize that behavior is both consistent and variable, regulated by both internal and external opportunities and constraints. However, alternative models of the organization of personality remain. One, the domain-specific view, suggests that people behave similarly in situations perceived to be similar, with different response patterns associated with different groups of situations. This emphasis on generalizations and discriminations made by the person among situations may be found in trait as well as social-cognitive views. Although it is true that these represent fundamentally different views (Wright & Mischel, 1987), we should not ignore the fact that many trait theorists suggest that people use broad situation categories to regulate their own behavior as well as their expectations of others (Epstein & Teraspulsky, 1986).

The domain-specific view, with its emphasis on equivalence classes or categories of situations, can be contrasted with what I would describe as a psychodynamic or general-systems view. Such a view suggests that many of the same person variables are always at work, though a slight shift in the organization of them can lead to dramatic changes in behavior. Approximating the character view, this view suggests that basically the same units of personality are at work in all situations though their relative importance and the nature of their organization may vary. The rules governing consistency and variability of behavior often are left unspecified by proponents of this model, in part because they tend to be more interested in the units of personality and their dynamic organization, and in certain relevant behavioral phenomena (e.g., defensive, neurotic functioning), than in the variable, often adaptive aspects of behavior. Although for the most part left unspecified, the critical variables often emphasized are the needs and anxieties brought into play in each situation.

At times, the domain-specific and dynamic-systems models may approximate one another and the differences between them *as models* may appear to be minor. This may be the case as social-cognitive theorists increasingly struggle with questions of pattern and regularity in personality functioning. Thus, for example, consider the following statement by Wright and Mischel (1987): "To the degree that demanding situations require competencies not readily available, they may activate these more generalized or rigid coping styles and thus provide conditions under which individual differences in coping behavior may be more predictable from dispositional judgments'' (p.1163). Although at times subtle, the differences between the domain-specific and dynamic-systems models are fundamental. Thus, whereas Wright and Mischel (1987) emphasize a variable such as threat or stress in influencing the presence of a disposition across situations, they still caution against the utility of broader extrapolations to other behaviors or efforts to predict to other domains.

Clearly the domain-specific model has merit to it, particularly as a corrective against alternative models that neglect the variable, adaptive aspects of personality functioning. It is important, however, to recognize that it is not the only model that can attend to such phenomena and that it has its own potential problems and liabilities. For example, if personality functioning is domain specific and organized in terms of categories of situations, then how are we to determine such categories of situations? Not only are there problematic aspects to the classification of situations across individuals, but there is reason to believe that the individual has multiple ways of classifying situations (Pervin, 1981). For example, at times the person may categorize situations on the basis of role similarity and at other times on the basis of similarity of affective tone, at times on the basis of skill requirements and at other times on the basis of the potential for meeting various motives or goals. And, to anticipate a later section, at times the person may be able to articulate the rules for classification whereas at other times be unable to articulate either all the situations that fall into a category or the basis for categorization! Finally, the domain-specific view may represent a static picture of the person as well as a disregard for consideration of how the person is able to shift from situation to situation, or from domain to domain, often exhibiting vastly different patterns of behavior, though still retaining some coherence of personality organization.

I turn here to a clinical illustration, that of a patient who clearly behaves differently at home, at work, and in the therapy session. This, of course, is adaptive. Within each setting he also behaves differently on various occasions, generally being kind and entertaining, but at times being critical, judgmental, and verbally abusive. The latter is likely to occur, *in each setting*, when he feels that he is not being valued or treated as special. Thus, there is a ''dynamic'' that comes into play in all three domains, but only under special circumstances. And, though it is relatively rare in each domain, the feelings and behavioral consequences are extremely painful to him. It is an important part of his personality.

To take another illustration, a patient begins a session with a description of the feeling that ''If something goes wrong, it's my fault. There's a kind of fatalism about things—ultimately something will go wrong, I'll be rejected, and it will be because of me.'' This feeling and belief are always a part of him, though they enter into some areas more than others and are more powerful at some times than at other times. They are particularly powerful when he experiences some disappointment or loss. Such consistency of feeling and belief is recognized not only in psychoanalysis, but in such cognitive views as Ellis' irrational beliefs, Beck's negative thoughts, and Meichenbaum's core operating principles as well.

These clinical vignettes are given to illustrate the point that a model of personality must recognize consistency, pattern, and organization *as well as* diversity. The issue here is not whether diversity exists, but rather how such diversity can best be conceptualized in a model of personality. An alternative view might involve dimensions such as level of arousal, positive–negative affect, or level of threat.[1] In fact, this emphasis is part of such differing models as psychoanalytic theory, Eysenck's trait theory, and Mischel's approach to dispositional constructs. Although recognizing diversity, such dimensions suggest a different approach to personality than that suggested by a domain-specific view—one that is more fluid and dynamic. One might be able to develop idiosyncratic categories of situations, but they would not be grouped on the basis of similarities we generally think of in terms of object classification, and they would be much more fluid or shifting as well.

SKILLS AND MOTIVES

For some time the area of motivation was neglected by psychology generally and personality psychology in particular. It is to the credit of Cantor and Kihlstrom that they recognize and consider the importance of motives in personality functioning. They set their useful concept of life tasks in the context of other goals concepts and indicate how the study of periods of life transition can provide insight into individual differences in adaptive behavior.

The goals concept is receiving increasing attention within the fields of personality and social psychology (Pervin, 1989). I believe that part of the reason for this is that it offers the potential for considering both cognition and affect, for considering both stability and change in personality functioning, and for conceptualizing individuals and social cognitions in parallel terms (Read & Miller, 1989). Within this context it is important to distinguish among the goals people have, the plans or strategies they use for achieving these goals, and the skills or resources they have for developing and implementing strategies.

Adaptive functioning involves setting achievable goals that are of value to the individual and the utilization of strategies for implementation that take into consideration resources within the individual and affordances (Baron & Boudreau, 1987) or opportunities offered by the environment. I focus attention here on a few questions that are in need of further consideration. First, how are goals

---

[1]Discussions with Irving Sigel have been helpful in developing this point of view.

to be defined and measured? It is important to distinguish between a goal and the plan (behaviors) utilized to achieve the goal. Also, it is important to recognize that goals are associated with affect; that is, whereas affect is associated with the process of coming closer to or moving further from a goal, it also is associated with the goal itself (Pervin, 1983). One may be aware or unaware of one's goals, and they may be measured at very general or situation-specific levels. Global motive measures and measures of more specific motivational mediators may be useful for different purposes. The issue of assessment of unconscious goals remains a more problematic question, regardless of the level of generality at which one chooses to consider them.

A second question in need of investigation is the acquisition of goals. It is here once more that I believe we need to pay careful attention to the affective nature of goals. Many goals become life tasks not just during a specific period but for major periods of a person's life. Thus, they have a power to them that is sustaining over extended periods of time. And, at times they have a power to them that leads to behavior that the individual and others would likely consider maladaptive. We come here, then, to a third question, which involves the nature of goal system functioning. As Cantor and Kihlstrom so vividly illustrate, generally the individual is concerned with multiple goals and is faced with the task of developing strategies for the simultaneous achievement of many goals, selecting among goals of greater or lesser importance and potential for fulfillment, and resolving problems of goal conflict. In the future we will need to learn more about both how goals are acquired and about how individuals become capable of greater or lesser integration of goal-system functioning.

CONSCIOUS, NONCONSCIOUS, AND UNCONSCIOUS GOALS AND KNOWLEDGE

Today there is increased recognition of the possible importance of psychological content and processes that are not available to awareness (Bowers & Meichenbaum, 1984). The authors address the issue of life tasks and declarative social knowledge that is not available to awareness, and Kihlstrom in particular has written with wisdom in this area. To a certain extent, however, I remain uncomfortable with the treatment given. Recognition is given to nonconscious self-concepts, but the emphasis is on their role in psychopathology (p. 46). Attention is given to the problem of introspective awareness, but the suggestion is made that "Fortunately, people find it rather easy to articulate their life tasks by means of simple and direct self reports" (p.80).

The authors are mainly interested in adaptive functioning, and it probably is the case that awareness of goals, self-concepts, and declarative knowledge is more characteristic of adaptive than maladaptive functioning. However, as noted previously, my own sense is that many important goals and self-representations may be unavailable to awareness, and that at times these nonconscious goals and self-representations function in adaptive as well as maladaptive ways. Let me turn here to two brief clinical illustrations, both involving potential self-representations (Markus' possible selves) that were useful to the individuals in keeping them goal directed and both of which also were associated with distress. The two cases involve individuals who focused on being successful and productive in part to avoid being like a representation of the father associated with negative affect—in one case a father who had considerable talent but continuously changed jobs and never remained focused in one direction; in the other case a father who was alcoholic, jobless, and ultimately was rejected by the family. In the first case, the motivation to be productive, and not like the father in that regard, had served him well until the point where a change in career focus seemed to be advantageous. At that point the risk of being nonproductive, associated with a shift in career, became onerous and the individual experienced both anxiety and depression. In the second case, the individual became unemployed because of technological changes in his area of expertise. A profound depression resulted in which he told his wife to divorce him and marry a worthwhile person, in part because he unwittingly experienced himself as being like his father. In both cases these self-representations had positive as well as negative implications, and in both cases the individuals were not conscious of the connection between these self-representations and their current distress.

In the preceding discussion I have used the term nonconscious, or the description inaccessible to awareness, in keeping with the terms used by the authors. But why not the use of the term unconscious? I guess that this is because of the possible surplus meaning that the term may have, inviting psychoanalytic ideas of repression and defense. However, by now there is a substantial body of literature that as a minimum suggests that such ideas need to be taken seriously. And, in any case, as Brody (1987) suggests, "a complete understanding of human behavior cannot be derived from the study of those events that are phenomenally present. That is, it is becoming increasingly clear that those events of which we are aware constitute a subset, and arguably a small subset, of the events that influence our behavior" (p.297).

CHANGE AND RESISTANCE TO CHANGE

The authors take a relatively optimistic view concerning self-control and mutability of personality. Although recognizing signs of rigidity in social intelligence, Cantor and Kihlstrom remain basically optimistic about the mutability of social intelligence (p.87). As a clinician, I am impressed with the unconscious goals and self-representations of people, with their inability to exercise volition, and with their difficulty in changing. I would venture to say that virtually every person struggles with some aspect of life over which they are unable to exercise volition—either something to which they feel addicted or something they "want" to do but cannot "get themselves" to do. In other words, my sense is that the blockage of will or self-control is a rather common phenomenon. And, my sense is that when it comes to important areas of one's life, particularly areas associated with strong affect and conflict, change is difficult and at times impossible.

I do not think that what is involved here is merely a difference between the authors and myself in optimism–pessimism, or a different reading of the literature, though both may be true. Rather, what is involved is a focus on different kinds of phenomena and a reading of different literatures. Thus, to me mutability is a question of degree and that more surface aspects of the self are easier to change than are more fundamental aspects, what Swann and Hill (1982) describe as the difference between self-images and self-concepts, and that affective aspects of the self may be more difficult to change than cognitive aspects (Swann, Griffin, Predmore, & Gains, 1987).

It is important to consider here the difference between skills and motives. At the time of reading this chapter I considered with three patients the question of viewing their difficulties, and the process of change, in skill terms. One contrasted skill in driving a car with living life, loving, and developing intimacy— there might be limits to developments in both, but the latter was far more difficult. A second was struggling with fears of embarrassment, and I discussed with him the potential for developing greater social skills. He noted that, whereas this made some sense, the fact was that he was terrified of embarrassment in areas in which he had considerable skill and that any sign of a deviation from the facade of competence represented an extreme threat to him. In a third patient we considered his becoming more skillful in recognizing times that his wife was busy and could not spend more time with him. Once more the issue was not just one of skill but of the wish to be special to her, for her to be "hooked" on him, and the threat that if he was not special then he was nothing at all.

Of course these clinical illustrations may be biased by the more general psychodynamic structure of the therapy, but it seems to me that what the patients are saying makes sense. And, of course one could consider these as cognitive distortions, which they are, but to describe them only as such is to miss the tremendous affective meaning associated with them. Thus, the question of mutability is not only one of optimism–pessimism; it is a question of what is to be changed and the barriers to change. A psychodynamic-systems view suggests that people often actively resist change because it is perceived as involving exposure to new threats, because it is perceived to involve giving up goals (wishes, fantasies) to which the individual has long felt deeply attached, and because it is perceived to represent a threat to the system as a whole. Such a view of the barriers to change is fundamentally different from that suggested by current cognitive therapists (Messer, 1983; Wachtel, 1982).

CONCLUSION; IS A RAPPROCHEMENT POSSIBLE ?

As indicated in the introduction, it is the power of the thinking of Cantor and Kihlstrom that draws one to consider some of the most fundamental issues facing personality psychologists. Within the therapy area, consideration has been given to whether a rapprochement is possible among differing views (Arkowitz & Messer, 1984). Within the personality area, attention is being drawn to similarities among phenomena emphasized by social-cognitive psychologists and psychoanalysts (Westen, 1988). It is time to take stock of some of these parallel developments and the potential for integration among them, as well as the barriers to integration that may be equally significant. Whereas different models of personality may be useful for understanding different phenomena or for making different kinds of predictions, it seems to me that personality psychologists need to be concerned with models that emphasize both the stasis and flow of behavior, the pattern and organization of personality as well as the domain-specific aspects of behavior.

REFERENCES

Arkowitz, H., & Messer, S. B. (Eds.). (1984). *Psychoanalytic therapy and behavior therapy: Is integration possible?* New York: Plenum.

Baron, R. M., & Boudreau, L. A. (1987). An ecological perspective on integrating personality and social psychology. *Journal of Personality and Social Psychology, 53,* 1222–1228.

Bowers, K., & Meichenbaum, D. (Eds.). (1984). *The unconscious reconsidered.* New York: Wiley.

Brody, N. (1987). Some thoughts on the unconscious. *Personality and Social Psychology Bulletin, 13,* 293–298.

Epstein, S., & Teraspulsky, L. (1986). Perception of cross-situational consistency. *Journal of Personality and Social Psychology, 50,* 1152–1160.

Messer, S. B. (1983). Resistance to integration. *Contemporary Psychology, 28,* 111–112.

Pervin, L. A. (1981). The relation of situations to behavior. In D. Magnusson (Ed.), *Toward a psychology of situations.* Hillsdale, NJ: Lawrence Erlbaum Associates.

Pervin, L. A. (1983). The stasis and flow of behavior: Toward a theory of goals. In M. M. Page (Ed.), *Personality: Current theory and research.* Lincoln: University of Nebraska Press.

Pervin, L. A. (1986). *Person–environment congruence in the light of the person–situation controversy.* Paper presented at the meetings of the American Psychological Association, Washington, DC.

Pervin, L. A. (Ed.). (1989). *Goals concepts in personality and social psychology.* Hillsdale, NJ: Lawrence Erlbaum Associates.

Read, S. J., & Miller, L. C. (1989). Inter-personalism: Towards a goal-based theory of persons in relationships. In L. A. Pervin (Ed.), *Goals concepts in personality and social psychology.* Hillsdale, NJ: Lawrence Erlbaum Associates.

Swann, W. B. Jr., Griffin, J. J. Jr., Predmore, S. C., & Gaines, B. (1987). The cognitive-affective crossfire: When self-consistency confronts self-enhancement. *Journal of Personality and Social Psychology, 52,* 881–889.

Swann, W. B. Jr., & Hill, C. A. (1982). When our identities are mistaken: Reaffirming self-conceptions through social interaction. *Journal of Personality and Social Psychology, 43,* 59–66.

Wachtel, P. (Ed.). (1982). *Resistance: Psychodynamic and behavioral approaches.* New York: Plenum.

Westen, D. (1988). *Social cognition and object relations.* Unpublished manuscript, University of Michigan.

Wright, J. C., & Mischel, W. (1987). A conditional approach to dispositional constructs: The local predictability in social behavior. *Journal of Personality and Social Psychology, 53,* 1159–1177.

10

The Importance of Goals in Personality: Toward a Coherent Model of Persons

Stephen J. Read
University of Southern California

Lynn C. Miller
Scripps College and Claremont Graduate School

Cantor and Kihlstrom have done a truly impressive job of starting to analyze important individual differences in terms of the strategies people use to approach life tasks. Further, the concepts of social intelligence and life tasks are useful ones for analyzing individual differences in social behavior. Because we feel that their theory has great promise for personality, we focus on two major goals in this chapter. First, we discuss several ways in which we think the theory can be expanded to provide a more complete model of individual differences and social behavior. Second, we examine in greater detail their concept of "intentional consistency." We think this idea has extremely important implications for the future direction of personality theory and we explore in greater depth some of those implications.

TOWARD AN EXPANDED THEORY

Cantor and Kihlstrom (this volume) focus on social intelligence as their primary construct for understanding individual differences: "From a cognitive point of view, the structure of personality is identified with the social intelligence repertoire used in interpersonal problem solving. Just as traditional approaches to personality are concerned with the nature and organization of personality traits and motives, so the cognitive approach is concerned with the nature and organization of social knowledge" (p. 17).

Social Intelligence is defined as consisting of the procedural and declarative knowledge that people possess. Thus, individual differences are to be understood in terms of differences between people in these two types of knowledge. Although this is clearly an important source of differences, it seems there are other factors that are equally important and that must be considered concurrently in a comprehensive theory of personality. We focus on two: goals and resources.

Goals and Resources

There is a long tradition in personality of conceptualizing individual differences in terms of the organization of goals and motives (Allport, 1937; Allston, 1975; Miller & Read, in press; Mischel, 1973, 1977; Murray, 1938; Pervin, 1983; Read & Miller, in press). Allport (1929), for example, has argued that "the only really significant congruences in personality must be sought in the sphere of conation. It is the striving of a man which binds together the traits, and which shows how essentially harmonious they are in their determination of his behavior" (p. 14).

It is true that Cantor and Kihlstrom frequently acknowledge the importance of goals in directing behavior and mention individual differences in goals. Nevertheless, given their identification of the structure of personality with the individual's social-intelligence repertoire, goals do not seem to be a central component of their analysis of individual differences. Yet we would argue that goals should be central to any attempt to conceptualize individual differences (Miller & Read, in press; Read & Miller, in press).

There are several ways in which their theory might benefit from a more wholehearted inclusion of goals in the analysis of individual differences. First, Cantor and Kihlstrom do not consider in detail how differences between people in terms of their salient goals may affect behavior. For example, in their research on social and academic life tasks they have focused on a group of honors students, for whom the academic life task is probably more important than is true for many other students. Cantor and Kihlstrom then emphasize differences in how these life tasks are pursued, but they do not examine in much detail whether there are differences between students in the importance of these life tasks. Yet it seems plausible on its face that many of the most important differences between students are in terms of which life tasks are most important. We have all had students who make us wonder why on earth they ever went to college, because for them the academic life task seems nothing more than an obstacle to the social life task of partying and making friends.

Second, Cantor and Kihlstrom do not consider in any detail the role that various relations among goals, such as intraindividual goal conflict, may play in individual differences (although they briefly mention the possibility of measuring them). Yet as Wilensky (1983) and Argyle, Furnham, and Graham (1981) have argued, knowledge of people's goal relations is critical for understanding their behavior. Two people may possess the same goal but exhibit different behavior, because they differ in whether they possess a second goal that is related to the first. For example, both a sociable and a shy person may have a strong desire for intimacy; yet they may behave quite differently because the shy person also has a very strong desire to avoid things like embarassment and social failure. The shy person might inhibit social overtures because of his or her desire to avoid embarassment, might take longer to respond (because there is a conflict), and/or might exhibit behavior that is a "blend" or compromise that doesn't maximize the achievement of either goal (e.g., listening attentively to another, which is less "risky" than disclosing intimately but moderately likely to encourage intimacy).

Further, a shy person's response might very much depend on whether their partner can reduce their fears of embarassment (e.g., with an accepting partner or "Opener"). When we examine such dyadic interactions the importance of the relations among the goals of the members of the dyad becomes apparent. In any relationship, whether and how we attain our goals depends on how they interact with the goals and perceived goals of our partner. For example, if we are interested in achieving emotional intimacy in a relationship, whether we attempt to achieve that goal depends on whether we think our partner has the same goal or is instead merely interested in having a good time.

Another important difference between people is in terms of the resources they possess. Social strategies and plans typically require certain resources to be carried out successfully. Resources include things such as cognitive abilities, money, time, physical attractiveness, physical strength, etc. Whether or not an individual possesses these or other resources will frequently have a major impact on his or her ability to carry out social plans, and thus on the apparent consistency and coherence of his or her behavior.

The preceding therefore suggests that we could have two people who are equivalent in social intelligence (that is they possess the same procedural and declarative knowledge) yet exhibit very different behaviors, because their operative goals or goal relations differ or because they differ in whether they possess the resources necessary for enacting their strategies. Because Cantor and Kihlstrom do not have a well-articulated model of goals and resources, it is more difficult than it could be with their model to determine the conditions under which people will and will not use particular social strategies. Also, because they do not deal with how goals may change as a function of such things as situation, interaction partner, and goal satisfaction, they have difficulty adequately capturing how people's behavior may vary across situations and time.

Clearly one of the major contexts in which people exhibit their differences is in interactions with others. At present, however, it is not clear how the constructs in Cantor and Kihlstrom's model can readily handle the dynamics of dyadic interaction. For example, how would the model handle the change and flow of goals within an interaction, the coordination of plans between individuals and how the resources of one individual become an important part of the plans of the other?

It is also clear that individuals in long-term relationships typically develop unique patterns of interaction, with emergent properties that often could not be predicted from knowledge of either person alone. Their model, as presented, does not deal with the process by which people form these relationships. Nevertheless, an expanded model of individual differences that includes both goals and resources as central concepts in conjunction with the procedural and declarative knowledge that make up social intelligence can provide insight into how such relationships develop (Miller & Read, in press; Read & Miller, in press).

One might argue that Cantor and Kihlstrom's theory is not intended to be a theory of social interaction and therefore it is unfair to suggest that their theory should deal with social interaction. However, as we pointed out, probably the most important arena in which people exhibit their differences is social interaction. Given this, it seems to us that a complete theory of personality must deal eventually with the problem of social interaction and relationship formation. Cantor and Kihlstrom are clearly aware of this issue, as demonstrated by several instances in which they discuss the coordination of interactions. We encourage them to develop this aspect of their model more fully.

We sense a latent tension in their model between the attempt to analyze personality in terms of social intelligence and a recognition of the importance of some kind of motivational construct such as goals. Cantor and Kihlstrom state that social intelligence is their primary concept for analyzing personality and individual differences. Yet they frequently introduce the concept of goals and acknowledge its importance. We suspect that Cantor and Kihlstrom feel the same tension we do. But, individual goals and motives, cognitive processes, and knowledge structures could all potentially be integral parts of a richer, more integrated general theory of personality. We are reminded of Allport's (1937) proposal of a dynamic theory of personality that "regards motives as personalized systems of tensions, in which the core of impulse is not to be divorced from the images, ideas of goal, past experience, capacities, and style of conduct employed in obtaining the goal. The whole system is integral . . . Only individualized patterns of motives have the capacity to select stimuli, to control and direct segmental tensions, to initiate responses and to render them equivalent, in ways that are consistent with, and characteristic of, the person himself" (p. 320–321).

In our work (Miller & Read, in press; Read & Miller, in press) we have suggested one approach to these issues. We have argued that individual differences can best be understood as chronic configurations of goals, plans, resources, and beliefs. Some of these configurations may be highly idiographic, whereas other configurations may be widely shared across people and may be culturally recognized by a trait label. Consistent with this analysis of individual differences, Werner and Pervin (1986), in a content analysis of most of the major global personality instruments such as the MMPI, the California Psychological Inventory (CPI) and the 16 PF, have shown that all these measures specifically inquire about three of these components: people's goals and preferences, their typical actions and behaviors, and their beliefs about themselves and others.

Further, recent research (Miller, Jones, & Hoffman, 1988) suggests that different configurations of goals are associated with different traits.

We feel that all four components are necessary for understanding individual differences because behavior is a function of all of them. A change in any one of the components may radically alter what an individual does.

Situations

How do people interface with the characteristics of situations? For Cantor and Kihlstrom this question would seem to be, how do we predict which aspects of an individual's social intelligence are expressed in, and interact with, a given situation? Cantor and Kihlstrom, in laying out the broad strokes of a reply, refer to work by Argyle (1981) on the social rules in situations. We would like to see this facet of the theory elaborated further. Argyle (Argyle, Furnham, & Graham, 1981), in fact, provides a much richer conception of situations, one that goes beyond an emphasis just on social rules. This conception would seem particularly appropriate for a model of social intelligence. Argyle et al. (1981) suggest that situations can be conceptualized in terms of a number of components, among them the goals afforded by the situation, the roles and rules associated with the situation, the resources available in that situation, and the plans and strategies that can be effectively and acceptably carried out in them. In support of the importance of considering the goals associated with situations, Pervin (1983) has shown that people's preferences for different situations are a joint function of what goals they see as relevant to those situations, the affective value of attaining those goals, and the perceived probability of attaining them.

This conception of situations would seem to be a remarkably fruitful one for a theory of individual differences that focuses on differences in social intelligence and that could also include a consideration of goals. It is remarkably easy to analyze, in detail, how the goals, plans, resources, and beliefs of individuals interact with the characteristics of situations when they are conceptualized in this form (e.g., Miller & Read, in press; Read & Miller, in press).

Life Tasks

Cantor and Kihlstrom focus on the notion of *life tasks* as their primary concept for organizing people's goals. As they use the concept it does not generally seem to function as a way of conceptualizing individual differences, although sometimes they talk as if it could. Nevertheless, the concept of life tasks does capture an important way in which important social goals are organized around specific periods and contexts in people's lives.

However, it seems to us that the concept of life task also has some important limitations. Cantor and Kihlstrom need to expand their theory by providing a richer and broader framework for thinking about the organization of goals. There are numerous ways in which goals can be organized (Read & Miller, in press), at a variety of different levels of abstraction. Life task only captures a limited range of the possible ways in which goals are organized (for example, see Markus & Nurius, 1986, on "possible selves"). For example, life task does not seem like a particularly useful and appropriate unit of analysis for understanding the change and flux of goals within the context of an ongoing dyadic interaction, such as on a first date. Granted, going out on dates is part of an important life task, it does not seem that the concept of life task itself can capture the dynamics of the evening as it progresses. Life tasks seem best suited for capturing the organization of goals and strategies that are organized around particular broad periods in people's lives.

Also, life tasks seem to combine a number of different components into one unit, combining the rules, roles, plans, resources, and goals afforded by a particular context and life period. In addition, it seems to blend the individual's own interpretation or construal into this single, undifferentiated unit. Because the life task tends to be treated as an undifferentiated unit, it is much harder than it should be to determine how an individual's goals and social intelligence interact with the characteristics of the life task.

Cantor and Kihlstrom do argue that individuals respond on the basis of their own interpretation of the life task, but they do not really discuss on what that interpretation is based, other than a general notion of previous life experiences. Further, they do not always clearly separate the individual's construal of the life task from the life task itself.

Another concern about the model is that it does not deal to any great degree with how people choose which life tasks to pursue. Whereas some life tasks seem to be inescapable and pursued by everyone, other life tasks are optional. Not everyone goes to college or graduate school and not everyone decides to get married or to have children. How do we understand individual differences in pursuit of life tasks? Surely differences in social intelligence are not sufficient to let us understand such differences in choices. As we argued previously, we would also seem to need a theory of goals and resources.

Also, this framework does not really deal with how people may move between life tasks. For example, what factors govern how people move between life tasks within a particular period of time? How do we decide that we have finished for the time being with our academic life tasks and now is the time to deal with our social-life tasks? And what factors govern how people move between life tasks in different periods of time?

Units and Levels of Analysis

Part of the point we are trying to make concerns the appropriate level of analysis that will allow one to develop a model powerful enough to understand a wide range of social phenomena. Whereas social intelligence and life tasks capture important aspects of individual differences and social behavior, they seem somewhat inflexible, and sometimes incomplete. There are many aspects of social behavior that would not be easily captured in terms of these units. We would argue that Cantor and Kihlstrom's analysis needs to be supplemented to provide a set of units that can be combined in a number of different ways. For example, in the preceding we argued that the concept of life task can probably be decomposed into several components, and this decomposition would be quite useful in understanding the nature of life tasks and how different people respond differently to them.

Essentially, we (Miller & Read, in press; Read & Miller, in press) think that individual differences, situations, and life tasks can all be analyzed using very similar units, including goals, plans, resources, and beliefs, as well as other related concepts such as roles and rules. Analyzing these major elements of social behavior in a common language makes it much easier to think about the dynamic interplay of these elements, and how they can be combined into a process model that allows us to understand the specifics of ongoing dyadic interactions and relationships and how behavior coheres.

Coherence: Beyond Consistency

The "consistency" controversy has been an important one in personality for decades (Epstein & O'Brien, 1985; Magnusson & Endler, 1977; Mischel, 1984; Mischel & Peake, 1982; Pervin, 1983). But, according to Epstein and O'Brien (1985), there now seems to be some agreement that behavior "is simultaneously specific and unstable at the individual level [of particular acts] and general and stable at the aggregate level" (p. 533). Furthermore, people in their everyday lives do not expect to find cross-situational consistency at the individual level (Epstein & Terapulsky, 1986; Wright & Mischel, 1987).

We have argued (Read & Miller, in press) that what people—as perceivers of their own and others' actions—may be doing instead is trying to ascertain how sequences of action "fit together" to form coherent scenarios and "models" (see Read, 1987). Cantor and Kihlstrom's (this volume) notion of "intentional consistency" seems to be related to what we mean by "coherence." They argue that the "social intelligence approach involves many different types of consistency, but the most important of these is the consistency of action with perceptions and intentions [Kuhl & Beckmann, 1985]. Intentional consistency is apparent when people express their life goals and strive to achieve them, and when people act in accordance with their subjective impressions of the situation" (p. 43).

Cantor and Kihlstrom, in referring to "intentional consistency," have pointed out an extremely important and useful concept for personality. If there truly were no connections among perceptions, intentions, and actions, behavior would be little more than a collection of random acts. Understanding the connections among perceptions, intentions (or goals) and plans would seem critical to developing coherent models of sequences of actions. But what exactly do we mean by coherence? To get a better handle on this, let us consider how persons might develop coherent models of others. Such an analysis might provide insights not only into how people *perceive* coherence but might also provide insights into the *underlying* nature and structure of coherences that exist in persons. The following example of Mary, Anne, and John is adapted from earlier theory (Miller & Read, in press) and research (Read & Marcus, 1988). Consider the following two behavioral sequences.

1. Mary goes up to John and tells him she'll marry him now if they can elope immediately.
2. A woman tells Anne (who we know loves John) that John is about to "pop the question" and Anne gets all excited and thanks this woman.

If we saw only the first sequence of events, we might presume that Mary cares about John but for some reason—maybe she has other time constraints—she's in a hurry. If we saw only the second sequence of events, we might think "gee, maybe this woman shouldn't have told Anne that (she's being a bit of a busybody) but Anne seems to have appreciated the information, so maybe the woman in her own way was trying to be helpful." But, if we are told that Mary first told John she'd be willing to elope and then she told Anne that John was about to propose, our model of Mary is apt to shift dramatically (e.g., Mary is really manipulative and out to hurt Anne).

Notice that these actions can be "fit together," using principles such as parsimony (Miller & Read, in press; Read & Miller, in press) to build a coherent scenario about Mary that can provide the basis for inferences about her plans. For example, one plan might be to manipulate John into marrying her right away so that they will be married before Anne finds out. Another part of the plan may be to allow Anne to think that John really will marry her to give her "false hopes" so she'll be even more upset when she finds out he married Mary. These plans may be aimed at achieving a particular goal or set of goals (e.g., to hurt Anne).

The person perceiver (as actor or observer) may have trouble trying to fit this information in with other information about (or previous models of) Mary. For example, an observer may say something like, "but, I've never known Mary to be manipulative, she's such a caring person—this doesn't seem in character for her." Or Mary as the actor might say, "Why did I do that? That's not like me at all."

Although a variety of outcomes are possible, one possibility is that we may completely change our view of the person (or ourselves), organizing past actions to fit our new developing model of the person. For example, an observer might say something like the following: "Maybe Mary gave me a present when I was sick not because she cared about me, but because she wanted me to give her something. . . . right after that I did give her that antique lamp she had so admired. . . ." Such models serve as a basis for explaining current behavior (and retrospectively giving changing accounts or stories about causal sequences). They are also apt to be useful in making predictions about future behavior and testing alternative models (e.g., I'll bet the next time Mary does something nice for me, she'll be looking for some "hand out").

It is interesting that individuals appear to have and easily form fairly detailed models of persons (for example, shy individuals). These models may allow them to make predictions about how individuals may form very different "possible relationships" (same sex and dating relationships) with various others (Miller & Jones, 1988). For example, people may take into account what some of the resource limitations (access to social networks) of shy people might be and how individuals' patterns of goals, resources, and beliefs are likely to create "unique" relationships. They may also forecast "certain problems" arising with time.

There are a number of points to be made here. First, developing coherent scenarios (and models of persons) from sequences of actions may often depend on a great deal of inference and construction (and therefore depend on considerable knowledge). Second, people can form a "coherent" model even though the actions involved (proposing to John they elope and telling Anne that John is about to propose to her) may seem unrelated if not inconsistent. Third, actions from a variety of situations and contexts may be employed to add to or develop a coherent model of why particular people do what they do and why their behavior varies across situations (e.g., other salient goals, conflicting goals, resource limitations, etc). Information about cross-situational consistencies may be used by individuals in making inferences about how someone's behavior "fits together" from situation to situation, but it is but one class of information in an array of information that individuals appear to use in developing coherent models.

As Read (1987) has argued in a theory of attribution, person perceivers attempt to understand and develop models of sequences of actions by, for example, figuring out how the individual actions form a plan, and how this plan is tied to goals, and factors that initiated that goal. These models of extended behavioral sequences, models of other persons, models of themselves, and models of their unique relationships with others are apt to be constantly updated, especially when we first meet someone; they may be used to provide not only an explanation for why people are doing what they are doing but also to provide a means of predicting future behavior. In this way, individuals may "test" their "models" in future interaction. Or, individuals may "forecast" future relationships by imagining what a relationship might be like with someone else ("Nah, he'd be too into power for me . . . we'd always be fighting . . . better not go out with this guy he's "too cool" . . . all the "red flags" are going up). People may choose relationships where they perceive their goals, plans, beliefs, and resources will be compatible with their partner's, or where their goals may be facilitated by the partner.

Furthermore, individuals may plan their own behavior and simulate how their actions or interactions with others may turn out. In so doing they may ask themselves, "If I did that how might it be construed?" or "Would that really be me?", or they may reject plans that do not fit with goals or self-conceptions. What we suggest here is that coherence is important not only when people try to understand their own and others' behavior *after the fact,* but also when people *plan and enact* their behavior.

Understanding goals is central to a host of important phenomena in social and personality psychology from attributional processes to the actual planning and enactment of behavior. Thus, as personologists, understanding the connections between peoples' goals, plans, and actions is critical to understanding how "the system coheres" (Allport, 1937).

Let us now consider how the "social-intelligence" approach and more specifically the notion of "intentional consistency" addresses the broader issue of "coherence," and the implications of this approach for personality. As mentioned earlier, the notion of "intentional consistency" in which perceptions, intentions, and actions are linked would seem critical to understanding how behavior coheres. And, the knowledge structures needed to make the complex inferences that could connect acts together could easily be provided within the Cantor and Kihlstrom framework. Further, although mental representations of the connections between goals, perceptions, and actions could be uncovered in a variety of ways (see Read, 1987), we find Cantor and Kihlstrom's (this volume) focus on a specific "life task" (within which to examine the connections among the "life goal," strategies, and actions) an interesting possibility.

There are, however, several potential problems with the methodologies employed in studying life tasks that might make it more difficult for us to find coherences *across situations.* First, the typical methodological approach to studying "life tasks" involves finding a common task or goal in a particular environment for a group of people. Thus, individual differences in construals of the task and strategies employed are emphasized while seemingly holding goals constant. Whereas strategies are a very important structure for understanding sequences of actions, strategies (except their stylistic facets) are likely to be specific to particular goal configurations activated by persons in particular situations. Strategies are relatively unlikely to be cross-situational in their application. And, if individuals use different strategies in different situations (which seems likely), what structures *might* allow us to understand how these different strategies "cohere"? Goals are one possibility. However, if individual differences in goals (as units of analysis) are central to constructing coherent models of interactions and persons, then methodological approaches that hold goals constant would be problematic.

Although individual differences in personal goals are not being emphasized presently in the life-task methodology, there is no apparent methodological reason why individual differences in goals (e.g., avoiding rejection, avoiding failure, wanting to impress others, wanting respect, seeking knowledge, etc.) could not be extensively examined within life tasks and potentially related to patterns of goals in other life tasks. For example, in recent work concerned with sexual scripts in close relationships, different personal goals (e.g., avoiding rejection, impressing others, physical intimacy) were related to very different perceived obstacles to using "safer sex" (Miller & Bettencourt, 1988). Just as inferences about sequences of actions are apt to involve inferences about the goals of persons, personal goals offer a potential key (along with other possible structures) to examining how behavior seems to "fit" or be "out of character" in models of persons over time and across situations.

For personality, Cantor and Kihlstrom's notions of "intentional consistency" and "life tasks" provide exciting and useful concepts. Both seem to "fit" well with an interactional approach to personality (Magnusson & Endler, 1977) in which we attempt to understand the "mediating system's way of selecting, interpreting, and treating information as a basis for coherent behavior across situations" (p. 17). But, we would argue that as we (as personologists) continue in our mutual "life task" of understanding personality we consider whether our units of analysis are flexible enough to allow us to (1) analyze everyday social interaction, and (2) find coherence in behavior across situations as well as within them.

REFERENCES

Allport, G. W. (1929). The study of personality by the intuitive method. *Journal of Abnormal and Social Psychology, 24,* 14–27.

Allport, G. W. (1937). *Personality: A psychological interpretation.* New York: Henry Holt.

Allston, W. P. (1975). Traits, consistency and conceptual alternatives for personality theory. *Journal for the Theory of Social Behavior, 5,* 17–48.

Argyle, M. (1981). The experimental study of the basic features of situations. In D. Magnusson (Ed.), *Towards a psychology of situations: An interactional perspective.* Hillsdale, NJ: Lawrence Erlbaum Associates.

Argyle, M., Furnham, A., & Graham, J. A. (1981). *Social situations.* Cambridge, England: Cambridge University Press.

Epstein, S., & O'Brien, E. J. (1985). The person–situation debate in historical and current perspective. *Psychological Bulletin, 98,* 513–537.

Epstein, S., & Terapulsky, L. (1986). Perception of cross-situational consistency. *Journal of Personality and Social Psychology, 50,* 1152–1160.

Magnusson, D., & Endler, N. S. (1977). Interactional psychology: Present status and future prospects. In D. Magnusson & N. S. Endler (Eds.), *Personality at the crossroads* (pp. 3–31). Hillsdale, NJ: Lawrence Erlbaum Associates.

Markus, H., & Nurius, P. (1986). Possible selves. *American Psychologist, 41,* 954–969.

Miller, L. C., & Bettencourt, B. A. (1988). *Goals and traits: Predictors of different obstacles to negotiating safer sex.* Unpublished data. Scripps College, Claremont, CA.

Miller, L. C., & Jones, D. K. (1988). *I wonder if they would hit it off? Contemplating possible relationships.* Unpublished data. Scripps College, Claremont, CA.

Miller, L. C., Jones, D. K., & Hoffman, V. (1988). *Traits as goal-based structures.* Unpublished data. Scripps College, Claremont, CA.

Miller, L. C., & Read, S. J. (in press). Inter-personalism: Understanding persons in relationships. In W. H. Jones & D. Perlman (Eds.), *Perspectives in interpersonal behavior and relationships* (Vol. 2). Greenwich, CT: JAI Press.

Mischel, W. (1973). Toward a cognitive social learning reconceptualization of personality. *Psychological Review, 80,* 252–283.

Mischel, W. (1977). On the future of personality measurement. *American Psychologist, 32,* 246–254.

Mischel, W. (1984). Convergences and challenges in the search for consistency. *American Psychologist, 39,* 351–364.

Mischel, W., & Peake, P. K. (1982). Beyond deja vu in the search for cross-situational consistency. *Psychological Review, 89,* 730–755.

Murray, H. (1938). *Explorations in personality.* New York: Oxford University Press.

Pervin, L. A. (1983). The stasis and flow of behavior: Toward a theory of goals. In M. M. Page (Ed.), *Nebraska Symposium on Motivation 1982* (pp. 1–53). Lincoln: University of Nebraska Press.

Read, S. J. (1987). Constructing causal scenarios: A knowledge structure approach to causal reasoning. *Journal of Personality and Social Psychology, 52,* 288–302.

Read, S. J., & Marcus, A. (1988). *Metarules in the construction of causal explanations.* Unpublished manuscript, University of Southern California, Los Angeles.

Read, S. J., & Miller, L. C. (in press). Inter-personalism: Towards a goal-based theory of persons in relationships. In L. A. Pervin (Ed.), *Goal concepts in personality and social psychology.* Hillsdale, NJ: Lawrence Erlbaum Associates.

Werner, P. D., & Pervin, L. A. (1986). The content of personality inventory items. *Journal of Personality and Social Psychology, 51,* 622–628.

Wilensky, R. (1983). *Planning and understanding: A computational approach to human reasoning.* Reading, MA: Addison-Wesley.

Wright, J. C., & Mischel, W. (1987). A conditional approach to dispositional constructs: The local predictability of social behavior. *Journal of Personality and Social Psychology, 53,* 1159–1177.

11 The Fate of the Trait: A Reply to Cantor and Kihlstrom

Robert J. Sternberg
Yale University

Richard K. Wagner
Florida State University

Hold the casket! Trait theories are not ready to be buried quite yet. Sure, the patient is ill, but we would like to suggest that euthanasia is premature. Let's try one more medication before knocking the patient off. There may still be something worth saving.

We agree with Cantor and Kihlstrom that trait theories of personality and social intelligence have not fared well, and that one can go quite far without them. Cantor and Kihlstrom, among others, have shown how far one can go. Nevertheless, we believe that social intelligence and related skills can be understood through the analysis of individual differences, if one takes into account the importance of person–situation interactions and recognizes, moreover, that some traits are likely to be idiographic rather than nomothetic.

In our reply, we discuss our research and that of our collaborators that shows, we believe, that with more sophisticated theoretical and methodological tools than have been commonly used in trait studies of social intelligence and styles of cognition it is possible to go somewhat further with an approach that is at least partially trait based than Cantor and Kihlstrom believe.

We discuss three interrelated programs of theory and research that show that the concept of stable individual-difference dimensions of social intelligence and styles is not yet ready for execution, euthanasia, or even a permanent rest cure. First, we discuss our work on practical intelligence and tacit knowledge, then our work on intellectual styles, and finally, we discuss a program of research on consistencies in styles of conflict resolution.

PRACTICAL INTELLIGENCE AND TACIT KNOWLEDGE

How do you communicate your ideas effectively so that you can sell others on them? How do you learn what the values of your institution are, and which ones to adopt for yourself? How do you decide when to accept an invitation to speak somewhere or decide instead that the engagement just isn't worth the time? For the past several years, we have been pursuing a program of research on a kind of intelligence of which we view social intelligence to be a subset, namely, practical intelligence. Our particular angle in this research has been to understand the role of an aspect of practical intelligence in real-world functioning, namely, tacit knowledge. By tacit knowledge, we refer to that body of knowledge one needs to know in a particular area of endeavor, such as a job, that is not explicitly taught and that often is never even verbalized. For example, no one ever explicitly teaches most of us how to communicate our ideas in a way that will sell them, nor does anyone explicitly teach us either the values of our institution or when to accept a speaking engagement, and when not to.

Our research has been motivated by Sternberg's (1985) triarchic theory of human intelligence, according to which intelligence comprises purposive adaptation to, selection of, and shaping of environments. Our particular concern in our program of research has been primarily with adaptation—figuring out the norms of a system and then implementing them in a self-conscious and sometimes selective way.

In our initial research (Wagner & Sternberg, 1985), we distinguished among three basic kinds of tacit knowledge: managing self, managing others, and managing one's career. All three of these would seem relevant to the concept of social intelligence discussed by Cantor and Kihlstrom.

Managing self refers to knowledge about how to to handle oneself on a daily basis to maximize one's productivity and at the same time maintain a healthy level of morale. Managing others refers to knowledge about how to handle superiors, subordinates, and peers. Managing career refers to knowledge about how to do the things that will advance one's career, and how not to do the things that will derail it. In our subsequent work, we have replaced the "managing career" category with one of managing tasks, to make the framework more general. We have also distinguished between tacit knowledge with global implications versus tacit knowledge with local implications. The former refers to that knowledge that will have long-run effects, whereas the latter refers to that knowledge whose effects will be more short term. Obviously, global and local tacit knowledge are best thought of as on a continuum rather than as two fully discrete categories.

How does one go about finding out the tacit knowledge people need to know? We decided that, for however domain general the ability to acquire tacit knowledge might be, the tacit knowledge itself was likely to be at least partially domain

176

specific. So we decided to learn about the tacit knowledge of two fields, one of particular interest to us, and the other of particular interest to a very broad spectrum of people. The first field was academic psychology, the second, business management. We interviewed individuals who had been nominated as very practically intelligent in these two fields and sought to learn for ourselves the tacit knowledge that partially underlay their success.

Our interviewees agreed on at least three things. The first was that IQ is not very important to on-the-job intelligence, for however important it may be to school success. This observation was consistent with both the triarchic theory and the literature on the prediction of job success from psychometric intelligence test scores. The correlation is typically at the level of about .2 (Wigdor & Garner, 1982). This low correlation should scarcely be surprising. For one thing, the tasks required on the job generally don't have much to do with people's ability to continue number series or to mentally manipulate geometric forms, except for specific occupations, say, mathematician in the first case or air-traffic controller in the second. For another thing, there is already a substantial restriction of range in the IQ test scores of people in most occupations. Indeed, for higher level occupations, the practitioners of these occupations could not even have been admitted to advanced training unless they did fairly well on the tests.

The second thing our interviewees agreed on was that what they had learned in advanced training wasn't particularly relevant to practical intelligence on the job. This intuition also seemed about right to us. Indeed, when one of us was in graduate school, he was told that the wave of the future was semantic memory, a field that now has gone to that great beyond where some people would like to put trait theories. But we believed that there was a different kind of value to advanced training, role modeling, that had nothing to do with formal knowledge taught in courses, and that brings us to the third point our interviewees made, the point of consensus.

This third point was that one thing that did make a substantial difference is what we have referred to as tacit knowledge. Generally, such knowledge is not taught formally in courses, although such courses exist, and one of us is teaching such a course to graduate students during the present academic semester.

Armed with these results, we devised tacit-knowledge tests for academic psychology and business management. What does such a test look like? Consider one question from the academic-psychology inventory:

It is your second year as an assistant professor in a prestigious psychology department. This past year you published two unrelated empirical articles in established journals. You don't believe, however, that there is a research area that can be identified as your own. You believe yourself to be about as productive as others. The feedback about your first year of teaching has been generally good. You have yet to serve on a university committee. There is one graduate student who has chosen to work with you. You have no external source of funding, nor have you applied for funding. Your goals are to become one of the top people in your field and to get tenure in your department. The following is a list of things you are considering doing in the next two months. You obviously cannot do them all. Rate the importance of each by its priority as a means of reaching your goals.

a. improve the quality of your teaching

b. write a grant proposal

c. begin long-term research that may lead to a major theoretical article

d. concentrate on recruiting more students

e. serve on a committee studying university-community relations

f. begin several related short-term research projects, each of which may lead to an empirical article

. . .

o. volunteer to be chairperson of the undergraduate curriculum committee

This question assessed management of self. The question also illustrates what we believe is an important theoretical point, namely, that the thinking skills of social intelligence are not qualitatively different in nature from those of academic intelligence. Rather, they are the same skills but applied to different information in a different domain in which the information may be stored and represented differently from that in a more academic domain. Thus, this problem is one about allocation of resources, a "metacomponent," or executive process in the triarchic theory of intelligence (Sternberg, 1985), one that needs to be applied in academic as well as social and other kinds of practical settings.

We administered our academic psychology inventory to more advanced and less advanced professors, graduate students, and undergraduates. Similarly, we administered the business management inventory to upper and lower level executives, business graduate students, and undergraduates. Our main findings were, we believe, of some interest.

First, on the average, tacit knowledge increases with amount of experience in a given field. However, it does not always increase. Some people who are quite advanced in a given field have relatively little tacit knowledge, whereas some beginners have surprisingly sophisticated tacit knowledge. These results indicate that what matters is not so much how much experience one has, but how much one has learned from it. In particular, what matters, we believe, is a person's ability to apply three processes of knowledge acquisition to his or her on-the-job experience: selective encoding, or deciding what new information is relevant for one's purposes; selective combination, or deciding how to combine that new information in a coherent and useful way; and selective comparison, or seeing the relation between new information and information one has already learned in the past.

Our second finding was that scores on our tacit-knowledge inventories were uncorrelated with scores on a conventional test of verbal intelligence. In other words, as specified by the triarchic theory and as observed by our interviewees, practical intelligence as manifested in tacit knowledge really does appear to be a different thing from the more academic kinds of intelligence measured by conventional tests.

A third finding was that scores on the tacit-knowledge inventories predicted real-world criteria of success about twice as well as do conventional intelligence tests. Our correlations were at about the .4, rather than the .2 level. The kinds of criteria we used were things like productivity, citation rate, and rating of institution, for the academic psychologists; and merit raises, number of people supervised, and whether or not the company of the examinee was in the Fortune 500, for the business executives. Obviously, none of these criteria is foolproof. Moreover, we agree with Cantor and Kihlstrom about the importance of assessing people's performance in terms of their own goals, whatever these goals may be. In future research, we hope to attain criterion measures that reflect our subjects' own idiographic value systems. In the meantime, though, we believe that our correlational results suggest at least some efficacy for our tacit-knowledge measures.

One concern that one might have is that our tests of tacit knowledge were not measures of practical or social intelligence, but rather of practical or social sellout. Such an explanation might account for why the tests predict job performance well: To do well on the tests, one has to sell out; to do well on the job, one has to sell out; and selling out predicts itself.

Wagner (1987) investigated this possible interpretation by having a group of subjects fill out the tacit-knowledge inventories not for how one should respond to do well in one's actual job, but in an ideal job. In other words, the subjects were instructed to respond as though they were answering for an ideal job as either an academic psychologist or business manager. If tacit knowledge is simply a measure of how far a person has gone in selling out, then this new set of results should be unpredictive of job success, because one is no longer answering for the actual job, but rather for the ideal one. In fact, the predictive power of the test was at least as good under these conditions as under the standard ones.

Another concern might be that the testing procedure is wholly domain specific. Cantor and Kihlstrom are sympathetic to the notion of domain specificity, but if the domain-specific view is carried to its limit, then it loses interest. One might need different inventories not only for each job, but for each level within a job, for each institution in which one might hold a job, and so on. So Wagner had undergraduates fill out both the academic psychology and business management inventories to assess whether there was, in fact, any generality—any trait-like ability to acquire and use tacit knowledge in more than one domain. The two scores were correlated at about the .6 level. In other words, there does appear to be some generality. At least some of the tacit knowledge in one field should carry over to another, and hence people who have more tacit knowledge in one field should be able to generalize at least some of it to another field.

Another concern one might have is whether it is possible actually to specify the tacit knowledge of a given field in any usable form. It is obviously a long distance from studying tacit knowledge to learning what it is. To address this issue, we have recently adopted what we refer to as a "rules-of-thumb" approach. In this approach, we specify tacit knowledge in terms of rules of thumb that are useful to know to perform well in a given field. We have already applied this approach empirically to studies of salespersons, where rules of thumb are quite important (Wagner, Rashotte, & Sternberg, 1988). We have found that more successful salespersons actually do know more rules of thumb and are better able to use them. Presently, we are extending this same approach to management, basing our rules of thumb on the triarchic theory. On this view, examples of rules of thumb would be to have a very good idea of what a problem is before trying to solve it, and making certain that the information one is using to solve a problem is actually relevant to the solution of that problem.

To conclude, we believe that the tacit-knowledge approach is a useful complement to the kind of approach taken by Cantor and Kihlstrom. The approach is theoretically grounded, practically useful in assessment, and susceptible to teaching through the instruction of students in the rules of thumb within a given domain of pursuit. But we have followed other lines of work as well that we believe are relevant to the kinds of problems Cantor and Kihlstrom have addressed.

INTELLECTUAL STYLES: THE THEORY OF MENTAL SELF-GOVERNMENT

Models in psychology have come from a variety of fields, such as biology, computer science, and physics. One potential source of models, although not a heavily used one, is government, or political science. In particular, one way to conceive of the mind is as a form of mental self-government. Theories of cognitive styles have generally been derived empirically, with no particularly underlying model. In contrast, we propose here a view of intellectual styles based on the notion of mental self-government (Sternberg, 1988). Whereas theories of intelligence deal with how much of various kinds of intelligence one has, a theory of intellectual styles deals with how one uses intelligence to interact effectively with the world.

Government has a number of aspects to it, several of which are function, form, level, direction, and leaning. We consider these aspects of government in describing a portion of the theory of mental self-government.

Among the functions of government, three stand out: the legislative, the executive, and the judiciary. The three branches of government provide a system of checks and balances for each other. Similarly, intelligence must legislate, execute, and judge. We believe that various people have different proclivities toward these three functions, although people are not wholly directed toward one or another of these styles but rather take into account their situation.

A person who is legislative in orientation likes to create his or her own rules, likes to do things his or her own way, prefers problems that are not prestructured or prefabricated, likes to build structure as well as content, and prefers activities that involve creating structure, such as writing papers, designing projects, and creating new business, educational, or other systems. Legislatively oriented people often go into occupations that enable them to make the most of their proclivity, such as creative writer, scientist, artist, sculptor, investment banker, policy maker, or architect.

A person with a leaning toward an executive style likes to follow rules, figure out which of existing ways to do things, and prefers problems that are prestructured or prefabricated. This individual likes to fill in content within an existing structure and prefers activities that enable him or her to do so, such as solving mathematics problems, applying rules to problems, giving talks or lessons based on others' ideas, or enforcing rules. The executive type will tend to gravitate toward occupations that allow the individual to exercise his or her proclivity, such as lawyer, policeman, engineer, builder (of others' designs), surgeon, soldier, or prosyletizer of others' systems.

A person with a judicial style likes to evaluate rules and procedures, as well as existing structures of any kind, and prefers problems in which one analyzes and evaluates existing things and ideas. This person prefers activities such as writing critiques, giving opinions on things, judging people and their work, and evaluating programs. The individual will seek a line of work consistent with the judicial proclivity, such as judge, critic, program evaluator, admissions officer, grant or contract monitor, systems analyst, or consultant.

Governments also differ in form. These forms correspond to different proclivities for engaging the intellect.

A person with a preference for a monarchic style will tend to be motivated by a single goal or need at a time, be singleminded and driven, believe that ends justify means and be likely to want to go full-speed ahead, damn the obstacles. This individual is likely to be an oversimplifier, and to be relatively unself-aware and intolerant. The individual is also likely to be relatively inflexible and to have little sense of priorities. He or she is, if anything, too decisive and systematic in seeking to achieve an overarching goal.

The hierarchical stylist is someone whose thoughts and actions tend to be motivated by a hierarchy of goals, with the recognition that not all goals can be fulfilled equally well and that some are more important than others. This person takes a balanced approach to problems and is less likely than the monarchist to believe that ends justify means. Competing goals are viewed as acceptable, and often the person is a complexifier, seeking to assign priorities to things that may not lend themselves to such assignments. The person tends to be self-aware, tolerant, and flexible, and to have a sense of priorities, which may or not be a good one.

The oligarchic stylist is similar to the hierarchical one, except that this person has trouble setting priorities. Competing goals are viewed as of equal importance, and this individual has trouble deciding what to do when. He or she is likely to be driven by goal conflict and tension, and to find that competing goals get in the way of task completion. The person is self-aware, tolerant, but often frustrated by his or her inability to set priorities.

The anarchic stylist is one whose thoughts and actions are motivated by a potpourri of needs and goals that are often difficult to sort out. This person seems to take a random approach to problems, and sometimes to be driven by a muddle of seemingly inexplicable forces. The person is likely to believe that ends justify means, and to be a simplifier. He or she is likely to be relatively unself-aware, and to be, if anything, too flexible because of difficulties in setting any kinds of priorities at all.

One can also distinguish between levels at which one prefers to attack problems. The global stylist is someone who prefers big issues, who ignores or eschews details, who is conceptualizer and is idea oriented, who likes to think abstractly, who can see the forest but sometimes not the trees, and who may have a tendency to get lost on Cloud 9. In contrast, the local stylist prefers details, deals well with these details, is oriented toward pragmatics, is relatively concrete and down-to-earth, and may lose the forest for the trees.

Government must also deal with both domestic matters and foreign affairs. Similarly, people must deal with intrapersonal and interpersonal matters, as recognized by Cantor and Kihlstrom in their discussion of how people manage both themselves and others. In the present context, some people are seen as having more of an internal style. They tend to be introverted, task oriented, socially less sensitive, interpersonally less aware, and preferring to work by themselves. In contrast, external stylists tend to be extraverted and people oriented. They like working with others and tend to be outgoing, socially sensitive, and interpersonally aware.

Finally, governments vary in their leaning, ranging from far right to far left. Similarly, people vary in this respect. We are not referring here to people's political beliefs, but rather to their style for using their intelligence. Some people like to adhere to existing rules and procedures, like to minimize change, prefer familiarity in life and work, and avoid ambiguous situations where possible. These conservative stylists differ from more progressive ones, who like to go beyond existing rules and procedures, like to maximize change, prefer unfamiliarity in life and work, and seek ambiguous situations.

Again, we wish to make clear that the theory of mental self-government does not state that people are one thing or another. Rather, they have preferences and thus will seek to use certain styles more often than others. The styles are crossed with each other, although we expect that there would be correlations among them; for example, legislative types would be more likely to be progressive than executive types.

At present, the theory is just a theory (Sternberg, in press): It has not yet been tested. However, we are currently collecting data to test the theory, and to compare it with other theories of cognitive styles. Subjects have been given questionnaires that ask them preferences for various activities across a wide variety of domains. However, within a given item, preferences are tested within domain. Thus, a given question might ask subjects whether they would prefer formulating an advertising campaign, implementing it, or evaluating it. Because the data are only now being collected, we are not yet able to report on them. Nevertheless, we believe that the mental self-government approach is one that is based on the notion that people do have traits (in this case, styles), but that these traits are flexible in their manifestation with respect to different kinds of situations. People are not bound but rather guided by their styles. But styles can be not only intellectual, but in other domains, such as in the domain of conflict resolution.

STYLES OF CONFLICT RESOLUTION

An important manifestation of social intelligence is in conflict resolution. Nowhere has this been more apparent than at one of the authors' host institutions, where a series of crippling strikes has resulted from the inability of the administration and unions to negotiate in what to anyone on the outside would appear to be a socially intelligent way. One possibility, of course, is that people are totally flexible with regard to styles of conflict resolution and resolve each conflict on its merits, without resort to any preferred style that they use even when it is not fully appropriate. But our observations of the world are certainly not in congruence with this belief: Rather, people seem to have preferred styles of conflict resolution, which they are likely to use whether they are appropriate or not. These styles might even be viewed as trait-like, although we believe that these styles, like intellectual styles, or intelligence, for that matter, are modifiable to some extent.

We have been involved in two sets of studies of styles of conflict resolution that have yielded results consistent with the notion that people have preferred styles of conflict resolution that they exhibit across situations.

In the first set of studies (Sternberg & Soriano, 1984), subjects each received a written text describing nine conflict–resolution situations. Three of the conflicts were interpersonal, three were interorganizational, and three were international. The conflicts were each described in some detail and had been rated in advance so that each party to the conflict would be viewed as having roughly equal merit in terms of the claims being made. Following each conflict were seven possible resolutions of the conflict. Subjects were asked to rate the goodness of each of the resolutions. Each of the resolutions for each of conflicts was, in fact, an exemplar of one of seven general styles:

1. physical action, in which the target party attempts to get its way through physical force or coercion directed at the other party;
2. economic action, in which the target party attempts to get its way through economic pressure directed at the other party;
3. wait and see, in which the target party decides to wait things out and see if the situation improves;
4. accept the situation, in which the target party decides to accept the situation as it is and make the best of it;
5. step-down, in which the target party attempts to defuse the conflict by reducing or negating its demands on the other party;
6. third-party intervention, in which the target party seeks some outside third party to mediate the conflict;
7. undermine esteem, in which the target party seeks to undermine the esteem in which the opposing party is held by other parties outside the conflict situation.

The result of signal importance in the present context is that not only were there widespread individual differences in preferred styles of conflict resolution, but these styles were highly correlated both within domain (e.g., interpersonal or interorganizational) and across domains. In other words, people did show consistency in their preferred styles of conflict resolution. People who preferred conflict-exacerbating styles generally did poorer on psychometric intelligence tests than did people who preferred conflict-mitigating strategies.

One might argue, of course, that people's consistency in what are basically hypothetical, experimenter-generated scenarios would have little to do with how they would handle either real-world conflicts, or conflicts that they themselves have experienced. Sternberg and Dobson (1987) sought to test this view. They had subjects generate their own conflicts and had the subjects evaluate a broader array of styles of conflict resolution than that previously described both for their own conflicts and for those of others. All the conflicts to be evaluated were real rather than hypothetical. The results came out as in the earlier set of studies: People showed styles of conflict resolution that were consistent across domains.

To conclude, the evidence from the two sets of studies on styles of conflict resolution suggests that although people do exhibit some flexibility in their styles of conflict resolution, they nevertheless have preferred styles that they seek to apply across different kinds of situations. Thus, one needs to take into consideration both situations and people's stylistic preferences.

CONCLUSION

We were very impressed by Cantor and Kihlstrom's analysis of social intelligence, and, indeed, we found little to quibble with. At the same time, we believe that Cantor and Kihlstrom are prematurely dismissive of the notion of traits. On the one hand, we agree that trait-based approaches have not always been fruitful, in part because they were too rigid, lacking in theoretical basis, and not sufficiently cognizant with respect to the importance of situations. But we believe that approaches to social intelligence can be worked out that take into account both the importance of situations and the importance of natural individual differences in persons, as well as the interaction between the two.

REFERENCES

Sternberg, R. J. (1985). *Beyond IQ: A triarchic theory of human intelligence.* New York: Cambridge University Press.

Sternberg, R. J. (1988). Mental self-government: A theory of intellectual styles and their development. *Human Development.*

Sternberg, R. J., & Dobson, D. M. (1987). Resolving interpersonal conflicts: An analysis of stylistic consistency. *Journal of Personality and Social Psychology, 52,* 794–812.

Sternberg, R. J., & Soriano, L. J. (1984). Styles of conflict resolution. *Journal of Personality and Social Psychology, 47,* 115–126.

Wagner, R. K. (1987). Tacit knowledge in everyday intelligent behavior. *Journal of Personality and Social Psychology, 52,* 1236–1247.

Wagner, R. K., Rashotte, C. A., & Sternberg, R. J. (1988). *Tacit knowledge in sales: Rules of thumb for selling anything to anyone.* Manuscript submitted for publication.

Wagner, R. K., & Sternberg, R. J. (1985). Practical intelligence in real-world pursuits: The role of tacit knowledge. *Journal of Personality and Social Psychology, 49,* 436–458.

Wigdor, A. K., & Garner, W. R. (Eds.) (1982). *Ability testing: Uses, consequences, and controversies.* Washington, DC: National Academy Press.

12 Social Intelligence and Adaptation to Life Changes

Abigail J. Stewart
University of Michigan

There is a beautiful irony in Cantor and Kihlstrom's (this volume) choice of life transitions as a natural laboratory for studying social intelligence as the "cognitive basis of personality" (p. 1). The irony is that it is in the course of life transitions that people experience themselves as most "socially stupid." Nevertheless, Cantor and Kihlstrom's choice is a sound one, resulting not only in the undoubted gains they point to themselves, for our understanding of social intelligence, but also in gains for our understanding of the consequences of life changes. It is to this latter issue—the implications of a social-intelligence approach for our understanding of life changes—that I address my comments.

TRANSITIONS AS CONTEXTS FOR STUDYING PERSONALITY

Cantor and Kihlstrom suggest that "Periods of life transition provide a nice real-world analogue to a laboratory task that balances familiarity and novelty of demands" (p. 12). This is clearly true from the perspective of an outside observer (thus, a first-year college student is confronted with many familiar interaction situations with peers and teachers, as well as many new ones). It is probably also true if one averaged the subjective experience of many different individuals in a given life transition (thus, for example, some college students see college as similar to previous experiences they have had, like camp, or trips to Europe, whereas others experience it as entirely new). Moreover, it is sometimes true if one averages an individual's views over time. For example, one college student reported that at the beginning "I just kinda sat around thinking a lot. I was pretty

worried about what was gonna happen to me, whether I would get along generally, whether I'd be able to make friends, whether I'd do well in school, whether
I'd–the whole thing. It was a big place, new city. I'd never been there . . . and
the whole new atmosphere, just getting used to it." (quoted in Stewart & Healy,
1985, p. 124). That same student said that a little later "I was a little surprised at
how easy it was" (p. 125). (It is perhaps worth noting that this student was
clearly preoccupied with precisely the two "life tasks" Cantor and her colleagues have identified as the central concerns of the college students they
studied: social and academic competence.)

Nevertheless, it may be important to differentiate among various experiences
of life transition, both within and across individuals. Thus, for example, the
adaptive challenge being faced by a student who finds college a radically "new"
and unfamiliar environment (not one balanced in novelty and familiarity) may be
crucially different from that faced by a student who finds it relatively similar to,
say, prep school, even if both of them view the central tasks as falling into the
same broad categories. Similarly, the white, middle-class student faced with a
new but broadly supportive college environment faces a different challenge than
the black, middle-, or working-class student in the "same" college. There may
be very different pressures operating to facilitate and constrain the acquisition
and use of both declarative and procedural social knowledge for these different
students (see Fleming, 1984). Thus although life transitions do have normative,
or consensual, definitions, they also have many private or individual meanings,
which may, in turn, be important factors in the individual's definition of, and
success at accomplishing, life tasks within the transitional situation.

Even within individuals, timing may be important in systematic and predictable ways; it may affect not so much the content of a life task, but the strategies
used to accomplish it, and the specific goals adopted within a relatively narrow
time-frame. In research carried out with a number of colleagues over a number of
years, I have explored a sequence of psychological stances toward the external
environment that seem to be adopted in the course of adaptation to changed
circumstances (see Stewart, 1982; Stewart & Healy, 1985; Stewart, Sokol,
Healy, & Chester, 1986; Stewart et al., 1982). These psychological stances are
quite diffuse, including an affective tone, an orientation toward other people,
toward authority figures and peers, as well as a posture toward personal action.
They are, however, entirely *internal* and do not have direct or simple behavioral
consequences. Thus, an individual who has adopted a "passive" stance toward
personal action may nevertheless *behave* in a vigorous and forceful way; the
internal stance is informative about how the person feels and may affect the way
in which an action is carried out, but it is not—especially in adults—itself
predictive of particular behaviors. Some early research, and especially recent
research by Healy (1985, 1988), has suggested that these psychological stances
do, however, have more direct consequences for cognitive performance. Integration of Cantor and Kihlstrom's perspective and the developing work on the

cognitive consequences of the psychological stances we have been studying seems a promising avenue for enriching both research programs, and filling out our understanding of the psychology of change.

THE SEQUENCE OF PSYCHOLOGICAL STANCES IN THE COURSE OF ADAPTATION TO LIFE CHANGES

On the basis of a broad review of the crisis and role transition literatures, some broad consistencies in individuals' responses to a wide range of both sudden and anticipated life changes were identified (see Stewart, 1982). A number of accounts included an emphasis on the notion of adaptation to change, pointing at the same time to the stressful nature of transitions and individuals' eventual accommodation of them (see, e.g., Scott & Howard, 1970; Whitlock, 1978). Building on this broad base, we identified a series of psychological stances toward the environment that may define individual differences among people under stable conditions, but which are adopted more or less in turn (but not in any strictly sequenced way) after major changes in external circumstances (ranging from personal losses such as bereavement, role transitions such as marriage, and travel).

In the first instance a person faced with changed circumstances—say, me on a trip to Europe—adopts a "Receptive" stance. I will feel, when I am in my new situation, as if I am in a familiar, but past, mode of operating—perhaps a mode I had, or thought I had, outgrown. I will be aware of feeling confused and bewildered, even a bit sad. I will feel helpless to take action, and eager to find others—peers or especially benevolent authority figures—to take care of me. I will feel more like a confused child than I usually do—I will feel "socially stupid." Despite this fact, I will collect my luggage, change currency, find a taxi, and check in at a hotel; I will appear to be a reasonably good approximation of a competent adult to an outside observer. Moreover, I will feel grateful and pleased about the attention and assistance I am given and will be both interested in and positively disposed to whatever I learn about my new situation.

Assuming that all goes as hypothesized, over time I will adopt a more "Autonomous" stance. I will at this time begin to experience the external environment as frustrating; I notice that both peers and authority figures are not in fact meeting my needs. My affective state will be apprehensive and indecisive, but I will begin to experience some impulse to take limited actions to straighten out problematic situations. I will have, then, an increased sense of the need for me to exercise some agency, at the same time that I have an increased sense of the external environment as inadequate. This stance is the "Terrible Twos" of adaptation to change. For the traveler it is the time when a culture seems strangely comfortless, different, and inadequate.

Over time the negativism and anxiety of the Autonomous stance gives way to a more confident, and more hostile, Assertive one. I feel angry, rebel against the stupid corruption of authorities, and feel superior to less active peers. I am inclined to take risks and to be concerned only about making errors of judgment that might lead to failure. The traveler who has adopted this stance feels hostile to, and belligerent about, the obviously incompetent and ignorant people being encountered in an environment to be challenged and mastered—Pollyanna becomes the Ugly American.

Ideally, this stance too will pass, and an Integrated stance is adopted. The monolithic emotions of the previous stances give way to complexity and ambivalence; authorities are seen as limited in their powers, other people are viewed as fully individual partners in mutual relationships, and emotionally involving work is experienced as a possible form of action. Travelers adopting this stance are for the first time able to pay less attention both to the environment and to their own needs and begin to be able to "get some work done" and form genuine relationships. The environment is experienced, then, as relatively neutral (neither overwhelming nor oppressive), and the individual is a locus of competent action, but not domination.

Empirical Evidence for the Sequence of Stances

First using an empirically derived scoring system for coding TAT stories (Stewart, 1982) and later using a modified scoring system to code personal documents (Stewart, 1986; Stewart & Healy, 1984), psychotherapy transcripts (Sokol, 1983), and interview responses (Stewart, 1987), my colleagues and I have accumulated considerable evidence in support of the hypothesized sequence of stances in the context of children's school changes and parents' divorce, adolescents' transitions to high school and college, and adults' marriage and parenthood transitions, and experiences following divorce and bereavement, as well as in the course of psychotherapy.

In general, results support the notion both that in the immediate postchange period adults and children adopt the Receptive stance, and that over time that stance gives way to the other stances. Case analyses (Stewart, 1986; Stewart & Healy, 1984) have suggested that the sequence of stances is often as hypothesized. However, most of our larger studies have involved only two points in time (bereavement and psychotherapy are exceptions); therefore, it has not been possible to explore the degree to which adoption of each stance in turn characterizes most individuals' experience. We have observed a small average tendency for women to adopt the Autonomous rather than the Assertive stance (which may be less sex-role normative for women), and for men to do the reverse (Stewart & Healy, 1985; Stewart et al., 1986). After a relatively long period within any particular situation, most children and adults seem to adopt those two stances, or some mixture of them, as a relatively stable orientation to the environment.

It does seem, then, that life changes do precipitate an emotional reorientation and a sequence of psychological adaptation. The early reorientation seems to involve a high degree of focus on the environment and a relative suppression of the individual's agency. Over time, the focus shifts, moving through a period of high focus on individual agency, to a point when the individual and the environment may be seen as in some kind of equilibrium. If this sequence is genuinely one aspect of an adaptive process, there may be some value to the heightened salience of the environment, and reduced emphasis on individual action in the early postchange period. Similarly, there may be some value in the gradual and eventually exaggerated agency that follows, though ultimately it should be most useful for individuals to achieve the kind of neutral relationship with the environment that characterizes the Integrated stance. Some of our research and theoretical efforts have explored the adaptive significance of the particular stances and of the sequence as a whole.

The Adaptive Value of the Sequence of Psychological Stances

One possibility we have explored is that adoption and retention of the Receptive stance during the immediate postchange period allows for cognitive processing of more information or more "data" and therefore facilitates cognitive development. We have also assumed that later postchange adaptation should facilitate successful integration of that information. Thus, over time, the adaptive sequence should lead both to acquisition of a solid base of information (primarily during the Receptive stance) and integration of that information (as a result of later stances). Analysis of changes in college students' capacity to structure information over time supported our argument that retention of the Receptive stance at the beginning of college facilitates cognitive growth by senior year (Stewart & Healy, 1985).

A second prediction deriving from our approach is that over time in a new situation individuals should be increasingly able to "decenter," or to take a less egocentric view of the external environment. We have seen evidence of this in terms of a detailed case history of the course of one individuals' adaptation (Stewart & Healy, 1984), as well as in the literature on changes in college students' "maps" of their physical environment (which are increasingly abstract and differentiated; Wapner, Kaplan, & Cohen, 1973).

A third aspect of adaptation we have considered is the consequence of repetition in the sequence. Individuals clearly differ in how many successful adaptations they have already made to new situations; moreover, adults differ, on average, from children in this regard. We have argued that experience with successful adaptation should generally facilitate relatively more rapid progress through the sequence. In addition, we have suggested that cognitive and personality differences between adults and children should have consequences for their respective adaptations. Thus, adults should have a stronger sense of their own agency in the course of life changes; more anticipation of the experience of adaptation, including more knowledge of themselves; and more capacity to self-monitor and compare responses to past experiences. These hypotheses have been explored in some life history data (Stewart & Healy, 1984, 1985).

In addition, Healy (1985, 1988) has argued that Receptivity should facilitate some cognitive processes (e.g., acquisition of information) but interfere with others (e.g., integrative structuring of information). In a comparison of divorcing parents and comparison parents not divorcing, he found that both being in a transition and adoption of the Receptive stance interfered with performance on integrative tasks but did not negatively affect all cognitive processes.

The research conducted or proposed to date has had as its inspiration a broadly cognitive developmental perspective, which assumes that cognitive (and perhaps diffuse cognitive and affective) disequilibrium is uncomfortable but motivates adaptive efforts and cognitive development. This perspective has been useful, but it is clear that the social-intelligence perspective is not necessarily inconsistent with it and can offer different—perhaps greater—specificity in the hypotheses and operationalizations.

A Social-Intelligence View of the Sequence of Stances

In Cantor and Kihlstrom's terms, we might think of the various stances as having implications for both declarative and procedural knowledge. Thus, the Receptive stance might be one that permits the acquisition of new declarative knowledge. A transition is a situation in which, by definition, one lacks some declarative knowledge one needs; this is in part what makes it an interesting situation for studying social intelligence. It may be, though, that successful acquisition of new declarative knowledge flows best from adoption and retention of the Receptive stance. That stance allows even competent adults to attend to the many details of their environment that have most often become "ground" to their activity; this attention is obviously a prerequisite to learning. At the same time, the opportunity to learn more about oneself by observing one's reactions to a new situation may increase self-consciousness. The lack of a broad base of data about themselves and about others in the same situation, combined with the hyper-vigilance toward the environment may actually reverse the usual attributional bias and result in a tendency to make more environmental (rather than self) attributions than are warranted. In addition, the novelty of the situation should increase the likelihood of an individual experiencing responses that are inconsistent with the previously developed "self-schema." This is, then, a time for a high degree of felt inconsistency in one's own behavior and responses, and a sense of one's identity as relatively plastic. During this time an individual's vision of the self in the future ("possible selves") should be equally formless. However, it may be that during this period individuals will experience new recall of past experiences as the self-schema weakens and provides a less powerful focus to autobiographical memory, and new experiences provide the potential occasion for new associations to lost memories.

Moreover, other peoples' judgments or opinions will be maximally important to an individual in the Receptive stance. Thus, new situations increase our vulnerability to conformity and other normative pressures. This vulnerability permits our learning of the norms operative in the new situation and should lead us to adopt as "life tasks" for ourselves the tasks most "demanded" or sanctioned in the situation. Finally, the preference for inactivity, and the wish to be cared for by others, should reduce the likelihood of dangerous or "stupid" mistakes and increase the likelihood of useful social bonds being created. It is clear, then, that adoption of the Receptive stance should facilitate some kinds of socially intelligent functioning and interfere with others.

Obviously, though, the Receptive stance wears thin over time. It may result in information overload, with relatively unassimilated, undigested facts about a situation combining with an increasingly unattractive and even potentially dangerous dependency on peers and authorities. Our learned and socially sanctioned aversion to dependency and the internal need to structure and organize information may be the motivations behind the shift toward greater autonomy and eventually toward assertion. These stances facilitate first activity, and then risk taking, certainly leading to acquisition of some additional declarative knowledge. More importantly, though, the felt need to take action should facilitate exercise (and potentially development) of certain cognitive "procedures" more inconsistent with the Receptive stance. Thus, these cognitive processes involving integration of information, and active operation on information, should be enhanced by autonomy and assertion. In addition, increasing focus on the self as a locus of action should facilitate increasing confidence (particularly in the Assertive stance) in the stable content and structure of self-knowledge, and decreased concern about others' views. At this time "life tasks" and "possible selves" should be extremely important vehicles of self-expression. Thus, they should be far less socially defined and should reflect more fully the increasingly differentiated and structured self-knowledge. More generally, the self-schema should operate with increased intensity in the context of these stances. In fact, this may be a time in which the stability and agency of the self is overvalued, and in which therefore more person attributions about one's own behavior are made than are warranted. In addition, autobiographical memory may become more stable or "canned," with few recovered memories and even loss of memories inconsistent with the powerful self-schema. Thus, both the relative enhancement of agency and the deficit in attention to the environment, and avoidance of more "passive" cognitive operations, may be consequential.

The final, integrated stance is the one that should permit the individual free access to declarative and procedural knowledge as it pertains to the situation. It is this stance, then, which might be thought of as maximizing "social intelligence" in the sense of the capacity for flexible, bias-free responses to a situation. In addition, the self-schema may be less "totalitarian" than in the preceding stance but still more potent and stable than in the Receptive stance. Some new and inconsistent autobiographical memories may be tolerated, along with knowledge of other kinds of inconsistent aspects of the self. Attention to and interest in the environment, other persons, and the self should attain some equilibrium or balance.

Overall, Cantor and Kihlstrom's notion of social intelligence is a powerful framework within which to think about the consequences of the psychological stances we have been studying. It permits articulation of a number of clear and interesting hypotheses about differential cognitive functioning in the course of adaptation to life changes. At the same time, it is clear that what we know about the sequence of stances may have some consequences for thinking about social intelligence.

Consequences of Stances for Thinking about Social Intelligence

If the hypotheses linking stances with aspects of social intelligence discussed previously are correct, it is clear that information about how people function in the context of life transitions is at once enormously interesting and extremely limited. According to the argument spelled out here, assessments of social intelligence obtained in the first phase of adaptation should tend to be systematically biased towards: knowledge of details, self-consciousness and egocentrism, a relatively weak self-schema, over-attribution of causality to the environment, recovery of new autobiographical memories, high valuation of social ties, and conformity to social norms and values. The later phases (often the final ones at least for the U.S. samples we have studied) should be equally biased towards hierarchical structuring of information, with attendant loss of detail, operation of a powerful and selective self-schema, intense engagement in purposive striving, over-attribution of causality to the self, exclusion or loss of inconsistent autobiographical memories, relatively low valuation of social ties, and low conformity to social norms.

To the extent that a given research program exploring some aspects of social intelligence depends on collection of data from individuals at a single point in the course of adaptation to a major life transition, these overall systematic biases may affect the findings. Two different studies, or the same project at different points in time, could be affected in opposite ways. Conversely, to the extent that a research program on social intelligence builds in attention to subjects' situation in terms of adaptation to change, it should be in a position to specify when certain effects (e.g., the tendency toward false consensus, which should be stronger in the Receptive stance when a less differentiated view of others is held, but when others' views are highly significant) will be stronger or weaker. Similarly, some specific predictions about some aspects of social intelligence (e.g., the relative power of the self-schema, the relative individuality of life tasks) may be derived from our understanding of the consequences of psychological stances.

Studying People in Transition: Gains and Losses

It is clear that there are many advantages to studying individuals undergoing role transitions or other major life changes. Their coping strategies are challenged, they are often newly open to growth and change, and their energy and attention are focused and directed. Precisely for these reasons, studying individuals in transition results in some costs. In fact, individuals do probably adopt some relatively stable, even rigid, strategies for coping, some of which are not optimally functional. Thus, by studying individuals in transition we will tend to overestimate individuals' capacity and average tendency to change, and to be variable (or inconsistent) in responses. In addition, some declarative and procedural knowledge may be wholly or largely irelevant in transitions, but relevant and valuable in stable conditions. Under conditions of transition, individuals are maximally influenced by their environment, and minimally "in control" of it; thus, research on people in early stages of transitions may systematically overestimate the power of the external environment and underestimate individuals' agency. The environment's influence may also be more diffuse or random (less the result of the individual's selective attention and value) than it otherwise is.

Finally, it may be that studying people in transition, but a bit further along, we run the risk of overestimating individual's purposive striving (e.g., pursuit of life tasks) or intentionality. It is in the course of transitions, according to the stance theory, that individuals will for awhile find themselves enormously interesting and salient. At this time, individuals will generate (and may attempt to implement) personal visions and plans, but these goals and purposes may be at least somewhat less important over time, as attention to the environment, the self, and other people assume some balanced, relatively stable relationship—at least until the next major life change!

REFERENCES

Fleming, J. (1984). *Blacks in college*. San Francisco: Jossey-Bass.
Healy, J. (1985). *Emotional adaptation to life transitions and cognitive performance*. Unpublished doctoral dissertation, Boston University.
Healy, J. (1988, March). *Emotional adaptation to life transitions: Implications for cognition*. Paper presented at a conference on Emerging Issues in Personality Psychology, Ann Arbor, Michigan.
Scott, R., & Howard, A. (1970). Models of stress. In S. Levine & N. A. Scotch (Eds.), *Social stress*. Chicago: Aldine.
Sokol, M. (1983). *A content analysis of psychotherapy: Measuring emotional perspectives*. Unpublished doctoral dissertation, Boston University.

Stewart, A. J. (1982), The course of individual adaptation to life changes. *Journal of Personality and Social Psychology, 42,*1100–1113.

Stewart, A. J. (1986, November). *Social change and individual change in women's lives.* Paper presented at a conference on Women's Development at Mount Holyoke College, South Hadley, Massachusetts.

Stewart, A. J. (1987). *The course of adaptation to bereavement.* Unpublished final report to Radcliffe College.

Stewart, A. J., & Healy, J. M., Jr. (1984). Processing affective responses to life experiences: The development of the adult self. In C. Malatesta & C. Izard (Eds.), *Emotion in adult development.* Beverly Hills, CA: Sage.

Stewart, A. J., & Healy, J. M., Jr. (1985). Personality and adaptation to change. In R. Hogan & W. Jones (Eds.), *Perspectives in personality* (Vol. 1, pp. 117–144). Greenwich, CT: JAI Press.

Stewart, A. J., Sokol, M., Healy, J. M., Jr., & Chester, N. L. (1986). Longitudinal studies of psychological consequences of life changes in children and adults. *Journal of Personality and Social Psychology, 50,* 143–151.

Stewart, A. J., Sokol, M., Healy, J. M., Jr., Chester, N. L., & Weinstock-Savoy, D. (1982). Adaptation to life change in children and adults: Cross-sectional studies. *Journal of Personality and Social Psychology, 43,* 1270–1281.

Wapner, S., Kaplan, B., & Cohen, S. B. (1973). An organismic-developmental perspective for understanding transactions of men and environments. *Environment and Behavior, 5,* 255–289.

Whitlock, G. E. (1978). *Understanding and coping with real-life crises.* Monterey, CA: Brooks-Cole.

13 Social Intelligence and Personality: There's Room for Growth

John F. Kihlstrom
University of Arizona

Nancy Cantor
University of Michigan

We thank our commentators for their thoughtful, constructive, and largely positive critiques of our work on social intelligence. We were particularly pleased to find that many of the responses were not really critiques at all, but more like responses in the spirit of our enterprise, that pick up on various issues and pursue them further than we have. To us, that means that the social-cognitive approach to personality is engaged in a healthy process of growth and development. But that is not to say that the commentators have not raised a number of important criticisms as well. In the space available to us we want to provide some sense of our own perspective on the new issues and attempt to clear up some misunderstandings.

INTELLIGENCE AND SOCIAL INTELLIGENCE

The term *social intelligence* was selected deliberately, but in the end it has caused us no end of trouble and misunderstanding. People naturally confuse our notion with the more familiar concept of "social IQ." This is a confusion that is not confined to academic psychology. Just as we were preparing our response to the commentaries, the *New York Times Magazine* (July 3, 1988) carried an installment of William Safire's syndicated column, "On Language," discussing the various meanings of the word *intelligence.* Safire distinguished between the common attributive meaning of the noun, as a modifier of words like *test* and *quotient,* and the more recent use, as described by H. E. Meyer in his recent book, *Real-World Intelligence:* "information that has not only been selected and collected, but also analyzed, evaluated, and distributed to meet the unique policy-making needs of one particular enterprise. . . In short, intelligence has become a management tool.''

That's how we use social intelligence: not so much as a thing that people *have* in varying quantities, like height or weight, or even the practical intelligence of Sternberg and Wagner, but rather an ever-evolving resource—a fund of information, and a set of operating procedures that people *use* (and disagree on) in managing their lives. Intelligence, as a rich and diverse fund or resource isn't a static or unidimensional entity; it is the essential ingredient of the active, creative, evolving side of personality. Just as the most interesting thing about self-esteem is not whether you have it or not, but how you use and maintain and enhance it (whatever *it* is); intelligence is a resource to be cultivated and we are all gardeners first and foremost—all engaged in making sense of ourselves and of our worlds.

Sternberg and Wagner seem to prefer an attributive concept of social intelligence when they discuss practical intelligence as a means of achieving success in some domain in life and propose that practical intelligence is a quantity that people possess in varying amounts, and which teachers can inculcate in students. But from our point of view, social intelligence is something everyone has—not just young PhDs or MBAs on-the-make. We don't dispute the value of their approach (though we doubt that our readers, as ostensibly successful academics, would agree on the answers to their test question–and we wonder how a person who isn't identified with a coherent program of research ever got hired by a prestigious department), but we think they are too sanguine about their results on consistency. Putting aside the question of whether correlations of 0.30 or 0.40 are modest or substantial (see also Baron), a correlation of 0.60 between practical intelligence tests for making-it-in-psychology and making-it-in-business won't make the case for consistency. From a logical point of view, the fact that people who know the ''correct'' answers in one domain also know the ''correct'' answers in the other does not mean that practical intelligence in one domain actually carries over into the other. To make that claim, one needs evidence that the same answers are correct in the two situations. But we don't really want to carp about the degree of consistency and predictability in behavior: Our approach considers them to be empirical questions rather than pretheoretical assumptions; and besides, Sternberg's theory of practical intelligence doesn't require them.

Specificity and Generality

As several of the commentators noted, we do, however, emphasize specificity over generality in the analysis of personality. We see a number of virtues in starting an analysis from the ''bottom-up''; though we certainly have nothing against finding generality. First, the specificity approach is consistent with the architecture of human cognition, and ours' is a cognitive theory of personality. Linville and Clark thoughtfully elucidate the fine-grained structure of declarative and procedural knowledge. Second, the problem-solving process that underlies what Bergen and Dweck aptly called the actualized side of personality starts with individuals' appraisals of particular problems or tasks in specific settings. Given this framework, it makes most sense to start with analyses of reactions to context-specific tasks, as one might start with a chess master's handling of certain prototypic game situations. Of course, it is frequently preferable to consider several situations at once in light of a common task that the person sees in them. This process of aggregation, however, must still be taken with care, and thus the delineation of equivalence classes of situations is a central part of the assessment technology of a cognitive approach (e.g., Cantor et al., 1987; Wright & Mischel, 1987). Those equivalence classes frequently change for groups of individuals over time, as one of us has seen in a longitudinal study of the transition to college life, and almost always there are important interindividual differences in the sets of specific situations that are seen as mapping onto a life task (see Cantor & Langston, 1988; Zirkel & Cantor, 1988). Nevertheless, principles of generalization, based on individuals' perceptions of similarity of *task* across situations, fit well with our approach.

In fact, the social-intelligence view is not embarrassed by findings of generality—as a learning theory it is built on principles of generalization such as those described by Linville and Clark. We simply do not want to assume generality without testing its empirical validity for individuals in their particular life contexts. Whereas findings of discriminativeness and *specificity* are often dismissed by others as bothersome noise or unreliability of measurement, evidence of *generalization* is not theoretically inconsistent with the social-intelligence perspective. In that respect, despite its acknowledged complexity and more than occasional vagueness, we see a social-intelligence theory as in principle more parsimonious than traditional trait-based alternatives.

We look for generality in personality in the schemata, tasks, and strategies that individuals repeatedly bring to bear in their different life situations. Several commentators point to ways in which these consistencies are built. As Stewart and Pervin note, the autobiographical record provides a flexible source of self-continuity, and self-schemata can "expand" to accommodate quite a diverse array of self-data. Likewise, as Read and Miller and Emmons and King emphasize, individuals often have a penchant for seeing their most salient tasks and concerns as relevant to a broad collection of life events and situations; people also then choose to be in those task-relevant situations as often as they can. (Smith & Rhodewalt, 1986, provide a beautiful illustration of this generalization process in their analysis of the "hostile" world view and stress-engendering strategy of Type A individuals.) Linville and Clark suggest that strategies can easily be (over)generalized, sometimes from "ignorance" (as when a general principle is used to handle a novel situation or a traumatic event), and at other times because of automatic reliance on strategic "expertise" (as when the novel features of a task are ignored in favor of a more familiar interpretation). In this vein, it seems critical to underscore, as they do, the extent to which this process of strategy generalization can sometimes be good for people—e.g., it helps when facing a crisis to operate by analogy to past events, even if only to bring oneself past the initial panic and immobilization. Whereas, at other times, individuals might be better off containing their impulse to rely on well-worn, familiar strategies, even when those strategies are quite effective in some situations. For example, effective use of defensive pessimism probably requires that a person makes fine distinctions between situations in terms of their anxiety-provoking properties, to identify those achievement contexts that simply are not worthy of exerting much preparatory effort (Cantor & Norem, 1988). Strategy generalization can lead to rigid, inflexible, or even self-destructive consistency; a consistency that is typical of much *mal*adaptive responding.

Social Intelligence and "Success"

Several of the commentators suggest that we have not made sufficient efforts to test and to apply the social-intelligence approach in clinical contexts. Carver and Scheier, for example, chide one of us for conducting research on "successful" students; whereas Pervin warns us that we may be overestimating flexibility in personality by ignoring clinical cases of resistance and unawareness. These critiques are very well taken and appropriate. A theory has to start somewhere, and we chose to start with the adaptive behavior of undisturbed, mature individuals. Although we agree that it is incumbent on theories of personality to address clinical material eventually, we don't see any principled reason to *start* with psychopathology. Some theories of personality, such as Freud's and Eysenck's, have made good use of clinical material, but in so doing they too have risked some generalizability. To take an example: even if Freud's insights into Dora, Schreber, and their confreres were accurate, that doesn't necessarily have anything to do with the rest of us. From our point of view clinical cases are *special* cases, and special cases—almost by definition—are going to be unrepresentative of the norm. In particular we suspected that analyses of clinical cases might miss some important features of social behavior. A chief feature of the interpersonal behavior of many individuals is that it can be flexible and optional rather than rigid and obligatory. The social-intelligence view, like its counterparts in the cognitive-social-learning tradition, seeks to explain this discriminativeness; and we preferred therefore to start with people who more often than not vary their behavior to fit the "requirements" of the situation. As these commentators wisely note, however, it is now time to venture into these other domains.

Although we do appreciate the prod in the clinical direction, at the same time we want to emphasize that observation of mature, undisturbed people also often reveals the breakdown of flexibility in social behavior. For example, Cantor has observed considerable struggle, pain, and self-defeating behavior on the part of those "successful" honors students. Unfortunately, they do not always achieve their goals, feel good, or flexibly adapt their behavior to increase pleasure and decrease pain. In many respects, these students have taught us as much about the limits on adaptive social behavior as about its actualization.

Social Intelligence and Prescriptions for Living

In a related vein, many of the commentaries contained a plea for this approach to take more of the traditional role of intelligence theories to evaluate individuals and to prescribe solutions to problems in living. Baron, for example, notes that our approach is only descriptive and feels that we should pay more attention to the normative and prescriptive aspects of theorizing; that is, we should have a theory of character that informs people what goals they should have "on reflection" and how to achieve them. Baron may well be right, but his complaint is based on a view of social intelligence that is somewhat different from ours'. He argues that intelligence is an evaluative concept, and that the criteria for social intelligence should be prescriptive rules that bring people to those good goals that they would have on reflection.

This is not exactly what we mean by social intelligence. From our point of view, social intelligence consists of the cognitive resources—the knowledge and skills—that people bring to bear on social problem solving. Our attempt is to begin from a morally neutral stance, focusing on a person's goals (proximal and distal) and the cognitive means by which he or she achieves them. This is not because we disavow the study of self-defeating and maladaptive social intelligence; but rather because everything we know about social intelligence makes us very cautious about adopting uniform standards for success or for moral worth. To adopt a normative or evaluative point of view necessarily involves imposing the investigator's constructs and values on the subject, and this we are hesitant to set out to do, though we all end up doing some evaluation in the end. It seems important to come to those evaluative conclusions about the effectiveness and worthiness of individuals' goals and strategies only after having the chance to view the person in action for some time, and to listen to his or her viewpoint. Perhaps this is what Baron intended, and if so then we applaud the suggestion of standards derived "on reflection." We fear, however, that too much evaluation goes on in our field, *before the fact,* and without sufficient understanding of the individual's perspective. Moreover, we suspect that too often the evaluation enterprise takes over, clouding our view of the complexity inherent in most strategic "solutions." In our experience, there is rarely a strategy that is all "good" or all "bad" for all people; and furthermore, strategies that seem to work well at one point in time sometimes become, over time, less appealing as *the* solution to a pressing life problem. The problem with evaluative standards is that they don't typically encourage people to be flexible and to change their minds.

Thus, we agree with Baron in principle that psychologists should be able to help people to anticipate the goals that they would want to achieve on reflection. Nonetheless, we see this as a much trickier, more time-consuming task than he does. First, to evaluate the effectiveness of a strategy for an individual, a thought experiment has to be played. The costs of using the strategy have to be compared against those that would accrue from not using it. In this regard, for example, some defensive pessimists would be immobilized by anxiety without their strategy (Cantor & Norem, 1988); and most socially anxious individuals would probably stop socializing altogether from fear of embarrassment, without the self-protective security afforded by a social-constraint strategy (Langston & Cantor, 1988; Read & Miller, this volume). Cost-benefit analyses on life-task strategies are not easy to perform. Second, as Baumeister notes, the things that we do that turn out to be "good" for us are often buttressed by illusions that we hold about the self and others; and these are not likely to be the prescriptions for behavior adopted on detached or "wise" reflection. Pervin underscores the illusions that clients hold about themselves and about their real goals and motives. We want also to raise the possibility that psychologists will give bad prescriptive advice because we will not necessarily see clearly what the best solution will turn out to be. In this regard, we think that the best advice is for constant monitoring and updating: People mainly need to be encouraged to be flexible. It may simply be too risky to prescribe a standard course.

Therefore, we shy away from the normative and evaluative standards that most would associate with the study of social intelligence. When we evaluate, we try hard to take a relativistic stance, evaluating individuals' goals and strategies against a self-standard as much as against a social criterion. Taking this stance is by no means easy, and we have been guilty frequently of taking the simpler path of normative comparisons. It is a great deal simpler to say that defensive pessimism is bad because optimists experience less stress, than to say that the pessimists are still better off than they would be without the strategy. Similarly, there is little doubt that "extraverts have more fun" than do the socially anxious individuals who embrace a social-constraint strategy. Nonetheless, those anxious people are still striving for their social goals; it is not altogether clear that they would do so without that "self-defeating" strategy. So we want to try to be true to this relativistic stance, even though we don't always succeed in avoiding promoting uniform standards of adaptive behavior.

There is, however, one prescription that we too believe comes close to being generally applicable. Both Baron and Stewart stress the importance of individuals' roles as agents of choice in framing tasks and choosing strategies that facilitate active confrontation with the environment. Our prescription is to heighten that sense of choice and active confrontation whenever possible; even in the face of real social-environmental (or biological) constraints on behavior. A heightened sense of self-agency and of self-focused reflectiveness may well be a critical precursor to important personality change (Carver & Scheier; Stewart, this volume). In fact, this is surely part of the reason for feelings of panic and of challenge experienced in times of traumatic stress, transitions, therapy, personal failures, or social censure, when there is at least the hope of effecting some real change (e.g., Stewart; Linville & Clark; Pervin; Read & Miller, all this volume). If as Baumeister notes, striving for self-agency is a major aspect of the process of giving meaning to life, then it can only help to encourage that process (Bandura, 1986). Therefore, a "complete" theory of personality and social intelligence must not shrink from participating in this one prescriptive enterprise.

What Are the Individual's Life Tasks?

A number of commentators appear to agree that our analysis is good as far as it goes, but that certain important things have been left out. This seems to be particularly true of our treatment of life tasks. We are criticized, somewhat paradoxically, for not being attentive enough to the larger meanings and origins of life tasks, and at the same time for ignoring the idiographic variation in the role played by age-graded life tasks in the lives of individuals. Our reaction to these critiques is mixed. We think that we give more attention to each of these considerations than may have come across in our target chapter, and yet there is clearly room for improvement here.

First, as to the broader meanings of life tasks: Baumeister thinks our analysis is incomplete, and that people have life tasks that go beyond the kinds of issues outlined by us and by Klinger and by Plutchik. We were impressed by his analysis and do agree that people need a purpose in life, and a sense of efficacy, legitimation, and moral worth, and that these needs (among others, like competence motivation; Harackiewicz, Abrahams, & Wageman, 1987) are important aspects of personality. It is not difficult to see these broader pursuits at the basis of many of the life tasks and strategies that we observe on the part of college students. In fact, it is reasonable to see our approach as organized around the need for meaning—the need to make sense of life; and self-esteem maintenance is certainly a core task served by individuals' strategies. We don't doubt the relevance of these global categories of life tasks; and we think that some tasks, such as the search for legitimation and moral worth, do get too little attention in our work.

Still, we would be skeptical of a system that strived too relentlessly to link individuals' life tasks to only a few "basic" and abstract pursuits. By way of illustration, we are more comfortable with the diversity of Erikson's scheme of age-graded psychosocial tasks than with Freud's rather exclusive reliance on sex and aggression as the core human concerns. Here, as in most cases, we take the position that more is better; and when one of us, for example, smoothes over some of this individual variation in the service of nomothetic comparisons on age-graded life tasks, it is not without awareness that this is a compromise (Cantor, 1988). (We also wish to note in passing that we were a little perplexed by the idea raised by Emmons and King that a life-task approach somehow induces an achievement orientation towards motivation and behavior. In this regard, we see our work as following in the tradition of Erikson, 1950, and of Murray, 1938. Life tasks, like Brian Little's 1983 personal projects, guide individuals' purposive striving and problem solving in numerous different life domains. The domains of applicability of tasks and projects surely range at least from work to play and from intimacy to health, and probably elsewhere as well.)

In empirical work, we think that it is vital to stay as close as reasonably possible to the specifics of individuals' life-task concerns. We do think, however, that a theoretical scheme such as that provided by Baumeister can lead one to study important domains of life tasks that might otherwise be ignored. Emmons and King urged us to attend to the origins of life tasks in goals that have evolutionary significance (as in the work of Cantor's colleague, David Buss, 1986); and we have tried this in forging theoretical links to Plutchick's model. Here too, we can see considerable value in focusing on these adaptive pursuits as part of a hypothesis-generation process—e.g., mate-selection strategies become especially interesting if you believe that reproductive success is a central human goal. However, as Baumeister argues, delineation of such "basic" evolutionary goals cannot replace analysis of the diverse meanings that are overlaid on those shared goals. In this way, Buss's (1985) analysis of actual mate-selection strategies follows this dual-level approach to the meaning of evolutionary tasks. Somewhat more generally, Vallacher's and Wegner's (1987) analysis of action identification—i.e., of "what people think they are doing"—provides a framework for uncovering levels of meaning in human behavior, as Baumeister rightly notes.

This discussion brings us then to the other, flip side of the critique of our treatment of life tasks: the view that we ignore idiographic variation in favor of nomothetic analyses of age-graded tasks. In particular, Emmons and King and Read and Miller criticize the work of Cantor and her colleagues (e.g., Cantor et al., 1987) for failing to emphasize sufficiently interindividual variation in the *importance* and *meaning* of particular age-graded life tasks. Although we see their point, the critique does not seem entirely justified. It is certainly true that we do try to find ways to combine individuals' different construals of age-graded life tasks in order to see the diversity of their "solutions" to those tasks (e.g., college students try to "get good grades" or to "make friends" in very different ways). But we also try to point out that those strategic solutions are anchored in importantly different interpretations of the task-at-hand, with different underlying personal goals to be met (e.g., the defensive pessimist is working to harness anxiety before the test and the optimist is busy protecting the self after it; one shy person focuses on potential risks of social embarrassment, whereas another works on assertiveness). With full awareness of the pitfalls of nomothetic aggregation, we have generally tried to be guided by our data as to the appropriateness of making those simplifying assumptions. This approach doesn't work perfectly, and we certainly do miss many of the nuances of the meaning of goals to particular individuals. At the same time it is not the case that we routinely gloss over such idiographic variation.

Actually, Cantor and her colleagues have found that age-graded life tasks vary in the extent to which individuals uniformly attach importance to them (Cantor & Langston, 1988). For example, not surprisingly, most of their college-student sample were very involved in "getting good grades" and in "making friends," and they were in substantial agreement as to the activities and situations that tapped into these academic and social goals. (They differed, nonetheless, in their appraisals of the ease or difficulty of achieving their task goals, and in the strategies that they embraced to work on these shared tasks.) In contrast, the life task of "being independent, on my own, away from family," a traditionally important age-graded task for college students, really seemed to mean very different things and to serve very different functions for different students (Zirkel & Cantor, 1988). Accordingly, analysis of this life task has remained more closely focused at the idiographic level of task construal, and on variations in task involvement.

For some students, this is a life task that they acknowledge but one that they almost "relegate" exclusively to the realm of mundane life activities—activities such as "doing my own laundry" or "managing my money," which they also feel are relatively easy to accomplish. In turn, this life task does not appear to serve as an organizing force in their life activities, nor does progress on this task predict much about their subsequent adjustment to college life. This pattern is very different, however, for another group of students in the sample (approximately one-third of the sample). These students, the "independence schematics," are very engrossed in this life task, imbue those mundane activities with more personal meaning and significance than does the typical student, and choose to be in activities that they view as relevant to striving for independence more frequently than most students. In turn, their feelings about their progress on the independence task are critically important to their later experiences of stress and satisfaction in college and even influence their satisfaction with academic success. For these students, the task of independence serves as a pivotal organizing force in their lives, influencing not only their general well-being but also their reactions to and activities in their other important life tasks (see also Stewart & Healy, 1985).

The analysis of these different patterns of striving for independence at college show clearly the necessity of taking into account individual differences in meaning and centrality of age-graded life-task goals—differences that several commentators pointed to as fundamental components of goal-based theory and assessment in personality research (Emmons & King; Read & Miller; Pervin). We wholeheartedly agree with the desire to remain faithful to these goal-based individual differences. We also find it intriguing that the tasks themselves seem to differ somewhat in the amount of important idiographic variation that they actually reveal.

What Prospects for Assessment?

A number of commentators(Bergen & Dweck; Carver & Scheier; Emmons & King) expected us to have more to say about the problem of personality assessment. This expectation was natural given the title of the target chapter (frankly, we are running out of variations on the terms *personality* and *social intelligence*); and it is also natural in view of the dominance of traditional trait- and motive-based approaches to personality, for which assessment is central. But interesting theories of personality do not have to be focused on assessment: Freud, for example, never considered developing a questionnaire or projective technique.

Nonetheless, personality assessment has its rightful place, of course, and in our separate research programs (on defensive pessimism or hypnosis, for example) we have often been concerned with the measurement of individual differences on one dimension or another (Cantor & Norem, 1988; Register & Kihlstrom, 1986). One of us has contributed to some fairly detailed proposals for converting laboratory cognitive tasks into instruments for clinical assessment (Kihlstrom & Nasby, 1981; Nasby & Kihlstrom, 1986); he has also applied those methods to the study of both universal structure and idiographic content in autobiographical memory (Kihlstrom & Harackiewicz, 1982). Meanwhile, the other has been engaged in a 4-year longitudinal assessment of students' tasks and strategies for mastering the transition through college (Cantor et al., 1987). In pursuing these patterns of goal-based individual differences she has drawn on a variety of methods familiar to our commentators: self-reports of tasks, activities, and plans; observer Q-sort profiles of strategies from videotaped interviews; experience-sampling reports of on-line life task activities and emotional reactions; task conflict grids in which students consider the interrelations between their various task goals (after Little, 1983), symptom checklists and self-reports of daily life stress, and more.

In these contexts, in the clinical and semiclinical memory laboratory and in the longitudinal field study, we too have strived for idiographic precision, whereas remaining ever concerned with reliability and validity of measurement. In contrast, for other kinds of questions (the structure of social categories, for example, or the mechanisms underlying the self-reference effect), these idiographic assessments were less relevant, because we wished to study general processes that are widely shared if not ubiquitous (Cantor & Mischel, 1979; Klein & Kihlstrom, 1986). Throughout this work, however, respect and attention has been accorded to the scientific study of individual differences. We assume that the comments of Emmons and King on the absence of such an assessment program in the cognitive social-learning tradition simply reflect inattention to our mentors' empirical work. In fact, we model our assessment approach after Mischel's studies of person and process variables in self-control and Bandura's analyses of the dynamics of self-efficacy motivation; interweaving, *as they do,* the experimental analysis of process variables with longitudinal data on personality in vivo (Bandura, 1986; Mischel, 1983).

But the social-intelligence viewpoint also necessarily puts severe constraints on the process of assessment. If, as we believe the evidence shows, social behavior is flexible across situations, and personality is continually constructed through social interaction, then personality assessments are going to have to be context sensitive as well. We really doubt that assessments of personality in the abstract, without regard for context, are of much practical or theoretical use. For example, even expressly clinical assessments have a specified purpose. People don't just come in off the street to have their personalities tested: rather, they subject themselves to personality assessment because they are having some problem in living. And a proper clinical assessment is geared precisely toward that problem and interprets the client's test performance in the context generated by it. The same responses, in the context of another presenting complaint, might have an entirely different meaning.

In a similar vein, we do not pursue this level of specificity in our analysis, charting a path, for example, from life-task construal to strategy to outcomes, simply to achieve descriptive completeness. We truly believe that understanding, not to mention predictive power, in personality psychology comes through recognition of complex cognitive-behavioral routes that bring individuals closer to their goals, and the data on defensive pessimism and on social constraint, among others, support this position. (The position is reminiscent of Freud's contentions about ego defense mechanisms; though we do not necessarily accept other aspects of his doctrine.) If we as a field focus only at the structural level of the "big five," then we risk missing much that is active (vs. reactive) and inventive (vs. stereotyped) about the concrete processes of human personality (Cantor, 1988). It is true that we should do both; but frequently the latter enterprise gets jettisoned, perhaps because it is expensive, messy, intensive, difficult, nonparsimonious, and so forth. It may also be very worthwhile.

On the idiographic–nomothetic issue, we admit that we back off, just as Allport had to. Our view, like Allport's (and Mischel's), dictates that proper assessments are idiographic—in which people are allowed to speak for themselves about their own lives and are not forced into the Procrustean bed of the investigator's favorite constructs. It's fine as humanistic doctrine, but, as Allport found out, it's difficult when it comes to getting research done. We want our research to tell us something that generalizes beyond the individual case, and in order to generalize some compromises have to be made. Sometimes we have to evaluate everybody according to the same (nomothetic) standard, accepting the fact that a certain amount of noise will creep in. This compromise with idiographic ideals is not an embarrassment, but it *is* something we have to worry about.

We can entertain some other compromises that keep us close to individual lives but permit a considerable degree of generality. One strategy is to study relatively homogeneous subject groups, like honors college freshmen, who are presumably all at pretty much the same stage of life, with many shared goals and common resources. Another, which veers close to the semiclinical, is to enroll the subjects as active collaborators in the research enterprise. One of us, for example, is very interested in the possibility that autobiographical memory is organized temporally into relatively large "chunks" of time. But how are these chunks to be defined? Periods of 5 years, beginning at birth? Preschool, elementary school, secondary school, college, career, and retirement? What about people who don't go to college? Or who went to college after raising a family? Or who don't have a career? Or have had lots of different jobs? The only way to determine a proper organizational scheme is by means of a sensitive inquiry at the individual level, as Stewart suggests, and the most likely outcome is that the best organizational rubric will be different for each person. That's fine by us, because the essential prediction is that, however autobiographical memory is organized at the individual level, the effects of organization on memory processing should be the same for everyone. We look forward to creative combinations of idiographic and nomothetic research strategies, but our mathematical colleagues are either going to have to come up with some innovative techniques for data analysis, or our reviewers are going to have to accept some statistical sloppiness.

Awareness and Control

Almost from the beginning of psychology, there has been an unfortunate misidentification of things cognitive with things conscious. The idea of people as (fairly) rational social problem solvers sometimes gives the implication that every social interaction is the product of deep thought, in which people consciously evaluate their goals and select their strategies, and leads to the image of the person as lost in thought at the choice point. Moreover, at least since Kelly (1955) introduced the notion of constructive alternativism, we have had to struggle with the interpretation that there is no objective reality, and that behavior can be changed by a simple act of thought. Pervin is especially concerned that we may be too glib about what is conscious, and too sanguine about the ease of behavior change.

Pervin is right that clinical work frequently involves people who seem not to know what they're doing, or who have insight but seem unable to change. And insofar as our approach is to have any clinical application (as indeed we hope it does), we should have something to say about that. In fact, as he notes, one of us has been centrally concerned with the nature of nonconscious mental life

(Kihlstrom, 1984, 1987, 1988). And information-processing concepts such as automaticity may provide some explanation for why some aspects of personality and behavior are difficult to change. This is work for the future, and we appreciate the prod.

Where's Emotion? Where's Motivation? Where's Temperament?

An even larger group of commentators (Baron; Baumeister; Bergen & Dweck; Emmons & King; Klinger; Pervin; Read & Miller)—in fact, almost everybody who talks to us—raises the question of where emotion and motivation fit into our scheme of things. It's a natural question, because sometimes cognitive psychology seems to treat emotion and motivation as beyond the pale. We want to make it clear that we think that emotions and motives are important, and that any comprehensive approach to personality and social interaction should have something to say about how cognition, emotion, and motivation relate to each other. There's no doubt in our mind that emotions and motives affect cognitive processing, just as some emotions and motives are cognitively constructed, and that the "trilogy of mind" (Hilgard, 1980) works as an integrated system to produce behavior. In other places (Kihlstrom, 1988; Showers & Cantor, 1985) we have tried to expand on this point of view. Integrating emotion and motivation with cognition is work for the future, but we agree that it's important work.

Thus, we think that a very reasonable agenda for the future is to try to hook these specific structures of social intelligence to more global or generalized individual differences in motivation and emotion. This agenda applies to all the structural units that we have considered: (1) self-schemata and autobiographical memories might be importantly linked to and shaped by generalized expectancies (Carver & Scheier) and by current psychological stances (Stewart); (2) current life tasks can and do serve diverse purposes, reflecting species-general evolutionary goals, culturally defined prescriptions or moral guides to individual life, or highly personalized sources of self-worth and of meaning (Baron; Baumeister; Emmons & King); (3) strategic preferences are likely to be very much influenced by individuals' chronic or transient states of arousal, activity level, sensation seeking, and emotionality (Carver & Scheier; Klinger; Pervin; Stewart). Nevertheless, the thrust of these analyses should still be to capture the many ways that common dispositions are actually expressed in personal tasks and strategies, rather than to label people as abstract types.

For example, in several commentaries the links between defensive pessimism and need for achievement, and between social constraint and social anxiety or shyness, were correctly noted. Yet, in this regard, the dispositional constructs of shyness and social anxiety have been intriguing researchers as much because of the richness and diversity of their expression, as because of their unitary structure or *direct* predictive power (Cheek, Melchior, & Carpentieri, 1986). The Langston and Cantor (1988) analysis of social constraint, as only one possible path from social anxiety to social dissatisfaction, is based on this "fuzzy sets" view of shyness (see also Arkin, Lake, & Baumgardner, 1986). The diverse meaning of motives like need for achievement or fear of failure in the actual lives of real individuals provides another good illustration of this point (Stewart, this volume; Veroff, 1983). Thus, it would certainly be accurate to say that the defensive pessimist's construal of achievement tasks reflects a need for achievement balanced by a fear of failure (as Emmons & King suggest). In fact, they exhibit many of the features of a fear of failure profile *before* testing situations (Norem & Cantor, 1986). The critical feature of their task construal, however, is that it calls forth a strategy for initially overcoming the debilitating effects of that fear of failure. For these individuals, defensive pessimism is an active response to anxiety and, as such, they look less and less like "classic cases" (of fear of failure), the more they use it effectively. For others, or at other times, defensive pessimism may be a strategy invoked more to engender anxiety than to harness it—i.e., to energize and guard against overconfidence (Brehm et al., 1983). In that case, the resemblance to a fear of failure profile is just that—a resemblance. Either way, the strategy follows from the person's specific construal of the achievement task; and it makes more sense when viewed in that way, rather than as a mere reflection of an abstract motive of need for achievement or of fear of failure, or of some combination of both.

Thus, on one hand we see much to be gained in linking social intelligence to some underlying stylistic and motivational structures. At the same time, we also see much to be lost in the analysis of personality without detailed follow-through on the specific and diverse ways that those common dispositions are expressed in different individuals' lives. We still see a need to keep doing what Carver and Scheier aptly labelled as *idiographic process* analysis. And it was for this reason that we made the plea for increased attention to the "doing" side of personality, as a complement to the somewhat more popular broad-based structural distinctions in individual difference research (Cantor, 1988; cf. Emmons & King).

A related question comes up about temperament. Carver and Scheier suggest that individual differences in activity level, emotionality, and sociability are biologically based, but we're not so sure that's the whole story. The literature on gender identity and gender role (e.g., Money & Ehrhardt, 1972) may provide a better model for understanding temperament than any simple theory of genetic/hormonal endowment. A neonate's activity level, emotionality, or gregariousness may be initially determined by his or her biological endowment, but these behaviors also occur in a social environment that either supports or modulates them. In Money and Ehrhardt's terms, the program for temperament passes, at birth, from the genes to the environment. Later, as children become aware of their actions, their impact on the environment, and others' expectations of them, they begin to regulate their own behavior in accordance with perceived social norms and their developing self-concepts. In Money and Ehrhardt's terms, the program for temperament is now continuously exchanged between the person and the environment. From this point of view, whatever continuities exist between child and adult temperament are as much a function of the environment and the person's self-concept as they are of some *autonomous* genetic/biochemical processes. Moreover, these are environmental effects that do not vanish with the wave of a behavior geneticist's hand. The program for temperament differentiation, like the program for gender differentiation, is uniquely structured in the specific interactions between child and parents and siblings and teachers; it is bound to be different for each child in the family, as behavior genetic studies of "nonshared environmental" effects reveal. So although it's true that a truly comprehensive theory of personality ought to have something to say about the biological substrates of temperament, it's also true that a theory of temperament ought to have something to say about cognitive and social processes.

Is This Really a Theory?

Baron raised the question of what kind of theory ours' is, and Bergen and Dweck ask how well it meets certain formal standards for a theory. It's a good question, and we're willing to concede that maybe ours' is only a viewpoint, or an approach, or a model. Whatever it is, it is also, as Bergen and Dweck note, a little vague here and there. By way of conclusion, let us at least try to clarify two problems.

Concerning structure: Social intelligence consists both in what the person knows about the self and his or her social world (declarative knowledge) and the skills, rules, and strategies by which he or she applies that knowledge to solve the problems encountered in social interaction (procedural knowledge). The only constraints on this structure are the constraints on the representation of knowledge in the cognitive system. We admit that this is not a simplifying structure, but we doubt that any *very* simple structure—like a three-or five-factor model of personality, for example, is any better. Moreover, some of the confusion between the "structural" and the "actualized" elements of personality in our model is intentional. We view the cognitive system as a fluid, evolving resource or fund; new life tasks and strategies, for example, are continuously constructed *in vivo*, and some of them then get "permanently" represented in the declarative and procedural structures of personality.

Concerning formal specificity: There's not a lot of rigor in the present account, if a theory's adequacy is measured by whether it can be translated into an operating computer simulation. It's too early for that, but when the time comes it seems likely that Linville and Clark will have been on the right track with ACT* or some related production-system architecture (like SOAR; Newell, 1988). In our view, social interaction involves problem solving, and personality contributes a repertoire of structured knowledge—declarative and procedural—that an individual can use in "solving" problems. Explicitly or implicitly, an ACT-like architecture pervades both our book and target chapter and appears in some of our other work as well (e.g., Kihlstrom, 1985, 1987). Even if our ideas are not expressed in LISP programs, in principle they could be. One of us, at least, is certain that an interesting computer simulation of an individual personality could be designed like an expert system, linking nodes and writing productions that would represent the individual's fund of knowledge in some domain, and that would effectively mimic his or her actual behavior in some domain. Here is another place where the idiographic–nomothetic tension rears its ugly head. The architecture of personality, in terms of how socially relevant declarative and procedural knowledge is structured, is universal. The particular content of personality, in terms of the social knowledge represented by nodes and productions, is highly idiosyncratic. A model of people-in-general will never adequately simulate an individual's behavior. But just let us tinker with the parameters a little.

REFERENCES

Arkin, R. M., Lake, E. A., & Baumgardner, A. B. (1986). Shyness and self-presentation. In W. H. Jones, J. M. Cheek, & S. R. Briggs (Eds.), *Shyness: Perspectives on research and treatment* (pp. 189–203). New York: Plenum Press.

Bandura, A. (1986). *Social foundations of thought and action: A social cognitive theory.* Englewood Cliffs, NJ: Prentice-Hall.

Brehm, J. W., Wright, R. A., Solomon, S., Silka, L., & Greenberg, J. (1983). Perceived difficulty, energization, and the magnitude of goal valence. *Journal of Experimental Social Psychology, 19*, 21–48.

Buss, D. M. (1985). Human mate selection. *American Scientist, 73,*47–51.

Buss, D. M. (1986). Can social science be anchored in evolutionary biology? Four problems and a strategic solution. *Revue Europeenne Des Sciences Sociales, 24*, 41–50.

Cantor, N. (under review 1988). From thought to behavior: "Having" and "doing" in the study of personality and cognition. *American Psychologist.*

Cantor, N., & Langston, C. A. (in press 1988). "Ups and downs" of life tasks in a life transition. In L. Pervin (Ed.), *The goals concept in personality and social psychology.* Hillsdale, NJ: Lawrence Erlbaum Associates.

Cantor, N., & Mischel, W. (1979). Prototypes in person perception. In L. Berkowitz (Ed.), *Advances in experimental social psychology* (Vol 12, pp. 3–52). New York: Academic Press.

Cantor, N., & Norem, J. K. (in press). Defensive pessimism and stress and coping. *Social Cognition.*

Cantor, N., Norem, J. K., Niedenthal, P. M., Langston, C. A., & Brower, A. M. (1987). Life tasks, self-concept ideals, and cognitive strategies in a life transition. *Journal of Personality and Social Psychology, 53*(6), 1178–1191.

Cheek,J. M., Melchior, L. A., & Carpentieri, A. M. (1986). Shyness and self-concept. In L. M. Hartman & K. R. Blankstein (Eds.), *Perception of self in emotional disorder and psychotherapy* (pp. 113–131). New York: Plenum.

Erikson, E. H. (1950). *Childhood and Society.* New York: Norton.

Harackiewicz, J. M., Abrahams, S., & Wageman, R. (1987). Performance evaluation and intrinsic motivation: The effects of evaluative focus, rewards, and achievement orientation. *Journal of Personality and Social Psychology, 53*(6), 1015–1023.

Hilgard, E. R. (1980). The trilogy of mind: Cognition, affection, and conation. *Journal for the History of the Behavioral Sciences, 16,* 107–117.

Kelly, G. (1955). *The psychology of personal constructs.* New York: Norton.

Kihlstrom, J. F. (1984). Conscious, subconscious, unconscious: A cognitive perspective. In K. Bowers & D. Meichenbaum (Eds.), *The unconscious reconsidered* (pp. 149–211). New York: Wiley.

Kihlstrom, J. F. (1985). Posthypnotic amnesia and the dissociation of memory. In G. H. Bower (Ed.), *The psychology of learning and motivation* (Vol 19, pp. 131–178). Orlando: Academic Press.

Kihlstrom, J. F. (1987). The cognitive unconscious. *Science, 237,* 1445–1452.

Kihlstrom, J. F. (1988). Cognition, unconscious processing. In G. Adelman (Ed.), *Yearbook of the encyclopedia of Neuroscience.* Boston: Birkhauser.

Kihlstrom, J. F., & Harackiewicz, J. (1982). The earliest recollections: A new survey. *Journal of Personality, 50,* 134–148.

Kihlstrom, J. F., & Nasby, W. (1981). Cognitive tasks in clinical assessment: An exercise in applied psychology. In P. Kendall & S. Hollon (Eds.), *Cognitive-behavioral interventions: Assessment methods* (pp. 287–317). New York: Academic Press.

Klein, S. B., & Kihlstrom, J. F. (1986). Elaboration, organization, and the self-reference effect in memory. *Journal of Experimental Psychology: General, 115,* 26–38.

Langston, C. A., & Cantor, N. (in press). Social anxiety and social constraint: When "making friends" is hard. *Journal of personality and social psychology.*

Little, B. (1983). Personal projects: A rational and methods for investigation. Environmental Behavior, 15, 273–309.

Mischel, W. (1983). Delay of gratification as process and as person variable in development. In D. Magnusson & V. P. Allen (Eds.), *Human development: An interactional perspective* (pp. 149–165). New York: Academic Press.

Money, J., & Ehrhardt, A. A. (1972). *Man and woman, boy and girl: Differentiation and dimorphism of gender identity from conception to maturity.* Baltimore: Johns Hopkins University Press.

Murray, H. (1938). *Explorations in personality.* New York: Oxford Press.

Nasby, W., & Kihlstrom, J. F. (1986). Cognitive assessment of personality and psychopathology. In R. E. Ingram (Ed.), *Information-processing approaches to clinical psychology* (pp. 217–239). New York: Academic Press.

Newell, A. (1988). *Unified theories of cognition.* The 1987 William James Lectures, Carnegie Mellon University.

Norem, J. K., & Cantor, N. (1986). Defensive pessimism: "Harnessing" anxiety as motivation. *Journal of Personality and Social Psychology, 51*(6), 1208–1217.

Register, P. A., & Kihlstrom, J. F. (1986). Finding the hypnotic virtuoso. *International Journal of Clinical and Experimental Hypnosis, 32,* 84–97.

Showers, C., & Cantor, N. (1985). Social cognition: A look at motivated strategies. In M. Rosenzweig & L. W. Porter (Eds.), *Annual Review of Psychology* (Vol. 36, pp. 275–305). Palo Alto, CA: Annual Reviews.

Smith, T. W., & Rhodewalt, F. (1986). On states, traits, and processes: A transactional alternative to the individual difference assumptions in Type A behavior and physiological reactivity. *Journal of Research in Personality, 20*(3), 229–251.

Stewart, A. J., & Healy, J. M., Jr. (1985). Personality and adaptation to change. In R. Hogan & W. Jones, (Eds.), *Perceptives on personality: Theory, measurement, and interpersonal dynamics* (pp. 117–144). Greenwich, CT: JAI Press.

Vallacher, R. R., & Wegner, D. M. (1987). What do people think they're doing. Action identification and human behavior. *Psychological Review, 94*,3–15.
Veroff, J. (1983). Contextual determinants of personality. *Personality and Social Psychology Bulletin, 9*,331–344.
Wright, J. C., & Mischel, W. (1987). A conditional approach to dispositional constructs: The local predictability of social behavior. *Journal of Personality and Social Psychology, 53*(6), 1159–1177.
Zirkel, S., & Cantor, N. (1988). *Independence and identity in the transition to college life.* Paper presented at Meetings of the American Psychological Association, Atlanta.

Author Index

Subject Index

223